MARIJUANA LEGALIZATION

WHAT EVERYONE NEEDS TO KNOW

MARIJUANA LEGALIZATION

WHAT EVERYONE NEEDS TO KNOW

JONATHAN P. CAULKINS
ANGELA HAWKEN
BEAU KILMER
MARK A. R. KLEIMAN

OXFORD
UNIVERSITY PRESS

OXFORD
UNIVERSITY PRESS

Oxford University Press, Inc., publishes works that further
Oxford University's objective of excellence
in research, scholarship, and education.

Oxford   New York
Auckland   Cape Town   Dar es Salaam   Hong Kong   Karachi
Kuala Lumpur   Madrid   Melbourne   Mexico City   Nairobi
New Delhi   Shanghai   Taipei   Toronto

With offices in
Argentina   Austria   Brazil   Chile   Czech Republic   France   Greece
Guatemala   Hungary   Italy   Japan   Poland   Portugal   Singapore
South Korea   Switzerland   Thailand   Turkey   Ukraine   Vietnam

Published by Oxford University Press, Inc.
198 Madison Avenue, New York, NY 10016

www.oup.com

Oxford is a registered trademark of Oxford University Press

Library of Congress Cataloging-in-Publication Data
Marijuana legalization : what everyone needs to know /
Jonathan P. Caulkins, Angela Hawken, Beau Kilmer, and Mark A. R. Kleiman.
p.   cm.
Includes bibliographical references and index.
ISBN 978-0-19-991373-2 (pbk.) — ISBN 978-0-19-991371-8 (hbk.)
1. Marijuana—United States.   2. Marijuana—Law and legislation—United States.
3. Drug legalization—United States.   I. Caulkins, Jonathan P. (Jonathan Paul), 1965–
HV5822.M3M2935 2012
362.29′50973—dc23   2011046822

1 3 5 7 9 8 6 4 2

Printed in the United States of America
on acid-free paper

To Charles R. ("Bob") Schuster,
who brought the ethics of the laboratory
to the corridors of power

CONTENTS

2. Who Uses Marijuana? 16

3. How Is Marijuana Produced and Distributed Today? 31

4. How Stringent Is Marijuana Enforcement in the United States? 42

12. Could One State Legalize Marijuana If the Federal Government Didn't?   184

13. How Would Marijuana Legalization Affect Me Personally?   198

14. Between Marijuana Prohibition and Commercial Legalization: Is there Any Middle Ground?   207

15. Can Industrial Hemp Save the Planet?
(Written with Christina Farber)   225

ACKNOWLEDGMENTS

Partial support for this work was provided by a Carnegie Mellon University seed grant funded by the Qatar Foundation. The views expressed imply no endorsement by any funder.

We received many useful comments and other assistance from friends and colleagues including Martin Bouchard, James Burgdorf, Shawn Bushway, Marjorie Carlson, John Coleman, Carolyn Coulson, Richard Cowan, Tom Decorte, Wayne Hall, Keith Humphreys, Sarah Lawrence, Robert MacCoun, Francis Matthew-Simmons, Erin Kilmer Neel, Rosalie Liccardo Pacula, Rajeev Ramchand, Peter Reuter, Jack Riley, Mark Ristich, Robin Room, Sally Satel, Eric Sterling, Chris Wilkins, Jenny Williams, Irmgard Zeiler, and a federal prisoner who prefers not to be named. Of course none of them bears any responsibility for our views.

Leba Sable and Jillian Kissee provided able research assistance.

Christina Farber coauthored chapter 15; we are very appreciative of her time and effort.

Angela Chnapko has once again been a wonderful editor, keeping us in line and on time. Ben Sadock provided another pitch-perfect copy-edit; Richard Comfort supplied the indexing wizardry.

For additional information about the book and the authors, please visit http://www.marijuanalegalization.info.

INTRODUCTION

Should marijuana be legalized? Public opinion in the United States couldn't be more evenly divided; the latest Gallup poll reports that exactly half of Americans say "Yes."

Marijuana is forbidden by international treaties and by national and local laws across the globe. But those laws are under challenge in several countries. In the United States, there is no short-term prospect for changes in federal law, but sixteen states allow medical use and recent initiatives to legalize production and nonmedical use garnered more than 40 percent support in four states. California's Proposition 19 nearly passed in 2010, and as we write a number of states are expected to consider similar measures in 2012.

There's more to the issue than a simple "yes" or "no" on a survey or ballot. Marijuana legalization turns out not to be a single question but a whole collection of questions.

Should people be allowed to use marijuana? If yes, does that mean only people with medical need, or social and recreational users as well? Adults only? In public, or only in private? Should selling marijuana be legal? Or semilegal, as it is in the Netherlands? If so, under what rules? At what price? With what taxes? Or should users be restricted to growing their own or joining noncommercial cooperatives? While the drug remains illegal nationally, does it make sense to legalize it locally?

This book is not intended to persuade you of any particular answers to these questions. The four authors don't even share a single view (see chapter 16), and none of us hold exactly the same view now as when we started writing. There is no shortage of advocacy on either side. Instead we hope to provide both sets of advocates with material for an honest and logically coherent debate, and give people who have not yet made up their minds the raw material needed to develop informed opinions.

Legalization, in whatever form, would create both good and bad effects, and the magnitudes of those effects are uncertain. (In some cases, even the direction is unclear: for example, no one knows whether increased marijuana use would lead to less heavy drinking, or to more.) Even if the facts were known with certainty—and they can't be, about a policy change so profound—there's no "objective" way of weighing gains in liberty and pleasure against harms such as disease and injury. Our goal is to present the issues and to sweep away some of the myths and fallacious arguments that have been offered on both sides of the debate.

We have been studying marijuana and marijuana policy for a combined total of nearly seventy years, but what we know is only a fraction of what is known, let alone the vast amount that remains unknown. A thorough understanding would draw on ideas from agronomy, anthropology, botany, chemistry, history, international relations, law, management, medicine, economics, neurology, operations analysis, pharmacology, philosophy, policy analysis, political science, psychology, public administration, sociology, and statistics.

In the face of this complexity, we have done our best in this book to lay out the issues as clearly as we could. The rest is up to you.

PART I

MARIJUANA AND PROHIBITION TODAY

1

WHAT IS MARIJUANA AND WHAT WOULD IT MEAN TO LEGALIZE IT?

What is marijuana legalization?

Marijuana is the most commonly used illegal drug in the world; various forms of the drug have been used for thousands of years for their medicinal, social, and aesthetic effects.

International treaties and the laws of almost every country forbid growing, selling, and possessing marijuana. That makes lawbreakers out of more than 125 million people who have used marijuana in the past year, and those who supply them. It creates illicit markets with a total value in the tens of billions of dollars per year. Some of that illicit activity leads to violence and to the corruption of public officials. Millions of users each year are arrested for possessing the drug, and smaller but substantial numbers of traffickers go to prison.

The question of legalization concerns whether to change the laws to make it legal to produce, sell, and possess marijuana, and, if so, what rules should apply.

Full legalization would replace black market production and distribution with an aboveboard industry. There could still be rules and regulations, just as there are rules and regulations governing production and distribution of alcohol and automobiles and avocados. But the bulk of the trade would be populated by farmers and merchants and retail clerks, not by criminals.

There are many ways to liberalize marijuana policy short of full legalization. Use could be allowed but production and sale still forbidden. Use and sale of small quantities could be allowed but production and wholesale distribution still forbidden; that's the current policy in the Netherlands. The penalties for possession of small amounts could be reduced and treated as civil rather than criminal matters (an option called "decriminalization"). Production, sale, and use could be permitted only for medical purposes. Or they could be restricted to noncommercial channels, with users growing their own or forming cooperatives.

Likewise, legalization could be accompanied by more or fewer restrictions on sale and use. Alcohol may be sold only to adults and only by licensed sellers, while caffeine—in the form of coffee or cola drinks—is sold without restriction. Thinking about marijuana legalization, then, involves an exercise in policy design. Repealing current laws is simple in concept; figuring out what might replace those laws is more complex.

For most drugs in most countries at most times, legalization is a political non-starter. That is not the case for marijuana, especially in the United States. A recent poll reports that half of all Americans support legalization, and California's legalization initiative (Proposition 19) came fairly close to passing in 2010. Petitions are circulating in other states for ballot measures to allow commercial marijuana production for nonmedical use. The odds of such an initiative passing in at least one state over the next decade seem to be no worse than even.

What is marijuana?

"Marijuana" is the American term for the dried flowers and leaves of the plant *Cannabis sativa*. The flowers contain concentrated amounts of mind-altering chemicals known as "cannabinoids"; the leaves that have become the symbol of marijuana contain lesser quantities of the same chemicals. "Hashish" is made by extracting the cannabinoid-rich trichomes—tiny hair-like structures produced by the plant. Different plants produce different amounts and mixtures of cannabinoids; these vary with the genetics of the plant, with growing practices, and even with the timing of the harvest.

Most of the rest of the world refers to marijuana as "herbal cannabis" and hashish as "cannabis resin," with "cannabis" being a catchall term that includes both products. Scientific papers mostly use the same language. However, this book generally employs the vocabulary more familiar in the United States, using "marijuana" except when referring specifically to other forms of the drug or to the plant itself.

How does it feel to get high?

The sensation of being under the influence of marijuana varies based on the type and quantity consumed, the person and his or her purposes in using, and the social circumstances—what the late Harvard psychiatrist Norman Zinberg described as "drug, set, and setting."

Since sellers have a strong interest in understanding the viewpoint of consumers, advertising themes can offer insight into what products are "about." Purely illegal products aren't generally advertised, but hundreds of retail dispensaries supply marijuana products to the hundreds of thousands of California residents with doctors' letters "recommending" marijuana to them for (at least purportedly) medical use. Dispensary advertisements reflect the sellers' beliefs about the range of experiences marijuana users are seeking. One website describes the popular Purple Kush as "soothing & relaxing" and "great for sleep, pain, stress, & nausea." Sour Diesel, on the other hand, is said to provide "an uplifting & visual experience" that is "great for mood & appetite." There is also Dutch Crunch, which is claimed to have "mood enhancing qualities" and to encourage "clear-thinking and productivity."

Science has little to say about the feelings generated by marijuana intoxication and about how those feelings compare with the feelings generated by other drugs. The marijuana experience is complex; while most drugs taken for other-than-medical use can be classified either as central-nervous-system (CNS) stimulants (such as caffeine, cocaine, amphetamines, and MDMA) or as CNS depressants (such as alcohol and the opioid pain relievers including morphine, oxycodone, and heroin), marijuana is neither a stimulant nor a depressant. While most psychoactive drugs used for pleasure influence one or more of three sets of nerve receptors—those for dopamine, serotonin, or GABA—the chemicals in cannabis react with a pair of receptor systems (CB1 and CB2) unique to them and to a naturally occurring neurotransmitter called anandamide (from the Sanskrit word for "bliss").

The effects of those interactions are multiple and oddly assorted: focusing attention on sensory experience, impairing short-term memory and the "executive function" in ways that interfere with absorbing complex information and managing divided attention (an effect which, for some, might boost creativity), enhancing appetite, and making users more receptive to humor. Especially with low-potency varieties, naive users may not experience the desired subjective effect until they have "learned to get high." The effects are not always pleasant: at high doses, users can experience intense anxiety and panic attacks. (The positive and negative effects of marijuana are discussed in chapters 5, 6, and 7.)

What are the active ingredients in marijuana?

Until recently, most discussion about the effects of marijuana focused on a single chemical: delta-9-tetrahydrocannabinol, better known as THC. THC is the main psychoactive ingredient in marijuana, and the one most responsible for its intoxicating effects.

THC is just one of more than sixty cannabinoids found in marijuana. Different parts of the plant, plants of different genetic strains, and plants grown under different conditions contain different mixes of these chemicals.

The effects of the other cannabinoids are less well understood than those of THC. They do not produce a high in the absence of THC, but they interact with THC to affect its impact in a variety of ways: enhancing or attenuating it, speeding up or slowing down its onset, and influencing how long the effect lasts.

One compound drawing increasing attention from both scientists and medical marijuana providers is cannabidiol (CBD). CBD is not intoxicating—CBD alone doesn't produce a high—but some claim it may calm the anxiety sometimes produced by high doses of THC. It may even have antipsychotic activity. Some research suggests that marijuana with a better balance between CBD and THC is less risky than the high-THC, low-CBD strains that now dominate the upper end of the marijuana market. A recent RAND study by James Burgdorf and his colleagues shows both great variation in ratios and a strong trend toward more THC and less CBD over time in samples seized in California.

But most marijuana users—even those who know what CBD is—cannot detect its presence or absence in the material they use, and few sellers—even the dispensaries selling marijuana for medical purposes—have their products tested and labeled by chemical content. Learning more about the effects of this ratio and how it varies from one form of marijuana to another could improve knowledge of the mental health and public health consequences of marijuana consumption.

The change in thinking about the roles of THC and CBD suggests that more surprises may be in store as scientists learn about the roles of some of the other compounds in marijuana. Research in this area remains in its infancy.

What are sinsemilla, "commercial-grade" marijuana, hashish, and hash oil?

Potency, measured by THC concentration, varies greatly depending on the plant's genetics, how it is grown, which parts of the plant are used, and how it is prepared. Because of these differences, both participants in the market and enforcement agencies distinguish among different forms of cannabis products. More potent products, as measured by higher THC content, tend to cost more.

The stalks and stems of the plant have almost no psychoactive content; the leaves have some, the flowers ("buds" or "flowering tops") still more, and the tiny hair-like trichomes on the flowers the most of all. Consequently, marijuana that contains large proportions of stems and leaves is less valuable than marijuana consisting mostly of the flowering tops.

Cannabis plants are either males producing pollen, or females, capturing pollen and producing seed. Female plants produce a sticky resin that traps grains of pollen from the air. Marijuana growers have learned that unpollinated females keep producing more and more resin, thus increasing the cannabinoid content of the product. Flowers that are never pollinated never produce seed; therefore the high-potency marijuana produced by keeping females unpollinated is seedless: in Spanish, *sin semilla*. "Sinsemilla" typically runs between 10 percent and 18 percent THC, or about three times the level of the conventional "commercial-grade" marijuana that comes from pollinated plants.

Hashish, made by pressing together the resinous trichomes, can exceed 40 percent THC. Produced mostly in Asia and North Africa and popular in Europe, hashish has a special mystique, connected with its use by Baudelaire and other nineteenth-century French bohemians. Some users claim it has qualitatively different effects from sinsemilla, perhaps due either to the sheer concentration of THC or to the higher

CBD content of the North African hashish usually used in Europe.

The very potent product called "hash oil" is produced from marijuana by chemical extraction; it has nothing in common with hashish save the name and its high potency. Its use is not widespread, but it is available in some medical marijuana dispensaries in the United States.

What is "ditchweed"?

"Ditchweed" is at the other end of the potency spectrum. As the name implies, it is typified by wild weeds growing on the sides of roads. The average THC content of ditchweed is below 1 percent, giving it little value as an illicit drug. Although there is no active market for ditchweed, eradication of uncultivated plants accounts for an overwhelming share of domestic cannabis eradication by U.S. law enforcement, simply because weeds are easier to find than carefully concealed growing operations. This illustrates how misleading statistics on marijuana can be: eradicating hundreds of tons of ditchweed has no practical impact on drug use.

Has marijuana been getting more potent?

Yes, by quite a bit, though not nearly as much as some government and media accounts would suggest.

The potency of any cannabis product depends on its concentration of cannabinoids, and in particular THC. By that measure, potency is much higher today than it was in the 1960s, when marijuana first found a mass market in the United States. Much less is known about changes in the levels of other cannabinoids, but CBD content seems to have fallen as THC content has risen.

Selective breeding and better growing methods (e.g., indoor hydroponic gardening) now make it possible to produce far more potent marijuana than most of what was used on college campuses in the 1960s. Also, much of the marijuana sold in the 1960s and 1970s consisted of a mixture of the stems and leaves, with only an occasional flowering top. So the growth in potency results not only from advances in cannabis agronomy but also from changes in market practices.

Over just the past fifteen years, potency levels measured in U.S. seizures have more than doubled. That is mostly because sinsemilla accounts for a much greater proportion of the analyzed seizures than in the past. But even if we look at potency for sinsemilla and commercial-grade marijuana separately, average THC levels within each category have increased by about 50 percent.

The United Kingdom has also recorded potency increases in herbal cannabis, as have the Netherlands and Italy. But measuring changes in potency, both within and across countries, is fraught with methodological problems. Most potency estimates are based on seizures, which may not be representative of what is consumed.

Overall, the claim made in drug-prevention programs that "this is not your grandfather's marijuana"—with its implication that baby boomers who recall using the drug safely should not be complacent about its use by their grandchildren—has a solid basis. However, reports of super-powerful samples (THC levels greater than 25 percent) describe outliers. These samples exist, but they're hardly typical, even of sinsemilla.

Is higher potency bad?

While there's some dispute over how much potency has increased, there's even greater dispute over how much it matters.

In purely commercial terms, higher-potency marijuana is more valuable because a user needs less of it to attain any desired high. A user trying to minimize cost per hour of intoxication should be willing to pay about twice as much for marijuana that is twice as potent, and there does seem to be a price gradient based on potency, though other factors also influence price. But if more potent pot just meant that users smoked half as much, the main result would be a beneficial one: less throat irritation, and perhaps less lung damage, from smoking. (Another benefit for users is that higher-potency marijuana reduces the amount of time it takes to get high, which reduces the probability of getting caught.)

But there are three reasons to worry that more potent pot tends to lead to higher highs, and a greater incidence of bad effects such as panic attacks.

First, marijuana users, especially those without experience, may have no reliable way of judging the potency of the material they consume. A user who smokes a "joint" weighing a half gram will clearly get higher if that joint is 15 percent THC than if it is 5 percent THC.

Even users who don't smoke a fixed amount of material, but try to "titrate"—smoking enough to get the desired effect and then stopping—may find it more difficult with higher-potency marijuana simply because each individual puff contains such a large dose of intoxicant: it's easier to take about ten "hits" than it is to take precisely three.

Second, the intensity of the subjective "high" is determined by the rate of change of the blood concentration of the drug as well as by the maximum level attained. Smoking high-potency pot compresses the time over which cannabinoids enter the brain, thus generating a more intense intoxication for any given amount of chemical.

Third, as noted above, a very high ratio of the anxiety-inducing THC to the anxiety-relieving CBD may put the user at greater risk of negative side effects, and THC/CBD ratios have been rising along with THC content itself.

So there's reason to think not only that pot has gotten more potent but that more potent pot—especially if it also has high ratios of THC to CBD—could be more dangerous.

The changing age-pattern of use constitutes a separate source of concern. The college students who experimented with marijuana in the 1960s were about five years older than the typical person initiating marijuana today, and earlier ages of initiation are associated with much greater likelihood of dependence and other problems.

How long does intoxication last?

The duration of the high depends on the potency of the drug, how much is used, how and in what environment it is used, and the user's history of marijuana use.

When marijuana is consumed in cigarettes ("joints"), less than half of the THC is inhaled and absorbed by the lungs; the rest is burned up in the smoking process or lost to the atmosphere. The THC enters the bloodstream and begins to reach the brain within seconds, but it takes longer for the concentration to build up; effects are typically perceived within a minute or two and peak after several minutes more.

Ingesting marijuana orally (e.g., eating marijuana-laced brownies) is less efficient: a smaller fraction of the THC ends up in the user's bloodstream. This fraction varies with what else is in the user's digestive system; the "bioavailability" of the active agents is much greater if marijuana products are con-sumed on an empty stomach. Compared to smoking, the effects of eating take longer to be felt, typically half an hour to two hours after ingestion. Both variable bioavailability and delayed onset undermine efforts to adjust the dosage level to get to some target high. That leads some users to eat more in the belief that the original dose wasn't strong enough, and this can cause problems. The effects of orally ingested marijuana also tend to last longer than smoked marijuana, because of slow absorption by the stomach. While a smoker who feels "too high" can stop smoking with the assurance of not getting much higher, a marijuana eater who starts to feel anxious still has to deal with whatever chemicals remain in the gut on their way to the bloodstream.

How long can marijuana use be detected?

Employers and criminal-justice agencies use chemical tests—primarily urine tests—to detect the use of banned drugs. For heavy users, marijuana remains detectable longer than most other psychoactive substances.

The body's fatty tissues store both some of the THC itself, and some of the metabolic by-products generated when the liver breaks THC down. Over time, the fat cells rerelease those chemicals into the bloodstream, though generally too slowly to have much subjective effect. Thus marijuana can be detectable in a user's system well after the high has abated, and there is no simple relationship between the amount of THC metabolite detectable in a user's urine and time since consumption. How long the chemical traces remain in the body depends on many factors, most notably the user's metabolic rate and the amount and frequency of marijuana use.

This variation makes marijuana testing a messy business. Most users will have detectable levels of THC in their urine within about thirty minutes of use. First-timers and infrequent users could expect to test positive for days after use, depending on how much they consume. Frequent users will typically have a much longer "detection window," because THC metabolites accumulate more quickly than they can be eliminated, and are released slowly. As a result, a frequent user could continue to test positive for weeks after he or she stops using.

Hair testing extends the detection window to months, and does so for many illicit drugs, not for marijuana alone. But hair testing—more complicated, more expensive, and slower to produce an answer—is much less common than urine testing.

Is medical marijuana the same as illegal marijuana?

Yes and no. It's the same plant, and it has the same chemicals in it; the molecules don't know whether they're legal or illegal, or why they're being used. In principle, medical users are taking a drug recommended by a physician to help some ailment, rather than trying to get intoxicated; in practice, that distinction tends to blur, especially in California. Some medical marijuana dispensaries, but not all, are more careful about what they sell than the typical illegal dealer: they test the material for pesticides, fungus, and mold, and sometimes label it for its content of the various active agents. High-potency marijuana and hashish seem to account for a larger share of dispensary sales than they do of strictly illegal sales.

There are also conventional, government-approved pharmaceuticals derived from marijuana. Synthetic THC in capsule form is an approved drug under the trade name Marinol. Sativex is roughly a 50/50 mixture of THC and CBD extracted from cannabis plants, prepared to be taken under the tongue, and sold legally as a medicine in some countries (but not yet in the United States). Unlike suppliers of either purely illegal or medical marijuana, the manufacturers of Sativex have standardized their product so that each dose has the same chemical composition.

What is synthetic marijuana (Spice or K2)?

Spice and K2—sometimes called "herbal incense"—are names of products that contain plant material mixed with synthetic chemicals whose effects are similar to those of cannabinoids. These drugs purportedly deliver a stronger high than natural marijuana—as reflected in the name "K2," which refers to the world's second-highest mountain. But their principal appeal is that they exploit a legal and chemical loophole. The U.S. Controlled Substances Act, and similar legislation elsewhere, outlaws the products of a specific plant (cannabis). It is possible to invent and synthesize similar chemicals that do not appear in the plant; these "designer drugs" thereby skirt the law. The Drug Enforcement Administration invoked its emergency authority to add (temporarily) five of these chemicals to the list of prohibited drugs, thus closing that legal loophole with respect to those specific chemicals, though not yet for similar compounds. The ban is likely to be made permanent, and could be augmented for new synthetics as they arise.

But in another way the chemical loophole will remain open for months or years. Synthetic marijuana is not included in most standard drug test panels. While a number of laboratories now are offering tests to detect the synthetics, most employers and criminal-justice agencies don't employ them yet. Moreover, the synthetics seem to be less fat-soluble and therefore will offer a shorter detection window. Thus some users are likely to continue to prefer the synthetics, despite their possibly greater health risks.

Additional Reading

Decorte, Tom, Gary Potter, and Martin Bouchard. *World Wide Weed: Global Trends in Cannabis Cultivation and Its Control.*

DuPont, Robert L., and Carl S. Selavka. "Testing to Identify Recent Drug Use."

Iversen, Leslie L. *The Science of Marijuana.*

Pollan, Michael. *The Botany of Desire.*

2

WHO USES MARIJUANA?

How many people use marijuana?

Globally, between 125 million and 200 million people use marijuana in the course of a year; that's 3–4 percent of the world's population aged 15 to 64, making cannabis by far the most widely used illicit substance. The amphetamine-type stimulants and the opioids come next, each with about a fifth as many users as marijuana. The prevalence of marijuana use in the United States is about three times the global average, though less out of line compared with other Western democracies. With almost 30 million Americans reporting use in the past year, marijuana use dwarfs that of any other illicit substance, and is dwarfed in turn by alcohol use.

Many American adolescents consume marijuana; 44 percent of 12th graders have tried the drug at least once, and 6 percent are daily users. The typical person who takes up smoking marijuana has just turned 16. This is similar to the typical age of first alcohol use, but lower than the initiation ages for other illicit drugs (for example, the median starting age for both cocaine and MDMA is 20). Marijuana use is highest among 18–25 year olds; their past-year rate (31 percent) is three times the U.S. average.

While national survey data show large numbers of marijuana users, the true number is even higher, because some respondents are reluctant to report their own illegal activities. A number of studies suggest that roughly 20 percent of marijuana users deny their use in these surveys, and one study involving adolescents and young adults puts the figure closer to 40 percent.

How is marijuana consumed?

Most commonly, it is smoked, usually in hand-rolled cigarettes, called "joints" but also in pipes and water-pipes called "bongs." In much of the world, marijuana is often smoked mixed with tobacco in hand-rolled cigarettes; that's not as common in the United States, but some U.S. users smoke "blunts": cigars in which the interior tobacco has been replaced with marijuana. While joints, bongs, and blunts all vaporize the active agents by burning the plant material—thus producing very hot smoke and many unhealthy combustion products—vaporizers rely on external heat, so users inhale a relatively cool vapor rather than smoke. This is less irritating to the throat and may also reduce adverse health effects.

As discussed in chapter 1, marijuana can also be added to foods or beverages. THC dissolves in fats and oils, and also in alcohol. Marijuana edibles are usually prepared by grinding the marijuana into a fine powder and then dissolving the powder into hot oil or butter. Any food that ordinarily contains fats can be prepared this way; among the more popular are marijuana brownies, cakes, or cookies. Dose management is a challenge when preparing an ingestible, and the preparer needs to ensure that the cannabis is spread evenly throughout the item. A potential downside of ingestibles is accidental consumption or overconsumption; one effect of marijuana intoxication is an increased appetite for sweet and salty foods.

Marijuana is sometimes prepared as a drink. "Green Dragon" is made from alcohol infused with THC (not to be confused with beer brewed with hemp seeds; those seeds contain no psychoactive chemicals). Marijuana can also be made into a tea, but (since THC is not water-soluble) the liquid needs to be milk or something else with fat in it.

The route of administration will affect the speed of onset and the nature and duration of the high in important ways: smoking hits harder and faster, while eating is slower and less predictable.

How has marijuana use changed over time?

While marijuana did not achieve mass-market status in the United States until the mid-1960s, historically it is among the oldest of the psychoactives. Archeological evidence of hemp cord dates back some 10,000 years, before the Neolithic Revolution and the invention of farming. The first recorded medicinal application was in China around 2700 BC. Early writings tell us that the Chinese were well aware of marijuana's psychoactive properties, but these were considered secondary to its value in healing the body. By contrast, marijuana use in India was not primarily medical; there are records of Indian religious use going back to 2000 BC. Hashish was known to the Arab world by the tenth century; while the Koran forbids alcohol, it makes no specific mention of marijuana. (Most Islamic scholars now consider marijuana to be forbidden.) Westerners were late adopters, with little interest in the intoxicating effects of marijuana until the early nineteenth century. Cannabis had been used for centuries as a medicine and fiber, but recreational use was first introduced to Western Europe by Napoleon's soldiers, who became acquainted with marijuana and hashish as intoxicants and painkillers while in Egypt. Napoleon was fearful of the threat he saw in this foreign habit and banned marijuana consumption. But the ban was ineffective, and returning soldiers introduced the drug to Europe.

Marijuana has had a peculiar history in the United States. In the Colonial era, cannabis was grown alongside tobacco, but for industrial use in making rope, cloth, and paper rather than as an intoxicating smokable product; in 1619 the Virginia Assembly passed legislation encouraging farmers to grow hemp:

> For hempe also both English and Indian and for English flax and Anniseeds, we do require and enjoine all house-holders of this Colony that have any of those seeds to make trial thereof the nexte season.

By the late nineteenth century, marijuana was a common ingredient in many medicines and was widely available, but widespread use of marijuana as an intoxicant began only in the early 1900s, when it was brought across the border by Mexican immigrants. By the 1920s it had been adopted by jazz musicians. Hostility to Mexican immigrants during the Great Depression spilled over to hostility toward what was thought of as a Mexican drug.

Government portrayals of the drug grossly exaggerated its negative effects. (The movie *Reefer Madness* is held up as the classic example of government anti-marijuana propaganda, but apparently falsely so; it is not clear either that the movie was government financed or that it was much watched before its resurgence in ironic form in the 1970s.) Marijuana's association with the predominantly African-American jazz culture further hurt its image among the white majority. By 1931, twenty-nine states had criminalized marijuana. The federal government encouraged all states to enact laws to control marijuana use through the Uniform State Narcotic Act of 1932; the Marijuana Tax Act of 1937 effectively made possession of marijuana as an intoxicant illegal. (It could still be prescribed as a medicine.)

Marijuana was part of the Beat culture of the 1950s, but use remained uncommon until the 1960s, when it was embraced by the hippie counterculture and spread rapidly across college campuses. The first U.S. survey of marijuana use was a Gallup Poll of college students in 1967, which reported a 5 percent lifetime prevalence of use. Marijuana use exploded from there. Within two years, the college student lifetime-prevalence rate had jumped to 22 percent, and by 1971 it reached 51 percent; by that time, high school students had also begun to use. In 1969, Stanford law professor John Kaplan published *Marijuana: The New Prohibition*, questioning the wisdom of keeping such a relatively benign drug illegal; that was followed in 1971 by Harvard psychiatry professor Lester Grinspoon's *Marihuana Reconsidered*. Those books helped generate a growing academic consensus, with some strong support among other opinion leaders and policymakers, that a primarily punitive approach to cannabis was misguided.

At the same time, President Nixon signed the Comprehensive Drug Abuse Prevention and Control Act of 1970, which included the Controlled Substances Act (CSA). The CSA served as the implementing legislation for the main international drug treaty (1961 Single Convention; see chapter 10), and is still the linchpin of federal drug policy. Among its many provisions, the CSA created a scheduling system which placed psychoactive substances (excluding alcohol and tobacco) into five categories largely based on their potential for abuse and medicinal value. Marijuana, along with heroin and LSD, was listed as a schedule I drug, defined as having high potential for abuse and no currently accepted medical use.

The 1970 Act also authorized creation of a National Commission on Marijuana and Drug Abuse, and President Nixon appointed former Pennsylvania governor Raymond Shafer to head the group, which included two senators and two representatives, and which became known as the Shafer Commission. Its report, issued in 1972 under the title *Marihuana: A Signal of Misunderstanding*, concluded:

> Neither the marihuana user nor the drug itself can be said to constitute a danger to public safety. Therefore, the

Commission recommends ... possession of marijuana for personal use no longer be an offense, ... [and] casual distribution of small amounts of marihuana for no remuneration, or insignificant remuneration no longer be an offense.

While the Shafer Report drew an immediate and vehement denunciation from President Nixon, its publication reflected the ongoing shift in elite opinion. The (rarely enforced) federal mandatory sentence of 2–10 years for marijuana possession was repealed, and many states followed suit; by the end of the decade, eleven states had decriminalized marijuana possession, and others reduced penalties. When President Jimmy Carter said in a message to Congress, "Penalties against drug use should not be more damaging to an individual than the use of the drug itself. Nowhere is this more clear than in the laws against the possession of marijuana in private for personal use," it seemed as if cannabis might be on the way to joining alcohol as a second socially sanctioned intoxicant.

Marijuana prevalence increased through the 1970s, reaching an all-time peak in 1979. More than 10 percent of high school seniors that year reported daily or near-daily use; that finding helped fuel the "parents' movement," which in turn helped bring an end to the era of liberalization. Perhaps the watershed event was the replacement of Carter drug policy adviser Peter Bourne, an advocate of marijuana decriminalization, if not outright legalization, with the more conservative Lee Dogoloff. Bourne was forced to resign due to reports about his own drug use and his illegally prescribing sedatives to a White House colleague. Ironically, the source of the story was one of the leaders of NORML, then the main marijuana-legalization advocacy group; the source was angry that Bourne was not pressing strongly enough for decriminalization.

With the advent of the Reagan administration, the 1980s saw increasing levels of anti-marijuana rhetoric. First Lady Nancy Reagan launched her "Just Say No" campaign, and officials perceived as "soft" on marijuana were forced out of their jobs. When marijuana use among high school seniors dropped throughout the 1980s, this was proclaimed—not necessarily correctly—as vindication of the hardline stance. Marijuana use then bounced back, nearly doubling during the early and mid-1990s, though still remaining below the levels reached in 1979–1980.

In 1996, California voters passed Proposition 215 (the Compassionate Use Act), allowing the medical use of marijuana by any patient with a physician's recommendation. This started a trend. By 2011, sixteen states and the District of Columbia, with a combined population of nearly 100 million, had enacted laws permitting medical marijuana use. These states' laws are at odds with federal law, which continues to prohibit possession, sale, and cultivation of marijuana (see chapter 12).

How much marijuana do users consume?

Users' consumption depends on where they live, what they are using, how long they have been using, and their reason for using. A typical joint in the United States contains just under half a gram of marijuana, and a single intake of smoke, or "hit," is about 1/20th of a gram. A joint of commercial-grade cannabis might get a recreational user high for up to three hours; one-third as much premium-priced sinsemilla might produce the same effect. A heavy user might use upwards of three grams of marijuana a day; the development of tolerance means that frequent users need more of the drug to get to a given level of intoxication than do casual users.

Many people who have used marijuana within the last year haven't used much of it. One-third report using on ten or fewer days, and more than half report that the last time they used it they got it for free (e.g., by sharing someone else's supply) rather than for money.

How much marijuana is consumed within a state, region, or nation depends on the relative numbers of lighter and heavier users as well as on the prevalence of the drug. Averaged over the two groups, it appears that consumption runs about 100 grams per user per year. With something fewer than 30 million American consumers, this rule of thumb would estimate national consumption at about 3,000 metric tons (MT). (A metric ton is 1,000 kilograms, or about 2,200 pounds, about 10 percent more than an English ton. Thus 3,000 MT is 3 billion grams or roughly 6 billion joints.) More detailed analyses—adjusting, for example, for likely under-reporting of an illegal activity on official surveys—suggest a figure closer to 4,000 MT. None of this is precise, but it's reasonable to think that U.S. consumption is probably between 2,500 and 5,000 MT per year.

Traditionally the bulk of marijuana appears to have been commercial grade, but in trying to calculate grams of THC consumed or hours spent under the influence, it matters greatly whether the high-potency fraction is 10 percent or 20 percent, since a gram of sinsemilla might have three times as much THC as a gram of commercial-grade cannabis. Alas, the share of high-potency cannabis isn't known with any precision.

Grossly inflated estimates of the quantity consumed are often heard. Legalization advocates and "drug warriors" agree on very little, but as economist Peter Reuter (then at RAND, now at the University of Maryland) pointed out many years ago, both find inflated estimates of production and consumption convenient for their rhetorical purposes. Fantastic quantities let legalization advocates project high potential tax revenues, and they let enforcement agencies justify requests for budget increases. Big numbers also suit journalists, who naturally prefer to write stories about what seem to be more important, rather than less important, topics.

Estimates from the production side are even weaker than the consumption data; for example, Peter Reuter has documented the capricious and implausible fluctuations in State Department estimates of production in Mexico. That creates additional scope for inflated estimates of the size of the market.

Can marijuana use lead to dependence or addiction?

Yes, but even among frequent marijuana users only a minority suffers from a substance abuse disorder.

"Addiction" is no longer a term in medical use; the technical terms are "abuse" and "dependence," where dependence is the more severe condition. Sometimes "addiction" is used to refer to dependence in its chronic, relapsing form.

Abuse and dependence are defined by the *Diagnostic and Statistical Manual of Mental Disorders* of the American Psychiatric Association, currently in its fourth edition (and thus called DSM-IV). To simplify, the DSM-IV definition of drug abuse is continued use of a substance in the face of adverse consequences. Dependence is defined as current use meeting three or more of the conditions:

1. Tolerance (needing more to get same effect)
2. Withdrawal (cessation causes a characteristic set of symptoms)
3. Using more than intended
4. Wanting to or having tried unsuccessfully to cut down on use
5. Spending considerable time obtaining and using the substance
6. Interference with important work, social, or other activities
7. Continued use despite knowledge of adverse consequences

Survey responses suggest that more than 8 million current marijuana users meet criteria 4 and 5; far fewer mention the other issues. For example, only 1.5 million report that their marijuana use is causing problems with work/school/home and with family or friends.

Taking all the criteria into account, the self-report data suggest that 2.7 million Americans met clinical criteria for marijuana dependence in 2009, and another 1.7 million met the criteria for abuse, so 4.4 million met the criteria for abuse or dependence (that's 1.7 percent of the population aged 12 and older). Estimates from Europe and Australia also find rates of marijuana abuse and dependence in the general population between 1 percent and 2 percent. This relatively small group accounts for a considerable share of total consumption.

But regular marijuana use does not necessarily indicate dependence. Only about 30 percent of those who are estimated to have used on more than half the days in the last year self-report symptoms that suggest a diagnosis of abuse or dependence. The corresponding figure for cocaine is 88 percent. Someone who uses cocaine every other day or more often is probably cocaine dependent; someone who uses marijuana every other day or more often is probably not cannabis dependent. In this regard marijuana resembles alcohol more than it does the "hard" drugs.

What are the typical patterns of marijuana use?

Broadly speaking, there are four types of marijuana users. There are experimenters, recreational users, and regular users, with the regular users further divided into those who do and those who do not meet criteria for abuse or dependence.

Among all those who have ever tried marijuana, the largest number are *experimenters* who have not (at least not yet) become regular users; 40–50 percent of people who have ever tried marijuana report a lifetime total of fewer than twelve days of use. This group is important numerically but unimportant in

terms of personal or social problems or in shaping the marijuana market.

Recreational users might use for an extended period, but usually only in a social setting, and never with much frequency or
intensity. Their primary motivation may be to share an experience with friends, boost confidence, reduce anxiety, enjoy
music, laugh, and relax. But cannabis is not a central fact in
their lives; more than half report consuming on a less-than-
weekly basis. Like experimenters, recreational users account
for only a modest share of total demand.

Regular users are in the minority, but they dominate market
demand; those who report using on 70 or more occasions in the
last year account for 90 percent of all reported days of use, and
perhaps an even larger proportion of the quantity consumed.
They split roughly 50/50 into those who meet the criteria for
abuse or dependence for some substance and those who do not
meet those criteria, but almost half of those meeting the criteria
do so for substances other than marijuana. E.g., in one particular
survey year the proportions were 53 percent not meeting the
criteria, 27 percent meeting the criteria for abuse or dependence
of marijuana, and 20 percent meeting the criteria for alcohol or
another illegal drug, but not for marijuana. (Mostly that is
alcohol; one-sixth of all marijuana use is reported by people
who met the criteria for alcohol abuse or dependence but did
not meet the criteria for marijuana abuse or dependence.)

How common is heavy marijuana use?

Relatively few people who try marijuana become heavy users,
but those heavy users consume most of the marijuana.

As mentioned above, almost half of the people who try marijuana report having used it fewer than twelve times total. In
any given year, the one-third of past-year users who consumed
on ten or fewer days account for only 1 percent of the
consumption, intoxication, and black-market revenues.

Conversely, the relatively small number of very frequent users account for a disproportionate share of those totals.

Household survey data suggest that about 6 million Americans aged 12 and over use marijuana on a daily or almost-daily basis; that fifth of past-year users account for at least 80 percent of the quantity of cannabis consumed, just as people who average two or more drinks per day account for 80 percent of the alcohol consumed. The even smaller group of heavy daily users, using multiple joints per day—the majority of whom meet criteria for cannabis dependency—consume a disproportionate share of this 80 percent. Heavy users not only use more frequently, they also tend to use larger doses. Current data aren't precise enough to tell us whether the share of all cannabis that goes to feed dependency is 40 percent or 50 percent or 60 percent, but that is the relevant range.

Figure 2.1 shows the frequency of marijuana use among those who reported using marijuana within the past year.

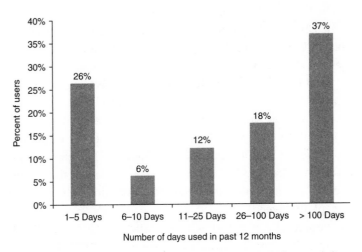

Figure 2.1 Frequency of Use among Americans Aged 12 and Over Who Used in the Past Year. *Data source: National Survey on Drug Use and Health, 2009.*

How does marijuana use vary across the country?

Marijuana is used all over the United States, with 6.4 percent of those aged 12 and older reporting that they used marijuana in the previous month. Regional variations are perhaps more modest than stereotypes would suggest: those living in the West (7.6 percent) and Northeast (7 percent) were only modestly more likely to be past-month users than those in the Midwest (6.1 percent) and South (5.5 percent). No state consumes at more than twice the national average; Alaska and Vermont are highest at about 11 percent, while Utah and Mississippi are lowest at about 4 percent. California comes in 13th at 7.7 percent.

What share of marijuana use is high-potency marijuana?

The large, nationally representative surveys do not ask users about the potency or quality of marijuana they use, but some insight can be obtained from chemical analysis of seizures and from the prices users report paying.

The Potency Monitoring Project (PMP), run by researchers at the University of Mississippi, analyzes the THC concentrations of cannabis confiscated in the United States. Most samples are classified as being either marijuana or sinsemilla (as opposed to ditchweed, hashish, or hash oil). While confiscated cannabis is not a representative sample of all cannabis consumed (and the samples sent to PMP are not even necessarily representative of all seizures), the trend seems clear: the proportion of samples classified as sinsemilla has grown from less than 10 percent before 2002 to over 40 percent today, and average potency has also been rising within each category (except ditchweed).

The second way to estimate how much marijuana is of high potency is to work backwards from users' reports of how much they paid. There are sharp differences between the price of lower-quality commercial grade and higher-quality sinsemilla.

In both the household survey and surveys of arrestees, 75–90 percent of respondents describe prices for their most recent purchase that are clearly below the range of prices typically charged for sinsemilla.

That proportion surprises some who think that these days "everyone" uses high-quality sinsemilla. It is important to remember, though, that connoisseurs are generally in the minority and that the average user may be more cost-conscious than the average person who writes about marijuana. Writers, including those who publish only on the Internet, tend to be better-educated than average. But college graduates account for only 14 percent of days of marijuana use reported in surveys versus 62 percent by people who have a high school education or less (including the 9 percent by those who are not yet 18). This wasn't always true; in the 1960s, cannabis use tended to be "upscale" demographically. But the bulk of marijuana consumed today is smoked by people both poorer and less educated than those whose views shape the public debate.

How much do users spend on marijuana?

Estimating spending seems like it should be trivial: just multiply consumption by price and you're done. Unfortunately, it's not that easy.

Survey respondents are so poor at answering questions about total spending that recent surveys ask only about the most recent purchase rather than about spending over a longer period. Further, quantity discounts complicate these calculations. An ounce of marijuana doesn't cost nearly as much as twenty-eight grams sold separately; the discounts are even steeper for pounds or kilos. What proportion of final sales are made at ounce-level prices rather than either gram-level or pound-level prices, is anyone's guess. The very heavy users who account for most cannabis consumption often buy in bulk and get volume discounts.

The standard reference on this question is a series of reports called *What America's Users Spend on Illegal Drugs*, produced by Abt Associates for the Office of National Drug Control Policy. Their most recent figure of $10.5 billion dates to 2000. In today's dollars that figure would be close to $14 billion. Beau Kilmer and RAND economist Rosalie Pacula, calculating the figure for 2005, arrived at an estimate of $20 billion in today's dollars.

Marijuana use has increased since 2005, so we would expect current retail expenditures to be larger. Reasonable estimates of the current total market value (medical plus purely illicit) might range between $15 billion and $30 billion; if the larger figure is right, the dollar volume of illicit marijuana transactions is now close to the dollar volume of illicit cocaine transactions; in the 2000 Abt report, cocaine accounted for half of all illicit drug revenues, with marijuana way behind.

Additional Reading

Kilmer, Beau, Jonathan P. Caulkins, Rosalie Pacula, and Peter Reuter. "Bringing Perspective to Illicit Markets."

Leggett, Ted. "A Review of the World Cannabis Situation."

Office of National Drug Control Policy. *Arrestee Drug Abuse Monitoring Program II.*

United States Department of Health and Human Services. *State Estimates of Substance Use and Mental Disorders from the 2008–2009 National Surveys on Drug Use and Health.*

3

HOW IS MARIJUANA PRODUCED AND DISTRIBUTED TODAY?

How and where is marijuana grown today?

Marijuana production is basically gardening. If marijuana were fully legal, it could be farmed, as industrial hemp is today in thirty or so countries around the world. But acres of marijuana fields are relatively easy to see and seize, so today in the United States it is mostly grown on a small scale.

Like tomatoes, marijuana can be grown outdoors or indoors, with or without soil. Some indoor production takes place in greenhouses, but growers often need to be more inconspicuous, so indoor production also occurs in basements, in individual rooms—sometimes hidden behind false partitions—and in "grow houses" (essentially single-family houses filled with plants). It is even grown in storage containers buried underground. Outdoor production likewise occurs in many places; the cannabis plant is hardy. But growing in federal parks and state forests ("guerrilla grows") is popular because there are few neighbors and there is no risk of having law enforcement seize the property on which the marijuana is grown.

Indoor growing is practical because yields per unit area are so high. Based on grow operations confiscated by Dutch police, horticultural scientist Marcel Toonen estimated densities of fifteen plants per square meter producing 33.7 grams of sinsemilla per plant per harvest. Assuming four harvests per year and a retail sales price of $375 per ounce (typical for sinsemilla in the United States), that implies revenues of $2,500 per square foot per year. So, marijuana grown on 1,000 square feet within a typical 2,000 square foot residential house could produce revenues of $2.5 million per year if sold as ounces, and more than $1 million per year even at wholesale prices.

In terms of cost per gram, per hour of intoxication, or per year of use, marijuana is much cheaper than cocaine or heroin. However, in terms of value per square foot at current U.S. retail (black market) prices, marijuana grown indoors can produce about five hundred times as much revenue per square foot as either coca or poppy crops do. Unlike cocaine and heroin, marijuana need not be extracted or refined; the dried plant material is the drug.

Marijuana can be and is grown almost anywhere. In places with less stringent enforcement (e.g., Mexico and Morocco) most marijuana is grown outdoors, with plants allowed to grow very large (producing just one harvest per year), yielding large quantities of commercial-grade marijuana of middling potency (4–6 percent THC). However, with the spread of higher-yielding varieties (e.g., via seed banks and clones) and readily available tips on growing at higher densities (notably via the internet), indoor growing—predominantly but not exclusively of higher-potency sinsemilla (10–18 percent THC)—has become increasingly common in industrial countries. Since illegal growers do not pay taxes or report their activities to government statistical agencies, it is very hard to estimate how much is grown in various places. We are reasonably confident that the majority of marijuana (by weight, if not by value) consumed in the United States is imported from Mexico; domestic production is the next largest source, with smaller amounts being imported from Canada, Jamaica, and a few other countries. Exact proportions are hard to pin down, but perhaps half to two-thirds comes from Mexico, one-fifth to two-fifths is produced within the United States, and the rest is imported from other countries. Since a larger share of U.S. and Canadian production is higher-potency, higher-value sinsemilla, those sources account for a larger share of the value than they do of the physical volume.

Within the United States there are good statistics on where law enforcement eradicates marijuana plants. California dominates for outdoor plants (74 percent of the 9.8 million plants in 2009) and to a lesser extent indoor plants (41 percent of the 300,000 indoor plants). Other prominent states include Washington (indoor and out), Tennessee (outdoor), and Florida (indoor). But we can't assume that seizure patterns mirror production or consumption patterns. For example, outdoor plants are much easier to discover than indoor plants, so one certainly should not conclude that 97 percent (9.8 million plants out of 10.1 million plants eradicated) of all U.S. production occurs outdoors.

How is marijuana currently distributed?

Cocaine and heroin distribution networks are long but fairly easy to describe. There are farmers in source countries whose products are processed through various stages, exported by professional smugglers, and then distributed through three to six distribution layers within the United States or other final market country.

Some marijuana is distributed in roughly similar ways, albeit with less processing in the source country and not so many distinct distribution layers within the United States. But some marijuana is homegrown by the user, and so is not "distributed" at all, or it is grown by a caregiver (in states with medical marijuana) or within a nonprofit co-op that shares marijuana among its members. (Chapter 14 describes how this happens in Spain.)

So there is no single distribution pattern.

Generally though, for imported marijuana the higher up the distribution chain one goes, the more marijuana distribution fits conventional notions of drug trafficking. While some Mexican marijuana is produced and/or smuggled by independent ("mom-and-pop") operators, most is smuggled by the extremely violent drug trafficking organizations (DTOs) that have been wreaking havoc on the Mexican people and institutions of government (see chapter 11 for more information on the DTOs). And in Canada, the Royal Canadian Mounted Police report that Vietnamese gangs and outlaw motorcycle groups are coming to dominate production in British Columbia.

The other end of the distribution chain could not be more different. Jonathan P. Caulkins and RAND economist Rosalie Pacula have observed that almost 90 percent of the National Survey on Drug Use and Health respondents report obtaining marijuana most recently from a friend or relative, and more than half report getting it for free. It is also common for heavier users to play the role of retail distributors without making it a principal source of income; they might purchase moderately large quantities and then sell to friends at cost, akin to the way one person might buy baseball tickets for a group and then get reimbursed for the cost of the others' tickets.

Thus, one end of the distribution chain can be enmeshed in brutal violence while the other is enmeshed in social networks and pleasantries. Even on the production end, the indoor growing rarely leads to violence.

How much is marijuana marked up between farm gate, wholesale, and retail?

The price of marijuana goes up markedly as it moves down the distribution chain from the grower to the user.

Commercial-grade marijuana of the sort produced in bulk in Mexico (4–6 percent THC) sells for $35–$50 per pound in

Mexico and $200–$500 per pound just inside the U.S. border. Within the United States, wholesale prices increase at a rate of about $400 per pound for every thousand miles away from the Mexican border, reaching $1,000–$1,400 per pound in the East and Northeast.

Prices per ounce for commercial-grade marijuana range from $70 to $230, depending on the location and number of ounces purchased. That reflects about a two-to-one markup relative to the pound price: an $800 pound package becomes sixteen $100 ounces. Similarly, buying in grams is more than twice as expensive per unit weight as is buying in ounces.

Of course quantity discounts aren't limited to illegal commodities; eight individual pints of milk cost about twice what a gallon costs. Nevertheless, marijuana price markups are substantial. So estimating the dollar value of the marijuana market by multiplying the total quantity consumed, in grams, by the price of one gram, is guaranteed to produce a wildly inflated estimate: since the lowest levels of distribution are mostly within social networks, with the supplier selling at cost or even giving the marijuana away, the final commercial transaction may more often be a sale at the ounce level. (Note: medical marijuana dispensaries are exceptional in this regard.) And if most final transactions are at the ounce level, the actual size of the marijuana market, in dollars, is only one-third to one-half as large as would be calculated by multiplying the gram-level price by 3.8 billion grams.

Prices for sinsemilla are higher across the board, but show similar markups. Growers might receive roughly $2,000 per pound (the "farm gate" price). Wholesale prices in California are typically $2,500–$4,000, with lower-level prices of $250–$400 per ounce (equivalent to over $5,000 per pound). Typically, an ounce of sinsemilla sells for one-tenth the pound price, meaning it costs 1.6 times as much to buy by the ounce as to buy by the pound. Gram prices are higher still.

Table 3.1 Excerpt of a Dispensary Menu in Northern California (Per gram price in parentheses)

	THC	Price in US Dollars		
		Gram	Eighth	Ounce
Sun Grown "Sweet Pea"	19.7%	12 (12)	35 (9.9)	240 (8.7)
Kush Blend	13.5%	14 (14)	45 (12.7)	295 (10.4)
Fire OG Kush	22.8%	15 (15)	50 (14.1)	325 (11.5)
Lemonade	14.2%	15 (15)	50 (14.1)	325 (11.5)
Jilly Bean	15.0%	16 (16)	55 (15.5)	360 (12.7)
U2 Kush	16.8%	16 (16)	55 (15.5)	360 (12.7)

Source: http://www.harborsidehealthcenter.com/menu.html (October 25, 2011)

Are prices lower in the Netherlands? California? Elsewhere?

Data collected by the United Nations Office on Drugs and Crime (UNODC) show prices are highest in affluent countries that do not have much domestic production (e.g., Japan, Singapore, and Hong Kong). The lowest prices are observed in less affluent countries in Africa, South America, and parts of Asia; cannabis resin (hashish) prices are particularly low in Pakistan and Iran, presumably because of proximity to Afghanistan, which is a major producer.

Within Europe, prices tend to be lowest in Spain, the United Kingdom, and some other parts of western and southern Europe. Prices are highest in the Scandinavian and Baltic countries.

Comparisons between Europe and North America are complicated by variation in everything from exchange rates to differences in the types and quality of marijuana. For example, cannabis resin is common in Europe but much less so in the United States, where herbal forms dominate.

Also, since the coffee shops in Holland are not allowed to advertise, we cannot simply pull their menus off the web as with dispensaries in California and Colorado. Yet data from the Netherlands Institute on Mental Health and Addiction suggest that the *nederwiet* sold in coffee shops in 2010 averaged 17.6 percent THC and was 8 euros (roughly $11) per gram. This seems only slightly less expensive than the dispensary price for equivalent potency in the United States.

Since marijuana is just a plant, why is it so expensive?

Marijuana is so expensive primarily because production and distribution are illegal, so they must be done surreptitiously and therefore inefficiently. Modern American agriculture is incredibly productive because it operates on such a large scale (much to the dismay of small family farmers) and harnesses technology, ranging from high-tech GPS systems in tractors to the hopper and conveyor a greenhouse farm might use to fill flats of seedling containers with soil. By contrast, marijuana production remains largely an artisanal activity dominated by batch processing in physical spaces not conducive to high productivity.

There is also inefficiency in distribution. A cashier and bagger at a grocery store make about one hundred times as many sales per person-hour as does a typical retail drug seller.

Wages are also considerably higher than those paid to typical agricultural workers. Marijuana producers pay a wage premium—even for low-skill tasks—because they can only employ people willing to take the risk of going to prison, and who can be trusted not to report their employers to the authorities. Stiffing a worker a dollar an hour is penny-wise and pound-foolish if the disgruntled worker can make an anony-mous call to the police.

People involved in drug distribution also have to be com-pensated for the risk of legal consequences. Miners and deep sea divers are paid a premium relative to above-ground construction workers doing otherwise comparable activities because of the greater risks of working in extreme environ-ments. Likewise, some of the money drug dealers make is better thought of as compensation for the risks they take rather than as pure wage income or profit.

However, compensation for risk is a smaller part of the story for marijuana than it is for other illegal drugs, such as cocaine (powder or crack) and heroin. To use the jargon of drug policy analysts, illegal drugs' prices are so high because of a combination of "structural consequences of product ille-gality" (meaning, inefficiencies created by having to operate covertly) and "risk compensation." For marijuana the struc-tural consequences are probably the greater part of the story, while for cocaine and heroin risk compensation may be more important, at least in the United States. Medical mari-juana dispensary prices are high in part for these same rea-sons; the production and wholesale distribution can still attract enforcement attention, even if retail dispensary sales do not. But there are other considerations as well. Although some medical marijuana dispensaries are merely fronts for supplying recreational use, others make a serious effort to provide a therapeutic service. They may offer higher-quality marijuana not just in the sense of having high THC content (that is, quality is not the same as potency) but also by providing predictable, controlled levels of THC and CBD, plants grown organically with no pesticides, etc. Likewise, some dispensaries provide ancillary services (e.g., consulta-tion and advice, free yoga classes). Those extras drive up costs relative to providing just marijuana as a recreational intoxicant.

Is marijuana really the nation's leading cash crop?

There is great irony in the idea that marijuana is the nation's leading cash crop, and the claim has been repeated so often as to have become dogma. Alas, the facts say otherwise. Analyses purporting to support the claim must contort the numbers, citing the retail price of marijuana but the farm-gate price of other products, or pretending that all marijuana consumed in the United States is sinsemilla, or ignoring the fact that most marijuana used in the United States is imported, or simply starting with implausible estimates of U.S. production.

One of the more frequently cited estimates comes from former NORML director Jon Gettman's 2006 report *Marijuana Production in the United States*. His estimate of $35.8 billion exceeds the Department of Agriculture figures he cites for corn ($23.3 billion), soybeans ($17.3 billion), and other crops. A $35.8 billion figure for marijuana farmers in the United States should raise a few eyebrows; it is larger than the best estimates of the *retail* sales value of *all* marijuana consumed in the United States—including the marijuana that is imported.

Broadly speaking, Gettman's $35.8 billion comes from multiplying a weighted average price of $1,606 per pound by production of 22.3 million pounds per year—most of which is consumed (10,000 metric tons per year) and a little of which is seized. (The details are actually a bit different because he does the calculations separately for indoor and outdoor plants, scaled in proportion to seizures.) Gettman claims that the $1,606 figure is conservative, because police value seized marijuana at $2,000–$4,000 per pound. Even leaving aside the incentives of police to present their seizures in the most favorable light, the figure is grossly unrealistic: $2,000–$4,000 is a wholesale, not a farm-gate, price, and it is the price of sinsemilla, while perhaps 80 percent of U.S. consumption consists of much cheaper commercial-grade marijuana.

As for the 10,000 metric ton figure, Gettman is right that it was published in various government reports, but it appears to trace ultimately to a Drug Availability Steering Committee (DASC) study. The DASC stated clearly that:

> the quantity of domestically produced marijuana that was available in the United States in 2001 is unknown. While the group did develop a methodology for determining such availability in the future, the uncertainty in the required data, some of which do not currently exist, is magnified by the model, and prevents the derivation of a credible estimate at this time.

However, DASC plugged in a set of "hypothetical values" (their words) meant only to illustrate how the arithmetic would be done if certain unknown parameters were to become known at some point in the future. The arithmetic yielded a range between 5,577 and 16,731 metric tons, whose rough midpoint of 10,000 metric tons has been magically transformed—through sheer repetition—into an estimate.

But that number simply doesn't make sense. Domestic production accounts for approximately one-third of U.S. consumption, so total consumption is three times domestic production. If domestic production were really 10,000 metric tons per year, then total consumption would be 30,000 metric tons per year, or 2,500 metric tons—2.5 billion grams—per month. Dividing 2.5 billion grams by 17 million past-month users would mean that the *average* (not the heaviest) user smoked almost 5 grams per *day*. If a joint contains about four-tenths of a gram, that would mean nearly *twelve joints per day*. When you get an answer that doesn't pass the giggle test, you know that (at least) one of your assumptions was seriously wrong. Since there aren't 17 million Americans who smoke marijuana from morning until night every day of their lives, there can't be a $35.8 billion domestic marijuana crop.

No one really knows the revenues from growing marijuana in the United States. A more credible baseline estimate would start with U.S. consumption of about 2,500–5,000 metric tons. Perhaps 15 percent of that is domestic production of commercial-grade marijuana with a farm-gate price of $600 per pound, and another 15 percent is sinsemilla worth $2,000 per pound at farm gate, most but not all of which is produced domestically. That suggests revenues from growing (as opposed to distribution, further down the chain) of around $2.1–$4.3 billion, rather than $35.8 billion. That would put marijuana in the top fifteen, but not the top five, cash crops, ranking somewhere between almonds and hay, and perhaps closest to potatoes and grapes.

Does marijuana production really use $5 billion worth of electricity in the United States each year?

No; this is another impossible number.

Evan Mills, a scientist at Lawrence Berkeley National Laboratory, generated the estimate that domestic marijuana production consumes $5 billion worth of electricity a year. The corresponding implications for greenhouse gas emissions sparked widespread media attention, even from such prominent thinkers as the authors of the Freakonomics blog. Alas, Mills started with the premise that U.S. production is 17,000 metric tons per year—at least ten times the true number.

Additional Reading

Decort, Tom, Gary Potter, and Martin Bouchard. *World Wide Weed*.

Kilmer, Beau, et al. *Altered State?*

Toonen, Marcel, Simon Ribot, and Jac Thissen. "Yield of Illicit Indoor Cannabis Cultivation in the Netherlands."

United Nations Office on Drugs and Crime. *World Drug Report* 2011.

4

HOW STRINGENT IS MARIJUANA ENFORCEMENT IN THE UNITED STATES?

Who gets arrested for marijuana possession?

All sorts of people, and in large numbers.

In 2010 there were more than 1.6 million state and local arrests for drug violations, constituting about an eighth of all arrests. More than half of those drug arrests were for marijuana offenses: 46 percent for possession plus 6 percent for marijuana sale/manufacturing. That's more than 750,000 arrests for marijuana possession. (Because some people are arrested more than once a year, the actual *number of people* arrested must be somewhat smaller.)

By comparison, there were 2.6 million arrests for public drunkenness, sales to a minor, driving under the influence, and other violations of liquor laws.

Figure 4.1 shows the number of marijuana-possession arrests over the last three decades; they have more than doubled over that period.

An "arrest" can mean many things, from handcuffs, a trip downtown, booking, and a jail cell to just getting a ticket or summons to appear before a judge. "Custodial" arrests—the ones with handcuffs—aren't usually counted separately.

Although the number of people arrested for marijuana possession appears strikingly high, nearly thirty million Americans use marijuana each year; only about 2.5 percent of users get arrested for possession in the course of an average year. Total days of use are estimated at about 3 billion per year, so there is about one marijuana-possession arrest per 4,000 days of use. Of course someone who uses over many years will face a much higher cumulative risk of eventually getting arrested.

Relatively few of those arrests result from police decisions to seek out and arrest marijuana smokers; most are by-products of other actions—mostly by uniformed officers rather than drug detectives—ranging from traffic stops to stop-and-frisks executed in the name of order maintenance. Sometimes marijuana charges replace other charges: if police find marijuana while responding to a domestic-violence complaint but the complainant is afraid to testify, a prosecutor might press the drug-possession charge instead. So 2.5 percent per year probably overstates the average arrest risk for someone who uses marijuana but otherwise does nothing to attract police attention.

Fluctuations in the number of marijuana arrests need not reflect either changes in the prevalence of marijuana use or changes in drug enforcement policy. A study by Bernard Harcourt and Jens Ludwig of the University of Chicago found that the pattern of marijuana arrests in New York City changed dramatically after the New York Police Department introduced "broken windows" policing in 1994. The broken-windows strategy is based on the premise that maintaining public order is as important as addressing other crimes, because reducing lower-level offenses makes neighborhoods seem safer and may prevent more serious crime. Harcourt and Ludwig found that arrests for smoking marijuana in public view multiplied 25-fold, from fewer than 2,000 arrests in 1994 to more than 50,000 in 2000. The goal behind the surge in arrests was maintaining public order, not suppressing marijuana use.

Order-maintenance policing is controversial. It has been associated with sharp declines in crime, but also with racially disparate impact. More than half of New York City's marijuana

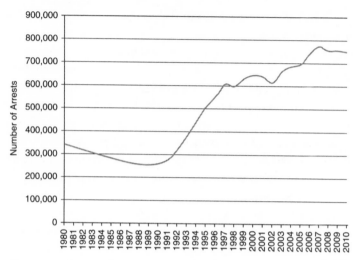

Figure 4.1 Arrests for Marijuana Possession in the United States (1980–2010). *Data source: Federal Bureau of Investigations: Uniform Crime Reports.*

arrestees in the last decade were black; only 14 percent were white.

Race is not the only risk factor. A study by Holly Nguyen and Peter Reuter of the University of Maryland found that men are more likely than women to be arrested for marijuana possession, and younger people than their elders. The disparities may reflect prejudice. For example, police officers tend to treat women more leniently than men, perhaps out of some sort of chivalry. But some part of the risk differences may be due to differences in the way that marijuana is bought and used. RAND behavioral scientist Rajeev Ramchand and his colleagues observed that—controlling for other factors—African American marijuana users were twice as likely to buy outdoors and three times as likely to buy from a stranger than other users, which might help explain part of why the marijuana arrest rate for African Americans is 2.5 times higher than would be predicted based on their prevalence of use alone. Nevertheless, such factors do not fully explain the disparities; the residual difference may hide a more sinister explanation.

What happens after those arrests?

Much less than some marijuana activists claim, but enough to represent a substantial cost of the current policies (and thus a potential gain from legalization or other policy changes).

In many jurisdictions, "arrest" for a misdemeanor such as marijuana possession typically means receiving a notice to appear in court, not being handcuffed and taken to a booking facility or a jail. These are referred to as "noncustodial" arrests; no one knows how many of the 750,000 annual marijuana-possession arrests are noncustodial.

Not all marijuana arrests lead to prosecution; prosecutors sometimes drop charges to focus their attention on more serious offenders. Even after conviction (usually by means of a guilty plea rather than a trial), what happens depends on the age of the offender, number of prior arrests, amount of marijuana possessed, and the jurisdiction: state laws vary, and even within the same state, local law enforcement practices can vary substantially.

Alaska has the most lenient statutory sanctions for possession of small quantities; possessing up to one ounce in a private residence is not considered a criminal act and carries no penalty. In California, Colorado, Maine, Massachusetts, and Nebraska, up to one ounce is considered a civil infraction or petty act that has no jail time attached, but users risk fines ranging from $100 (California and Colorado) to $600 (Maine). In some states, the fines increase for repeat offenders. Mississippi goes easy on first-time offenders, with only a fine of $100–$200 and no jail time. New York punishes possession of small quantities (twenty-five grams or less) with a $100 fine for a first offense, increasing to $200 for a second offense; third and subsequent offenses trigger a fine of $250 and jail time of up to fifteen days.

Florida is at the other extreme, with harsh laws for possession of small quantities of marijuana: carrying an ounce could in theory earn you up to five years in prison and a fine of $6,000. Again, actual sentences typically deviate from the written law; even in Florida, first-time offenders may be merely fined and put on probation.

Federal statutes also go relatively easy on first-time possessors of small quantities. However that leniency is largely symbolic since—outside federal lands such as the national parks and at the borders—federal agents rarely work cases involving anything less than hundreds of pounds of marijuana.

Possession of larger quantities of marijuana can be a misdemeanor or a felony depending on the amount being carried (the amounts vary by state) and the location of the arrest; many states impose stiffer sentences for possession in proximity to a school or recreation facility; as Will Brownsberger (then with the Harvard Medical School Division on Addictions) demonstrated, school-zone laws make the penalties systematically harsher in crowded urban neighborhoods than in less densely populated suburbs. Minnesota and Mississippi have the stiffest maximum penalties for possession of large quantities, imposing penalties of up to thirty years. Rhode Island has the strictest mandatory minimums: being caught with over 5 kg of marijuana will earn you twenty years plus a fine of $25,000–$100,000, and the sentence will double if possession occurs within three hundred yards of a school, playground, or park. But a "mandatory" sentence is mandatory only for the judge; prosecutors still have, and use, the discretion not to bring charges, or to bring lesser charges.

Although there is great variation across states in the severity of penalties for marijuana possession and sale, there is little systematic evidence of a relationship between statutory marijuana penalties and marijuana use, perhaps because of the large gap between the text of the laws and the sanctions actually imposed, which depend on risk of detection, probability of a sanction if detected, and magnitude of punishment if sanctioned.

Very few people convicted only of simple marijuana possession are incarcerated. The vast majority face a fine (very rarely over $1,000) or are placed into community supervision, where they are monitored closely, not so closely, or barely at all depending on the jurisdiction and their assessed risk for reoffending. On the other hand, those on probation or parole for other offenses, especially felonies, can, and sometimes do, go to prison if a drug test comes back "dirty." In one sense, you could say that those people were being punished for first breaking the law and then violating the rules of their conditional release rather than simply for using a forbidden drug. (Abstinence from alcohol can be a community supervision condition for probationers and parolees, even though alcohol is legal for nonoffenders.) But it's still true that some probationers and parolees are going to prison—or back to prison—as a result of smoking pot.

Even a simple possession arrest sometimes means spending a night or more in jail awaiting arraignment, and this constitutes a significant harm created by marijuana prohibition; spending time in jail is unpleasant, and much more dangerous than merely smoking pot.

Who gets arrested for marijuana dealing, production, and importing?

More than 100,000 people are arrested each year for growing or selling marijuana; that number, too, has been growing, though not as rapidly as arrests for simple possession.

Persons arrested for dealing marijuana tend to be young; half are under 23, with 18–23-year-olds accounting for about four-in-ten of all marijuana selling arrests. Juvenile sellers (aged 17 and younger) appear to face a lower risk of arrest than older youth and adults, perhaps because many younger

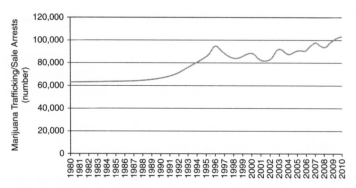

Figure 4.2 Arrests for Marijuana Trafficking/Sales in the United States (1980–2010). *Data source: Federal Bureau of Investigations: Uniform Crime Reports.*

"dealers" are schoolchildren selling to classmates or other members of their close social networks and therefore face less risk of detection than do professional dealers who sell to strangers in arm's length transactions.

Are federal marijuana sentences similar to sentences for heroin and cocaine?

No, not even close. Marijuana sentences are much lighter than those given for possessing or selling cocaine or heroin.

Federal mandatory minimum sentences are triggered (even for first-time offenders) for anyone caught with more than 100 grams of heroin, more than 500 grams of powder cocaine, or more than 28 grams of base cocaine (the category which includes crack). Table 4.1 describes federal penalties for marijuana; sentencing is based on quantities rather than dollar value or potency, and mandatory minimums for marijuana are reserved for amounts over 100 kilograms.

State penalties vary substantially and depend on the dealer's prior history and the amount possessed at the time of arrest. Except for a handful of states, selling—in some states,

Table 4.1 Federal Penalties for Marijuana Offenses

	First Offense	Second Offense	2 or More Prior Drug Felonies
50 kgs or less; or 1–49 plants	No more than 5 years. Fine of up to $250,000 if an individual, $1 million if not an individual.	No more than 10 years. Fine of up to $500,000 if an individual, $2 million if not an individual.	Life
50–99 kgs; or 50–99 plants	No more than 20 years. Fine of up to $1 million if an individual, $5 million if not an individual.	No more than 30 years. Fine of up to $2 million if an individual, $10 million if not an individual.	Life
100–999 kgs; or 100–999 plants.	5 year minimum, not to exceed 40 years. Fine of up to $2 million if an individual, $5 million if not an individual.	10 year minimum, no more than life. Fine of up to $4 million if an individual, $10 million if not an individual.	Life
1000 kg or more; or 1,000 or more plants	10 year minimum, no more than life. Fine of up to $4 million if an individual, $10 million if not an individual.	20 year minimum, no more than life. Fine of up to $8 million if an individual, $20 million if not an individual.	Life

merely possessing—even small quantities of cocaine and heroin trigger felony charges. By contrast, marijuana possession for personal use is often considered a misdemeanor or a civil infraction. Larger quantities would trigger a misdemeanor or a felony conviction, depending on the state. There's a great deal of discretion; for example, the San Diego U.S. Attorney's office routinely declines to prosecute marijuana cases involving less than 250 kg.

How many people are in prison for marijuana offenses?

About 40,000 state and federal prison inmates have a current conviction involving marijuana; perhaps half of them are in prison for offenses related to marijuana alone. The vast bulk of these inmates were involved in distribution; less than 1 percent of state and federal inmates are serving time for marijuana possession alone—and in many of those cases, the possession conviction was the result of a plea bargain involving the dismissal of more serious charges. Jacqueline Cohen of Carnegie Mellon University has shown that prisoners whose conviction charge was drug possession actually had more serious histories of violence than those convicted of violent crime; it takes an extraordinary criminal history to lead a judge to sentence someone to prison time for just possessing drugs, especially for just possessing modest quantities of marijuana.

Whether a marijuana arrest results in incarceration is influenced by many intervening variables: the quantity carried, the geographic location of the arrest, prior criminal history, and plea bargaining. One key determinant is criminal-justice status; an arrest while on probation or parole from a previous conviction is more likely to lead to incarceration than a similar arrest of someone who has no active criminal-justice status.

Not all kinds of marijuana sales carry the same risk of arrest or incarceration. Dealing that takes place discreetly behind closed doors, especially if embedded within social networks, carries little risk of arrest, in part because neighbors and passers-by don't notice and don't call the cops. The serious arrest risk comes from selling outdoors, and serious sanctions come from distributing large quantities (even if the defendant had only a small role within an organization transporting larger quantities) or having a weapon.

Patterns of drug dealing are not identical across races. In poor, urban, minority neighborhoods, marijuana dealing is more likely to take place outdoors. This makes marijuana dealers in those areas more vulnerable to arrest and incarceration.

How much does marijuana incarceration and enforcement cost?

The total cost of marijuana incarceration depends on how many people are behind bars because of marijuana and how much it costs to keep each of them locked up. Estimates are plagued by uncertainty in the number of people incarcerated *because of* marijuana's illegality, as opposed to being incarcerated with a marijuana conviction alongside other convictions for which the person would have been incarcerated anyhow. Reasonable estimates put total annual incarceration costs for inmates at state and federal facilities serving time on marijuana charges at about $1.2 billion: about 40,000 prisoners at about $30,000 per prisoner per year. The corresponding figure for people in prison *because of* marijuana charges—in the sense that but for marijuana's illegality they would be free—is perhaps half as large. To that figure must be added the cost of housing people in city and county jails who are awaiting trial, sentencing, or arraignment, or those who were sentenced to jail (rather than prison) on marijuana charges. If one assumed that half the 750,000 marijuana possession arrests are custodial (there is no data source that tracks this, so this calculation is purely illustrative), and arrestees average two days locked up before seeing a judge—that's an additional 750,000 jail days over the course of a year, or just over 2,000 cells, at a cost of about $60 million dollars per year. A total cost figure would have to include a host of other pre- and post-incarceration costs, such as policing, courts, and community corrections (probation, parole, and pre-trial release).

How much marijuana is seized and eradicated?

The DEA reports that in 2010 state and federal agencies eradicated almost 10 million outdoor marijuana plants and half a million indoor plants. Much of the indoor product seized is high-potency sinsemilla; much of the outdoor product is lower-value commercial grade, and a substantial chunk is worthless "ditchweed."

Lower-to-mid-level marijuana distribution tends not to be very violent in the United States, particularly as compared to distribution of the other major illegal drugs. But the 8,100 marijuana-related arrests were accompanied by seizure of 4,100 weapons, which suggests either that growing tends to be an armed activity—perhaps to defend the plants from "patch pirates" who steal the harvest from the growers—or that enforcement agencies are deliberately targeting the most violent growers.

Seven states, referred to as the "M7 states," account for about 90 percent of the marijuana cultivated in the United States. These states—California, Hawaii, Kentucky, Oregon, Tennessee, Washington, and West Virginia—are the focus of current eradication operations.

California leads in both cultivation and eradication. California accounts for just 6 percent of the outdoor sites but three-quarters of the outdoor plants eradicated.

Additional Reading

Federal Bureau of Investigation. *Crime in the United States 2010.*
Kleiman, Mark A. R. *Marijuana: Costs of Abuse, Costs of Control.*

National Drug Intelligence Center. *Domestic Cannabis Cultivation Assessment* 2009.

Ramchand, Rajeev, Rosalie Liccardo Pacula, and Martin Y. Iguchi. "Racial Differences in Marijuana-Users' Risk of Arrest in the United States."

Sevigny, Eric L., and Jonathan P. Caulkins. "Kingpins or Mules."

5

WHAT ARE THE RISKS
OF USING MARIJUANA?

Marijuana use has risks. Some are well established; some are probably real; some turn out to be mostly imaginary. The key domains include:

- marijuana dependence and creating a need for treatment
- overdose, fatal and nonfatal
- emphysema and other respiratory problems
- cancer
- secondhand smoke
- increasing the likelihood of future hard drug use (both the "gateway effect" among youth and the effect of marijuana dependence; see chapter 11)
- impaired mental health
- adverse education and employment outcomes
- automobile crashes
- effect of parental use on children

Why is it difficult to measure the consequences of marijuana use?

Estimating the extent of marijuana-related damage to users, their families, their neighbors, and the wider public is complex.

The hard truth is that the scientific community has not reached a consensus on many of these questions, so both sides of the legalization debate can refer to published studies that support their arguments and claim that the other side is ignoring the science. But the uncertainties are important.

One reason for the lack of consensus is that marijuana is not a standardized good—some studies are based on those who used commercial-grade marijuana; others have been conducted with populations that have had easier access to sinsemilla. To the extent that THC and other cannabinoids influence the outcomes of interest, this may explain some of the inconsistencies. The lack of standardization also makes it hard to precisely measure the amount of marijuana consumed, which in turn makes comparisons across studies difficult. Likewise some studies look for effects from any exposure to marijuana, however infrequent, while others focus on frequent or dependent use.

Much of the uncertainty comes from the fact that it is difficult to determine whether marijuana use *causes* negative consequences or just happens to be *correlated* with them. For example, it turns out that marijuana use is more common among people who drop out of high school, commit property crime, or use cocaine than among those who stay in school, do not commit crimes, and do not use cocaine. Thus marijuana is correlated with those outcomes. Does this mean that marijuana *caused* the outcomes? Not necessarily.

Uncertainty about causality also arises because of the classic chicken-or-egg question that comes up frequently in discussions about marijuana and mental health. While some argue that marijuana use aggravates mental health problems, others note that users may be using marijuana to self-medicate an already-existing illness. Both explanations may be correct—about different people, or even about the same person at different times.

Determining which relationships are causal is always difficult and sometimes impossible. The rules that protect the human subjects of scientific research forbid some of the controlled experiments in laboratories that might allow scientists to make clear causal attributions. For example, researchers obviously cannot take a classroom of 8th graders, offer pot to half of them, and then wait five years to see if those offered pot were more likely to drop out of high school.

How do researchers study the risks of marijuana use?

There are a variety of approaches for learning about the effects of marijuana. Some scientists ask marijuana users to smoke a few joints before taking the wheel of a driving simulator; others (after getting informed consent) simply inject THC into their subjects and observe how they react.

Much of the non-laboratory research uses a "longitudinal" design: following a group of individuals—often students or patients—for several years, and assessing whether those who use marijuana are more likely to experience certain outcomes (e.g., getting arrested for a property crime, being diagnosed with cancer). When researchers do find a correlation between marijuana and a particular outcome, they first look to see whether the marijuana use actually preceded the outcome of interest. If so, the researchers then try to control for other factors that could be driving the relationship. For example, one possible explanation for why kids who commit property crimes are more likely to use marijuana is that lack of parental supervision can contribute to both behaviors. Researchers can try to correct for such factors statistically, but each of those corrections is subject to error. Of course, even with the same parenting, some kids are more inclined than others to take risks. No matter how many of these "common cause" or "third-factor" explanations have been ruled out, there are always more that might be relevant, and researchers can only address so many questions in one study. Thus no single result can really nail down causation. However, if multiple studies from multiple countries covering different cohorts consistently tell the same story, it becomes harder to maintain there is no causal relationship.

Some researchers study jurisdictions where marijuana use is more common and examine whether certain outcomes are more likely in those areas; again, the arrow of causation could point in either direction. Economists have developed some clever strategies to address this issue, and they are always searching for policy changes and other "natural experiments" that influence marijuana consumption but not their outcome of interest.

Even when different studies on the same topic yield opposing results, that doesn't mean you should throw up your hands and conclude that the answer is simply unknown or unknowable. Some studies are simply better than others (e.g., superior research designs, larger sample sizes, longer time frames, use of advanced statistical techniques), and the answers from the better studies should carry more weight. Careful reviews of the research will take the quality of these studies into account when drawing conclusions about what the research says. It's harder to correct for the biases of researchers, funding agencies, and journal editors.

What is the likelihood of becoming dependent on marijuana?

Doctors have a checklist they use when they suspect that someone's marijuana use is causing problems (see chapter 2). A patient who exhibits three or more of these characteristics at any point in a twelve-month period meets the clinical definition for marijuana dependence. Of people in the United States who report having used marijuana at least once in the last month, one in eight met clinical criteria for marijuana dependence at some time in the previous year.

Asking "What share of current users have a drug problem?" isn't the same as asking "What's the risk of developing a drug problem for someone who starts using marijuana?"

Epidemiological studies by James Anthony and colleagues found that about 9 percent of those who had used marijuana wound up being clinically dependent on marijuana at some point in their lives, with males being at much greater risk than females. The comparable "capture rates" for alcohol and cocaine were 15 percent and 16 percent, respectively.

Anthony and his colleagues examined a cross-section of the U.S. population in 1990–1992, many of whom did not first use marijuana until they were adults for the simple reason that marijuana was not widely available when they were teens. (Marijuana did not become popular or widely available until the late 1960s and 1970s.) Initiating after young adulthood is now quite rare; in recent years 97 percent of new users were 24 or younger. Anthony reports that for those who first used marijuana before the age of 25, the probability of becoming dependent was considerably higher—15 percent, not 9 percent.

The larger figure is also consistent with evidence from three major longitudinal studies, two conducted in New Zealand and another in Australia. The New Zealand studies followed entire cohorts of children born in a city in a particular year and found that 9–10 percent of the cohort met the criteria for marijuana dependence at age 21. Adjusting for those who never tried marijuana at all, the probability of dependence at age 21 among those who did try it was over 13 percent. The Australian study tracked nearly two thousand youth into early adulthood and found that 20 percent of those who had used as adolescents exhibited dependence at age 24.

For the United States, 15 percent should not be considered an upper bound for dependence rates for today's youth. Among other reasons, the THC content of marijuana is higher now than it was in the 1960s through the 1980s; capture rates might be higher for those who start on today's more potent marijuana. A study by Wilson Compton and colleagues at the National Institute on Drug Abuse found that the risk of marijuana dependence increased throughout the 1990s in the

United States, especially for young black men and women and young Hispanic men. Since they did not find evidence of an increase in the frequency or quantity of marijuana used during the 1990s, they speculate that the increase in THC may be responsible for the increase in dependence.

How bad is marijuana dependency compared to dependency on other drugs?

Regardless of the particular substance or behavior, no one wants to experience dependence, or have a family member, friend, or colleague suffer through addiction. The uncertainty and disappointment associated with dependence—as well as the possibility of health and financial risks—impose important costs on users and their intimates.

Medical professionals essentially use the same checklist to determine whether someone has a drug problem no matter what the drug is, but not all abuse and dependency is created equal. Marijuana dependence does not, on average, create the same social and personal problems as alcohol or heroin dependence. For example, heavy marijuana users can experience withdrawal, but the physical discomfort generally pales in comparison to that experienced by those with serious addictions to heroin or alcohol. Withdrawal from alcohol can be more than painful; if not properly supervised, it can even be fatal.

Robin Room and his colleagues found that marijuana posed less addictive risk than tobacco, alcohol, cocaine, stimulants, or heroin, not only in terms of likelihood of dependence but also the degree of dependence, which they characterize as "weak." Their judgment is widely shared among experts. This finding does not deny that there are people who struggle to control their consumption or that marijuana dependence imposes a burden upon some users and their families; it just suggests that the intensity of marijuana dependence is generally less severe than dependence on some other well-known substances.

How many users seek treatment for problems with marijuana?

A large number of people, but a small share of heavy users.

In 2009, marijuana accounted for more than 350,000 drug treatment admissions in the United States. That's roughly 2 percent of all 17 million current users (defined as those reporting use in the month before being surveyed). This admissions figure has almost quintupled since 1992; marijuana is now second to alcohol and ahead of cocaine or heroin. This increase is not unique to the United States; in recent years Europe and Australia experienced more than a doubling in treatment admissions for marijuana and hashish.

Most of those receiving marijuana treatment are adolescents and young adults, with almost half (46 percent) of admissions involving those below the age of 21. By contrast, almost half (47 percent) of those entering treatment for cocaine were 40 or older.

There are a number of reasons why users enter treatment. Some enter on their own because they need help; some are nudged by their family, friends, counselors, employers, or lawyers; and others are ordered by their parents or the court to enter treatment. In fact, more than half of those entering treatment in the United States are referred by the criminal justice system. While some of these individuals would have eventually entered treatment anyhow, many are only there because they were court-ordered to be there; some of them, and some of the minors forced into treatment by parents or schools, may not in fact meet the clinical criteria for abuse or dependence.

On the other hand, this 350,000 figure does not count those who only attend 12-step programs (such as Marijuana Anonymous) or other self-help groups. Since no one takes attendance at such meetings, there are no precise estimates of how many people take this road to recovery. But the 2009 U.S. household survey estimates that more than 2.3 million people attended a self-help group for their illicit drug use in that year (1.7 million of them went for both illicit-drug and alcohol use). Of those people, 16 percent met clinical criteria for marijuana abuse or dependence in the previous year, though how many sought help specifically for marijuana use is unknown.

Does marijuana treatment work?

The intensity, and therefore costs, of treatment programs can vary dramatically. Outpatient programs can cost less than $1,000, while some residential programs cost tens of thousands of dollars per episode. In the United States, about 85 percent of marijuana treatment is provided by outpatient as opposed to residential programs.

Roughly half of those who enter marijuana treatment complete their programs (more for residential, less for outpatient). That may sound bad, but it is actually better than the corresponding rates for some other substances. Still, not even those who complete the programs were necessarily abstinent during or after treatment.

Most of the rigorous research on drug treatment has focused on substances other than marijuana; however, there are a growing number of randomized controlled trials specific to treating marijuana users. University of Connecticut psychologist Tom Babor and colleagues with the Marijuana Treatment Project Research Group found that adults assigned to treatment had lower rates of marijuana use 12 months later than did those who received no treatment. They also found that those assigned to the more intense treatment intervention had lower rates of marijuana use at follow-up than those receiving the less-intense treatment.

The story is not as clear for adolescents. A study by Michael Dennis, a psychologist at the Chestnut Health Systems, and colleagues randomly assigned marijuana treatment seekers into five different interventions. A decrease in use was detected for all five groups up to twelve months after entering treatment, but the authors found "only limited evidence that simply increasing the dosage of [marijuana] treatment had a differential effect on substance use and associated problems." The study did not include a no-treatment control condition, so it could not assess whether the interventions were better than none at all.

A review of the efficacy of outpatient marijuana treatment by Alan Budney, of the University of Arkansas Psychiatry Department, and colleagues suggests that incorporating contingency management (which provides small rewards for those who test clean for marijuana) into traditional interventions shows promise for reducing marijuana use. However, Budney and colleagues note that many community-based providers remain ambivalent about using contingency management because some are uncomfortable with providing incentives for abstinence; it also requires resources that many treatment centers do not have.

For the more expensive illegal drugs such as cocaine and heroin, studies show that even modestly successful treatment programs more than pay their way in reduced crime and other social costs. Since marijuana dependency tends to create fewer social burdens, and since marijuana treatment outcomes haven't been studied as closely, we do not yet have anything like a social benefit-cost analysis for the marijuana treatment effort.

Can users experience a fatal overdose from marijuana?

Even as late as the 1970s, the "drug prevention" literature made claims of marijuana-related fatalities. But those accounts fly in the face of what the science actually tells us.

Robert Gable of the psychology department at Claremont Graduate University estimated the "safety ratio" for various drugs (more formally the "therapeutic index"). Roughly speaking, this is the ratio of the average fatal dose to the average recreational dose. Bigger ratios mean greater safety.

The ratios for heroin, alcohol, methamphetamine, and cocaine range from about six to fifteen. A factor of six may sound like a pretty good margin, but not every person—or even every day or dose—follows the averages. There is no known fatal dose of marijuana; Gable estimates that if there is such a dose it must be at least one thousand times the amount typically consumed.

Gable's review only identified two deaths reported in the world medical literature that could possibly be attributable to a marijuana overdose, and University of Toronto pharmacologist Harold Kalant commented that these two deaths "probably involved individual risk factors without which the marijuana alone would not have been fatal."

There are, however, official statistics in the United States suggesting that marijuana can kill. The Centers for Disease Control's WONDER database reports that there were twenty-six deaths between 1999 and 2007 coded as mental and behavioral disorders due to use of cannabinoids—with ten different sub-categories. Half of the twenty-six deaths were attributed to dependence syndrome. It is unclear how to reconcile the Gable and Centers for Disease Control figures; that half the Centers for Disease Control–recorded deaths were attributed to dependence suggests that the proximate cause of death may have been something other than an overdose. But even if all twenty-six were overdose deaths, three deaths per year would work out to a rate of only about one per 10 million person-years of use (one in 10 million is roughly the death risk from taking a single commercial airline flight in the United States).

The fact that marijuana is not directly fatal does not mean it poses no acute risks. There can be interactions with other drugs. Notably, marijuana's capacity to prevent vomiting, which makes it appealing to some people undergoing chemotherapy, becomes a danger for those overindulging in alcohol, because vomiting is one of the body's defenses against poisoning.

Can users experience a nonfatal overdose from using too much marijuana?

Yes.

Tens of thousands of people end up in hospital emergency departments every year for reasons related to their marijuana use. The DAWN system (Drug Abuse Warning Network) estimates how many emergency department (ED) visits result from "accidental ingestions and adverse reactions as well as explicit drug abuse." In 2009, DAWN recorded more instances (or "mentions" to use DAWN's technical term) of marijuana (375,000 per year) than any other illegal drug save cocaine (425,000). The marijuana figure was almost double the number for heroin (215,000) and far more than MDMA (25,000). Nevertheless, marijuana is much more widely used than the others, so the probability of an ED mention per user is lower for marijuana than for cocaine or heroin.

For a long time people tended to assume the marijuana mentions all stemmed from interactions or just piggybacked on some other substance (e.g., heroin caused an overdose of someone who also happened to have used marijuana recently, but the marijuana use was incidental). And that is probably the right interpretation of the majority of the marijuana mentions. Nevertheless, for many tens of thousands of ED visits marijuana is the only drug mentioned.

Few of those marijuana emergency department episodes translate into hospital stays; the vast majority of patients are treated and released without ever being admitted to the hospital. When looking at all of the hospital admissions for California in 2008, RAND economist Rosalie Pacula found that there were only 181 inpatient admissions where marijuana abuse or dependence was the primary reason for hospitalization; however, when the analysis was extended to examine second, third, or fourth diagnoses, marijuana was mentioned in more than 25,000 of the admissions (still less than 1 percent of all California hospital admissions).

Does marijuana use cause emphysema and other respiratory problems?

Inhaling smoke on a regular basis is not good for one's lungs, regardless of whether the smoke came from the leaves of marijuana, tobacco, or, for that matter, maple trees.

Marijuana smoke contains many of the same irritants as tobacco smoke, and in a systematic review of the evidence on long-term marijuana smoking, Veterans Affairs epidemiologist Jeanette Tetrault and colleagues reported an association with increases in respiratory symptoms (e.g., cough, phlegm, and wheeze). However, they did not find a consistent association with pulmonary functioning. Studies examining the latter were more likely to account for tobacco smoking, but the authors argue that most of these studies used inferior measures of tobacco exposure.

The vast majority of research on the health consequences of marijuana focuses on smoked marijuana, but smoking is only one way to take the drug (see chapter 2). In addition to eating marijuana-infused foods or using cannabinoid-infused lotions, consumers can also use vaporizers that heat marijuana to a point where cannabinoids can be inhaled but below the point of combustion. Some research finds that vaporized marijuana contains fewer toxins than smoked marijuana, and a preliminary study suggests that moving from smoking to vaporizing marijuana may improve respiratory functioning among users. One possible benefit of marijuana legalization might be to increase the use of vaporizers rather than joints.

Does marijuana use cause cancer?

Marijuana smoke contains known carcinogens. What is not clear is whether exposure is great enough to cause cancer. Marijuana users typically inhale more deeply than cigarette smokers, but marijuana users consume far less marijuana than regular cigarette smokers consume tobacco: while a pack a day (20 grams of tobacco) is a typical cigarette habit, 4 grams a day is an extremely heavy marijuana habit. What is lacking is clear epidemiological evidence from population studies showing that groups who smoked marijuana had higher rates of cancer than otherwise similar groups that abstained. The published research shows mixed results.

A 1997 study by Kaiser Permanente researcher Stephen Sidney and colleagues followed 65,000 individuals for an average of eight years to examine cancer incidence. They found that using marijuana in the past or being a current marijuana user did not increase the risk of respiratory cancer. Another study by University of Utah professor Mia Hashibe and colleagues showed that marijuana does not increase the risk of lung or upper-aerodigestive-tract cancers, after accounting for cigarette smoking.

On the other hand, a study by Sarah Aldington and colleagues affiliated with the Cannabis and Respiratory Disease Research Group found that smoking the equivalent of a joint a day for a year increased the probability of lung cancer by 8 percent, after controlling for cigarette consumption. (That's 8 percent of the relatively low base rate for lung cancer, not an 8 percent chance of getting cancer.)

An international review by University of Melbourne sociologist Robin Room and colleagues found only one study suggesting that marijuana was positively associated with oral cancer—and the cancer risk was small. Other studies found no relationship. Room and his co-authors observe that "the findings from the case-control studies of lung cancer are more suggestive of higher risks, but the measures of cannabis use in these studies have been relatively crude and it is unclear how well these studies have been able to control for tobacco smoking."

Once again, it is important to note that these risks involve smoking; there are other ways to consume marijuana (see chapter 2).

In part, the answer to the cancer question depends on the level of proof one demands. There are literally hundreds if not thousands of careful studies using various methods that show that smoking tobacco causes cancer. The literature on marijuana and cancer does not even begin to approach that level of evidence.

However, tobacco is the exception, not the rule, in being so well studied and the number of cancers caused being so large. In many contexts we do not wait for epidemiological studies before drawing conclusions. Food manufacturers are not allowed to add known carcinogens to their products regardless of whether there are or are not epidemiological studies documenting an increase in cancer at the population level. On the other hand, cigarettes have not been banned, despite the overwhelming evidence that they cause cancer and a host of other ailments.

But the debate about marijuana and cancer is more complicated than just assessing whether or not smoking marijuana causes cancer. A number of studies suggest that some cannabinoids can inhibit the growth of tumors. (This is a separate issue from the use of marijuana in managing cancer symptoms and chemotherapy side-effects, discussed in chapter 7.) Most of this research has been done in the laboratory, with cells in petri dishes or with animals, and there are questions about how the results might translate to humans.

How much harm does secondhand marijuana smoke cause?

Since marijuana smoke contains carcinogens and other contaminants, it is possible that secondhand marijuana smoke could pose health threats to those who spend a lot of time around heavy users. Again, quantity matters: the average past-month marijuana smoker consumes less than 200 grams a year, while the average cigarette smoker goes through more than 100 grams (five packs) a week. Less smoke suggests less secondhand risk. While there have been thousands of studies on the impact of secondhand tobacco smoke, the literature is almost silent when it comes to secondhand marijuana smoke.

As long as marijuana remains illegal and drug tests are used in employment, schooling, and criminal-justice settings, there's another potential secondhand risk: that someone could test positive for marijuana after being around someone who was smoking marijuana. To address this question a chemist at Lehigh University led a study in the Netherlands which involved putting eight people into an unventilated passenger van and having four of them smoke one marijuana cigarette each. After an hour the passengers left the van, and their saliva and urine was tested for the next eight hours. While some THC was detected in the nonsmokers' saliva and urine, none of the nonsmokers exceeded the thresholds used to confirm marijuana use. This is consistent with other research suggesting that it is unlikely that passive exposure to marijuana will lead to a positive urine test (or unintentional intoxication). Thus, the problem of false positives is really only a concern for hair tests, and this has become less of a problem since tests now focus on detecting THC metabolites instead of THC itself.

Is marijuana a "gateway drug"?

Kids who use marijuana—particularly those who start marijuana use at a young age—are statistically much more likely to go on to use other drugs than their peers who do not use marijuana.

What is not at all clear, however, is whether marijuana use *causes* subsequent use of other drugs or whether it is merely a *signal* indicating the presence of underlying social, psychological, or physiological risk factors—such as weak parental supervision, a taste for intoxication, or a willingness to take risks—for both early marijuana use and later hard drug use. There have been some well-done studies with twins (comparing one who used marijuana with the other, who did not) that implicitly control for genetics and unmeasured family background, and some find evidence consistent with the gateway hypothesis. But once again, the question is how much of the correlation reflects causality.

Since most people have opportunities to try marijuana before they have opportunities to use harder drugs, marijuana use might precede hard drug use even if both are caused by the same underlying personality traits. Indeed, Andrew Morral and colleagues at RAND's Drug Policy Research Center have shown that such explanations are completely consistent with available data.

However, the fact that causal connections are not needed to explain the observed correlations does not mean there is no causal connection. At least two very different mechanisms might produce a causal "gateway" effect. One is the consequences of the drug use itself. For example, trying marijuana might increase the taste for other mind-altering experiences or lead users to revise their judgments about other substances, inferring that they are more pleasurable or less risky than previously supposed. The causal effect could also lie in social interactions. If acquiring and using marijuana leads to greater contact with peers who use and favor the use of drugs generally, those peer interactions might influence subsequent behavior. One version of this conjecture is that those peers could include people who sell other drugs, reducing the difficulty of locating potential supplies.

The same logic applies to the two drugs that typically come before marijuana in the developmental sequence: alcohol and nicotine. Early use of those drugs is a strong predictor of heavy marijuana use and of progression to harder drugs.

It also makes sense to distinguish between the very common use of marijuana and the less common heavy use of marijuana; their effects on later drug use are not necessarily similar. Drug dependency leaves its mark on the brain for some time after actual drug taking stops. It wouldn't be surprising if one of its effects turned out to be increased vulnerability to dependency on other drugs (or nondrug behaviors such as gambling). Since the evidence simply isn't in, a degree of humility is in order. That applies especially when we try to project our current knowledge—all of it gathered under prohibition—to the effects marijuana might have as a legal drug. The gateway effect could be stronger if the "vulnerability to dependency" story is right and if legalization turns out to increase the rate of progression to very heavy use, or weaker if the gateway effect stems from use of illegal marijuana bringing youth into contact with suppliers of other illegal drugs.

Few topics related to drugs have stirred more acrimonious debate than the gateway hypothesis. To the extent that there is any consensus in the professional literature, it is that claims about causal mechanisms rooted in marijuana's pharmacology have been overplayed in the past. But that doesn't prove that the problem is imaginary.

A parallel issue concerns the effects—if any—of using marijuana before the brain is fully developed. The associations are clear. For example, researchers at the University of Maryland report that adults who first used marijuana before age 15 were nearly five times more likely to meet clinical criteria for abuse or dependence of an illegal drug (marijuana or another illegal drug) as compared to those who first used marijuana when they were 18 or older. But as with the gateway hypothesis, it is very hard to know how much of the association is causally attributable to early marijuana use, as opposed to being merely a spurious correlation.

Does using marijuana cause schizophrenia and other mental health problems?

There is an emerging and highly controversial literature suggesting that marijuana use elevates the risk of schizophrenia and psychotic symptoms. Before exploring the evidence, it is important to clarify some terms.

There is a common misunderstanding that schizophrenia means having multiple personalities, but schizophrenia and multiple personality disorder are entirely distinct diagnoses. As far as we know, no one claims that marijuana use has anything to do with multiple personality disorder.

Rather, schizophrenia is a debilitating mental health condition characterized by persistent psychotic symptoms (e.g., auditory hallucinations or thinking that someone is controlling you), making it very difficult for those who suffer from the disorder to distinguish between real experience and illusion. It is often a life-long condition that can derail the lives of those who are diagnosed as well as their family and friends.

Relatively few people suffer from schizophrenia (past year prevalence for adults in the United States is 1.1 percent). However, many people experience psychotic symptoms at one point or another.

Psychotic symptoms are not benign, but there is a world of difference between experiencing bouts of some symptoms and having schizophrenia. And there are a range of schizophrenia symptoms, including not only hallucinations and delusions but also others such as jumbled speech and trouble paying attention that are not so terribly different than familiar and expected effects of acute marijuana intoxication.

Statistically, there is a strong association between marijuana use and the emergence of psychotic symptoms. But does that mean that marijuana use causes psychotic symptoms, that the symptoms cause people who have them to use marijuana, or that some third factor causes both?

Most of the research addressing this question follows individuals (usually starting in childhood) for several years and regularly inquires about substance use and mental health. A systematic review of these studies by University of Bristol psychologist Theresa Moore and colleagues examined the effect of marijuana consumption on symptoms associated with affective disorders such as depression and psychotic disorders such as schizophrenia. With respect to affective disorders, the authors concluded that the evidence was not consistent and some studies did not adequately rule out other explanations for the association. But they found stronger evidence implicating marijuana in causing psychotic symptoms. Pooling the results of seven longitudinal studies, they found that those who had ever used marijuana were more likely to experience psychotic symptoms in the future. The effect was stronger when examining more frequent users, thus suggesting a dose response. A more recent longitudinal study by Maastricht University Medical Center researchers Rebecca Kuepper, Jim van Os, and their colleagues concluded, "Cannabis use is a risk factor for the development of incident psychotic symptoms [and] continued cannabis use might increase the risk for psychotic disorder by impacting the persistence of symptoms."

But even if marijuana does increase the risk of psychotic symptoms, how important is that increase? Over a lifetime, between one in four and one in five people experience psychotic symptoms at least once. When Moore and colleagues pooled the results of the existing studies, they found that marijuana use increased the risk of experiencing a psychotic symptom by at least 40 percent, with the figure increasing for those who used marijuana more often.

There are other approaches for examining the relationship between marijuana and psychoses. For example, some researchers examine whether large changes in marijuana use (e.g., measured in household surveys) are correlated with changes in population-level rates of schizophrenia as reflected in registry data. Analyzing eight different age cohorts in Australia, Burnet Institute researcher Louisa Degenhardt and colleagues found that there was no evidence of an increase in schizophrenia during the thirty years when there was a steep increase in marijuana use.

The United Kingdom's Advisory Council on the Misuse of Drugs (ACMD) conducted its own analysis and found that the prevalence and annual incidence of schizophrenia and psychoses decreased from 1996 to 2005. Past-month use increased from 1996 to 2002, but then fell from 2002 to 2006. Based on its review of the literature, the ACMD concluded that the "evidence points to a probable, but weak, causal link" between cannabis use and psychotic disorders; however, the ACMD argued there is "unequivocal evidence that the use of cannabis by people with schizophrenia increases the likelihood of relapse, manifested by a worsening of symptoms and often accompanied by a refusal to continue treatment."

There have also been biological studies that randomly assigned subjects to different levels of intravenous THC (including a placebo). These studies find that THC increases the probability of experiencing psychotic symptoms for both healthy subjects and those with schizophrenia. In their review of the longitudinal and biological studies with humans, psychiatrist Deepak D'Souza and colleagues at the Department of Veterans Affairs conclude: "Taken collectively, exposure to cannabis is neither a necessary nor a sufficient cause of schizophrenia....More likely, cannabis exposure is a component or contributing cause that interacts with other known (genetic, environmental) and unknown factors." Based on the available evidence about marijuana and psychoses, Wayne Hall and Louisa Degenhardt go as far to say, "If we had similar evidence of an association between using a pharmaceutical drug and an adverse effect, the drug would either be withdrawn from the market or would only be prescribed with clear warnings about the risk to patients and prescribers."

As more work is done exploring the links between marijuana use and mental health problems, we hope more attention is paid to the amount and type of marijuana used. As noted in chapter 1, there is reason to believe that the ratio of THC to CBD in marijuana could affect the mental health consequences of consumption. That might suggest that contemporary marijuana is more dangerous than the marijuana whose use is reflected in historical statistics. On the other hand, it might also suggest that legalization with controls on potency and on cannabinoid ratios might lead to less mental illness in total than continued prohibition and a black market dominated by high-THC, low-CBD product.

Does using marijuana influence crime and delinquency?

The rate of marijuana use is higher among offenders than among nonoffenders, but the conventional wisdom in the academic community is that both behaviors are results of the same common causes, rather than that marijuana causes criminal offending. Heavy heroin and cocaine users who aren't rich may need to steal to support their habits, but while a heavy heroin or cocaine habit can consume $10,000–$15,000 per year, it's very hard to smoke up that much money in the form of pot—especially given the quantity discounts that heavy marijuana users often receive.

Marijuana use by itself does not tend to induce violent crime; in fact, some studies suggest the opposite effect. A review of the evidence in a National Academy of Sciences study on violence concluded, "The majority of the evidence in experimental studies with animals and humans, as well as most data from chronic users, emphasizes that cannabis preparations (e.g., marihuana, hashish) or THC *decrease* aggressive and violent behavior" (emphasis added).

As for other types of crime, Trevor Bennett, a criminologist at the University of Glamorgan, and his colleagues systematically reviewed thirty studies about drug use and crime and found the association was much stronger for hard drugs like crack, heroin, and powder cocaine than it was for marijuana.

While the association between marijuana use and general criminal offenses was positive and technically "statistically significant," the effect was small. In fact, one of Bennett's coauthors, David Farrington of Cambridge University, argued elsewhere that their results about the statistical association for marijuana should be thought of as inconclusive.

A number of longitudinal studies have examined the relationship between adolescent marijuana use and measures of future criminality. Those finding a positive correlation cannot escape the criticism that an unobserved third factor may be driving both results, but this does not mean that some of them are not more persuasive than others. In a particularly advanced statistical analysis, Johns Hopkins researcher Kerry Green and her colleagues found that in a cohort of urban African Americans, using marijuana more than twenty times before age 16 was positively correlated with adult property crime, even after accounting for dropping out of high school, progression to the use of harder drugs, and several other variables. The authors make it very clear that because of potential unobserved confounders, their results are *consistent with* a causal story but are not definitive evidence of a causal relationship.

Of course marijuana use under a prohibition directly causes crime and delinquency in the form of violations of drug laws. But it is important to distinguish that from effects on non-drug crime and delinquency when thinking about legalization because laws prohibiting marijuana possession would no longer apply to those above the legal age limit after legalization. Prohibitions on particular production and distribution practices may still exist, depending on the regulatory structure favored by the implementing jurisdiction. So marijuana-specific arrests will decrease after legalization, but they will not go to zero. As chapter 11 elaborates, there are about as many alcohol-related arrests (for public drunkenness, minor-in-possession, DUI, etc.) per dependent alcohol user as there are marijuana arrests per person dependent on marijuana.

Does marijuana use affect education and employment?

One of the many concerns about adolescent substance use is that it could lead to worse performance in school. If students come to school intoxicated, it may be harder for them to pay attention and learn. Some parents worry that substance use will increase the probability that their kids will get caught up with a crowd that does not take school seriously. There is also a worry that heavy substance use could have longer-term cognitive impacts that could limit school performance, and eventually lead to dropping out.

There is clearly a correlation between marijuana use and poor performance in high school, but the standard critique about causality generally applies to these studies. A review of this literature by researchers Michael Lynsky and Wayne Hall suggests that if there is a relationship (and they believe pot use does increase the risk of leaving school early), it is not because marijuana permanently impairs cognitive function; rather, it probably has to do with the social context in which marijuana is used. Specifically, they propose that early marijuana use appears to be associated with "adoption of an anti-conventional lifestyle characterized by affiliations with delinquent and substance using peers, and the precocious adoption of adult roles including early school leaving, leaving the parental home and early parenthood." More recent work by RAND statistician Dan McCaffrey and colleagues also suggests that the relationship between marijuana use and dropping out could be driven by an affiliation with deviant peers.

As for research on the effect of marijuana use on employment and worker productivity, the findings vary dramatically. Some studies find no effect; one finds that marijuana use reduces the probability of employment; one study finds that off-the-job marijuana use actually increases wages; and another shows that the same methodological approach yields precisely opposite findings depending on whether data from 1991 or

1992 are used. A review of this literature by Beau Kilmer and RAND economist Rosalie Pacula identifies a number of reasons for the disparate findings, including that these studies do not always examine the same age groups or use the same definitions of marijuana use. This is far from a settled question.

Does marijuana use cause automobile crashes?

Being stoned impairs driving performance. Even the pro-legalization National Organization for the Reform of Marijuana Laws includes "no driving" among its principles of responsible marijuana use.

The question is just how dangerous it is. The answer seems to be that driving stoned isn't as dangerous as driving drunk, but driving under the influence of both drugs is worse than either by itself.

That leaves open the question of how much marijuana adds to the risks of driving, both in terms of the risk of a crash and in terms of the contribution of marijuana to the overall rate of accidents and fatalities.

One of the difficulties in answering this question is that marijuana metabolites—unlike alcohol—stay in the body for a number of days after intoxication. If someone is in a traffic accident and has a positive urine test for marijuana, that shows past use but not necessarily current intoxication: to measure the current level of the drug requires a mouth swab or a blood test.

This is not just a problem for researchers studying drugged driving; it poses problems for law enforcement officers trying to assess whether or not someone was under the influence of marijuana at the time of an accident. Proving someone is under the influence can lead to longer sentences, increased fines, and possibly a treatment referral. To address this issue, some states passed zero tolerance per se laws which define someone as under the influence of a controlled substance if there is evidence of having *any* THC in their system, regardless of impairment. Thus someone could be punished for intoxicated driving as a result of marijuana use days before the incident.

The experimental research on marijuana-impaired driving examines how drivers under the influence of marijuana performed in driving simulators or on closed courses. Yale psychiatrist Richard Sewell and his colleagues reviewed this literature and concluded that

> use may impair some driving skills (automatic functions such as tracking)...but different skills (complex functions that require conscious control) are not impaired until higher doses, and cannabis users tend to compensate effectively for their deficits by driving more carefully. Unexpected events are still difficult to handle under the influence of marijuana, however, and the combination of low-dose alcohol and low-dose cannabis causes much more impairment than either drug used alone.

There is another line of research in the field known as culpability studies, which involves analyzing multi-car accidents and determining who caused the crash and who was the victim. After determining who caused the accident, researchers assess whether these individuals had drugs or alcohol in their blood, and then analyze whether marijuana increased the probability of being culpable in the crash. The early reviews of these studies did not find that those with cannabinoids in their blood were more likely to be culpable.

The more recent reviews of the epidemiological literature conclude that marijuana does increase the risk of traffic accidents. Room and colleagues argue that "better-controlled epidemiological studies have recently provided credible evidence that cannabis users who drive while intoxicated are at increased risk of motor-vehicle crashes." Similarly, a 2011 meta-analysis by Mu-Chen Li of Columbia University and colleagues finds that the risk of a crash rises in a dose-response fashion with the amount of THC consumed.

Does parental marijuana use influence child welfare?

The evidence is mixed about the effects of prenatal marijuana exposure—for example, on the child's birth weight; if there are such effects, they are probably slight.

Prenatal marijuana exposure can influence the development of the central nervous system; that has been shown both by studying the biological effects directly and by following the early lives of children whose mothers did and did not use marijuana while pregnant. The two major research projects which followed expectant mothers and their children after birth both found an association between prenatal marijuana exposure and poorer cognitive development, attention, and executive functioning. As always, it's hard to separate out the effects of marijuana on the fetus from the behavioral differences between women who keep smoking pot after getting pregnant and those who either don't smoke at all or stop. The fact that women who smoke marijuana are more likely to also smoke tobacco—a known source of fetal damage—further complicates the interpretation of the results.

One perhaps surprising finding from one of the studies is that prenatal marijuana exposure predicts the child's marijuana consumption at age 14, even after accounting for the parent's marijuana use when the child reaches that age. Whether or not this novel finding will be replicated in future studies remains to be seen.

As Harold Pollack of the University of Chicago has pointed out, parental substance abuse is as much a pediatric as an obstetric issue: the impact of the drug on parental (especially maternal) behavior after the child is born may be more important than the impact of whatever drugs reach the developing fetus.

There does not appear to be much research examining the effect of parental marijuana use on children.

As a pediatric issue, we know that there are at least 6 million kids under 18 who live with a parent who is a current marijuana user; more than 4 million of them live with a parent who used marijuana on more than one hundred days in the previous year and 1.2 million with a parent who meets diagnostic criteria for marijuana abuse or dependence.

While parental substance use is the main reason that kids are removed from their homes, the conventional wisdom is that marijuana is not an important contributor when compared to alcohol, cocaine, methamphetamine, and other drugs. That said, parents arrested for marijuana may attract attention from Child Protective Services, and in some states a misdemeanor marijuana conviction can create serious problems for those seeking to adopt or foster a child.

Current marijuana use by parents is associated with a greater risk of tobacco, alcohol, and marijuana use among their adolescent children; however, the jury is still out on whether this is a causal relationship.

Another potentially worrisome correlation was identified by UC San Diego sociologist Davis Phillips and colleagues. They found that SIDS deaths spike the day after April 20—which some users treat as a marijuana-smoking holiday—as they do on New Year's Day and on weekend. There are a number of hypotheses (e.g., parental caretakers are more likely to sleep in; exposure to smoke), but at this point there is no compelling evidence linking this spike to marijuana rather than other factors, such as concurrent alcohol use.

Additional Reading

D'Souza, Deepak Cyril, Richard Andrew Sewell, and Mohini Ranganathan. "Cannabis and Psychosis/Schizophrenia: Human Studies."

Hall, Wayne, and Rosalie Liccardo Pacula. *Cannabis Use and Dependence.*

Room, Robin, et al. *Cannabis Policy.*

Sewell, R. Andrew, James Poling, and Mehmet Sofuoglu. "The Effect of Cannabis Compared with Alcohol on Driving."

6

WHAT IS KNOWN ABOUT THE NONMEDICAL BENEFITS OF USING MARIJUANA?

Astoundingly little. Much is claimed, but little is known.

One thing is certain: hundreds of millions of people across the globe have enjoyed it. Users report that getting high is relaxing and pleasurable, and that it contributes to other pleasures, including food, music, dancing, art, conversation, humor, and sex.

Some believe that marijuana intoxication enhances their creative work in fields ranging from music to mathematics, or that the experience of having been stoned in the past gives them access, in their non-stoned hours, to a usefully different style of thought.

But even simple, easy-to-test claims such as "Marijuana users enjoy listening to Mozart more when they're stoned" lack anything approaching good scientific evidence to support them.

Of course, even if we knew more than we do about the benefits, we'd still need to know about the harms. The same drug can be both helpful and harmful: helpful at some times and harmful at others; helpful when used carefully but dangerous if abused; helpful to some people and harmful to others. Perhaps the least constructive—and certainly the most common—approach to writing about marijuana is to start from the desire to "prove" that it's either the source of all evils or the cure for all ills.

Why don't we know more about the benefits of marijuana use?

Studying the benefits of intoxication is inherently difficult; most of them are personal, subjective, and hard to observe. Marijuana intoxication is particularly challenging because marijuana users ingest a complicated mixture of psychoactive chemicals. And serious scholarship in the United States is hamstrung by administrative rules. Only one facility is allowed to grow cannabis for use in research, and that supplier is only allowed to provide the drug to the government. Scientists can't get legal supplies of research material without applying for what is technically (and administratively) a "grant" from the National Institute on Drug Abuse; that agency has not proven especially responsive to such requests from researchers interested in studying benefits rather than harms. If a special review panel decides that a proposal—for example, to study whether using a vaporizer would reduce lung damage compared to smoking joints—lacks "scientific merit," the researcher is out of luck. The study in question may have funding in hand and approval from an institutional review board for human subjects protection, but without a source of cannabis it's dead in the water. When the University of Massachusetts applied to start a competing facility that could have supplied researchers outside the grant process, the Administrator of the Drug Enforcement Administration (DEA) overruled the DEA's own administrative law judge and denied the application.

Thus, while virtually any adolescent has easy access to black-market pot, it's largely unavailable to research scientists. The rule is specific to marijuana: scientists studying heroin, cocaine, methamphetamine, or LSD don't have to jump through this particular hoop.

Even if there were no administrative barriers, the research itself would be hard. THC is the primary psychoactive agent, but as discussed in chapter 1, cannabis products also contain varying amounts of other psychoactive chemicals (e.g., CBD). The roles of the other agents, either on their own, in combinations, or as modulators of the effects of THC or CBD, are largely unstudied.

The ratios of active agents may also matter; the very-high-THC preparations that dominate the contemporary market for expensive marijuana tend to also have high ratios of THC to CBD. Users have a body of folklore about the varying effects of different strains, but except for some medical-marijuana dispensaries, few sellers are able to tell the buyers anything quantitative about the chemical content of their products. In recent years there has been considerable speculation that high-ratio products increase the risk of panic attacks and dysphoria. So asking about, or trying to study, the benefits (or harms) of marijuana generically is a little bit like asking what wine tastes like, as if merlot and champagne were interchangeable. Even for a single well-defined cannabis product, the effects still vary from individual to individual and from occasion to occasion.

It's possible to compare users to nonusers on a variety of dimensions, but such comparisons don't give usable estimates of the impact of marijuana use: those who choose to use the drug—especially while it remains illegal—surely differ systematically from those who choose not to use it.

We can study the immediate effects of being stoned, but those results don't tell us much about the lasting effects, and especially the effects of long-term heavy use. And of course the opinions of heavy, chronic users about the effects of their favorite drug need to be taken with a grain of salt, or maybe two.

Thus even under the best of conditions it would be difficult to study the benefits of marijuana use. Under conditions of illegality, "difficult" borders on "impossible."

Would we know more about the benefits if it were legal?

Legalization would remove some administrative barriers to doing research on marijuana, but it's not clear who would fund objective studies about nonmedical benefits. And the rules about protecting human research subjects would continue to make it difficult for scientists to offer marijuana to those who had never used it. In the absence of carefully gathered before-and-after data—ideally on subjects chosen at random to receive marijuana or not—it will remain hard to discover which of the impacts outlast the period of intoxication.

So legalization may not bring a wealth of reliable new knowledge; after all, most of what passes for "research" about (entirely legal) nutritional supplements and herbal remedies doesn't pass the giggle test. The licit marijuana industry might prove no more reliable a source of knowledge about marijuana than the nutraceutical sector is about its products, or than cigarette companies are about the effects of smoking.

Is there a "stoned" way of thinking?

Some of the argument about marijuana policy has to do with the adverse side effects of use: accident, health damage, and drug dependency. But that cannot fully account for the passion of some partisans on both sides of the question. Lurking in the background is the question of whether the *intended* effects of pot smoking ought to be regarded as valuable or harmful.

William Bennett, who as the director of the Office of National Drug Control Policy under George H. W. Bush was the first legislatively authorized "drug czar," once said of marijuana legalization, "Why in God's name foster the use of a drug that makes you stupid?" Since there is no evidence that occasional pot smoking permanently lowers IQ scores, presumably Bennett was describing the acute, intoxicated state and the changes in attitudes it might engender. In his view, those effects could be summed up as being "stupid."

At the other end of the spectrum, natural-health physician Andrew Weil's book *The Natural Mind* offers a spirited defense of what Weil calls the "stoned" way of thinking. He identifies "stonedness" with "states of consciousness other than the ordinary, ego-centered waking state" such as dreaming or meditative calm. "Straight" thinking, on this account, has five tendencies: dominance of the intellect; attachment to the senses and thus to external reality; attention to form over content, leading to materialism; a focus on differences rather than similarities; and "negative thinking, pessimism, and despair." Weil depicts straight thinking as literal-minded, linear, unsubtle, humorless, and hubristic (mistaking "our perceptions of reality for reality itself"), and as leading to such misguided (in Weil's view) activities as the use of insecticides and antibiotics, Western medicine, and political action.

Table 6.1 A Table of Oppositions

Straight	Stoned
Authoritarian	Permissive
Prose	Poetry
Straightforward	Subtle
Serious	Humorous
Conscientious	Creative
Hierarchy	Equality
Exchange	Gift
Business	Pleasure
Artificial or synthetic	Natural
Apollonian	Dionysian
Precision	Approximation
Analytical	Holistic
Sequence	Recursion
Certainty	Doubt
Football	Ultimate Frisbee
Frank Sinatra	John Coltrane
John Wayne	Jack Nicholson
Top ten lists	Tables of oppositions
To-do lists	
Lists of pros and cons	

The somewhat fanciful table on the opposite page tries to assign the members of various pairs of opposites to one side or the other of the "straight" vs. "stoned" division as Weil conceives it. It sets the stage for considering whether occasional marijuana intoxication is good or bad by trying to describe what mental processes, attitudes, and actions it is imagined to produce.

Is "stoned thinking" valuable?

Some might insist that one side of the table above is to be absolutely preferred to the other, but it seems more reasonable to seek an appropriate balance between the two. So if occasional pot smoking does indeed promote "stonedness" in this sense, then (nondependent) use might seem like a net benefit to those who think that contemporary society is too rigid and uptight and insufficiently tolerant and creative. It would seem like a net cost to those who think that our problems result more from an excessively permissive, insufficiently conscientious culture. And there is no reason to think that the "right" answer should be a constant over time, or across population subgroups. Perhaps this helps explain why sensible people can have such diametrically opposed—and passionately felt—opinions about marijuana use.

In philosophic terms, the attack on "straight thinking" reflects an often-stated critique of a certain kind of rationalism (often associated with Descartes) typical of both contemporary science and contemporary practice in business and statecraft. In terms of the psychology of personality, Weil's "Straightsville" would be characterized as having deficient openness, excessive negative affect, and too rigid a form of conscientiousness. In theological terms, legalistic traditions and organized religion tend toward the "straight" while mystical traditions and private spirituality tend toward the "stoned." In generational terms, the baby boomers and the cultural Sixties were "stoned," compared to the "straight" Depression/World War II and Korean War generations and the cultural Fifties (see table 6.1).

The culture war that now plays such a role in American political life has a "straight" vs. "stoned" dimension. And that is part of what makes marijuana and marijuana legalization so controversial, even in the absence of any strong evidence that smoking pot has any actual link with "stonedness" in Weil's sense.

But is Weil's description really about the effects of using marijuana, or does it rather portray the cultural and personality traits of the people who pioneered widespread marijuana use in the 1960s? In the 1960s, high school students who self-reported marijuana use were more likely than their nonusing peers to report that they planned to go on to college. Stereotypically, bookworms smoked pot while jocks drank beer. It was an easy leap, but not a valid one, from that observation to the idea that pot might make its users more reflective. Over the intervening years, pot has moved down the socio-economic ladder—the association between regular marijuana use and educational attainment is now negative—but perceptions about it may still be caught in a cultural lag.

The rise of the Sixties counterculture certainly was contemporaneous with the rise of marijuana use, but so many other things were changing at that time that it's hard to sort cause from effect. The same is true at an individual level: assuming for the purposes of argument that we find more "stoned" styles of thought among those who have used marijuana, is the right explanation that getting high leads to openness and intuitive thinking or that openness and intuitive thinking lead to getting high? The answer might vary from time to time, place to place, and group to group.

Thus it is entirely possible that the hopes of the advocates and the fears of the opponents are equally ungrounded.

Does marijuana use enhance creativity?

Maybe. Maybe not. Maybe for some people and some forms of creativity but not others.

Certainly some people believe that they are more creative under the influence, but those opinions cannot be accepted at face value; many people also believe that they sing better while drunk. On the other hand, the role of marijuana in the cultures of reggae, hip-hop, and Beat poetry is harder to dismiss.

The effects of marijuana on mental functioning are complex and poorly understood, but it is possible to lay out a sensible story for why they might enhance creativity. While the user is under the influence, chemicals alter the experience of time and the "gating" process that filters out most sensory input before it reaches consciousness. It also interferes with short-term working memory and the "executive function" that allocates attention across topics and activities: performance on what psychometricians call "divided attention" tasks degrades sharply. The person who begins a sentence and forgets what he was saying before reaching the end of it is a staple of stoned humor.

These alterations seem to enhance some kinds of sensual experience; colors, sounds, tastes, textures, and aromas may seem more intense, and may actually (this is not known) be more sensitively perceived. Slowing of the time-sense may allow more attention to the details of music, whether listening or performing.

Altered gating may occur at the level of thoughts as well as sensations. If creativity is defined as the capacity to make valid but nonobvious connections between seemingly disparate elements, then it is not hard to see how a less stringent set of filters might enhance it.

One of the most widely reported effects of marijuana use is increased susceptibility to laughter. Insofar as laughter depends on the perception of incongruity, it's not hard to imagine that laughter and creativity might be helped or impaired by the same things. But the mere possibility of a connection is not evidence; we don't actually know whether people who smoke pot really have more laughter in their lives overall.

Studies so far—admittedly, mostly studies with injected THC in laboratory settings rather than smoked whole marijuana in natural settings—have not found measurable gains in creativity.

Also unknown is the extent—if any—to which marijuana users can learn ways of thinking while under the influence that then become available to them while not actively high. If that were possible it would constitute an important potential benefit of marijuana smoking, and thus of marijuana legalization. That makes the failure of the current research enterprise to address such questions (or the broader question of "stoned thinking") all the more frustrating.

Can marijuana enhance athletic performance?

At first blush, or to anyone who remembers Zonker, the feckless, hapless Yale pass receiver from the early Doonesbury comic strips, this question seems far-fetched. But a recently published paper by two researchers at the National Institute on Drug Abuse and a physician at the World Anti-Doping Agency argues that marijuana is properly included in the list of drugs banned from competitive sports because using it might give some athletes an improper advantage on the playing field. Among the potential benefits they cite are improved concentration and reduced "anxiety, fear, depression and tension."

What role does cannabis play in worship?

Only a modest one.

Rituals involving cannabis seem to be quite ancient, but current ritual use is not widespread. Among Hindus, some devotees of Shiva regard cannabis use as pleasing to the goddess, and cannabis is used in some Sikh festivals. Cannabis is central to Rastafarian culture, though its relationship to worship services is obscure. Sufism has a long relationship with cannabis use.

A number of churches seem to have formed specifically to be able to claim a religious exemption from the drug laws; those claims have been rejected by the courts.

Overall though, the tension between the drug laws and religious freedom is not nearly so strong with respect to cannabis as it is with respect to the hallucinogens.

So there's no real evidence of any benefits?

It's fair to say that evidence of measurable nonmedical benefits, and especially of lasting benefits, remains equivocal, and mostly not up to the standards used in evaluating claims of medical efficacy. But that laboratory-and-dataset approach is only one way of looking at the value of an activity. The other way—characteristic of economics rather than psychology or biomedical research—is to look at behavior in the market. Tens of millions of people enjoy using marijuana, as evidenced by their willingness to pay even the inflated prices generated by illicit markets and to face the legal risks and social stigma associated with being "drug users." Why? Answering that question may be complicated for those who are dependent, but it is simple for the majority of users who are not. Primarily they use it because they enjoy it.

But neither domestic law nor international treaty recognize enjoyment as a reason to allow the use of otherwise banned drugs.

Why should mere pleasure count as a benefit?

Why *shouldn't* pleasure count as a benefit? Marijuana dependency is a real problem, and the demand for marijuana by those dependent on it isn't evidence that it benefits them. But that doesn't mean that the pleasures of ordinary use are imaginary, or that getting stoned somehow shows a defective character.

Some will protest that pleasure is all well and good, but it should not enter the equation when there is a real risk of serious injury or death. That line of reasoning should not persuade anyone who skis, climbs mountains, or rides motorcycles, or, for that matter, drinks alcohol. We have long known how much football, at every level from high school to the Super Bowl, damages its players' knees; now we're learning more and more about how much it harms their brains. Yet would anyone propose making football illegal?

Economists have a straightforward way of evaluating the benefits consumers receive from the things they buy and use: the principle of "willingness to pay." Clearly, anyone who buys something is willing to pay its price rather than go without it. But many people who buy at the market price would have been willing to pay more, if necessary. The difference between the actual price of a good and the maximum a consumer would have been willing to pay for it is called the "consumer's surplus."

The problem of drug dependency makes the evaluation of consumers' surpluses more difficult. Marijuana, like any other drug when used as part of a pattern of dependent behavior, may actually create "consumers' deficits" (a concept unknown to orthodox economic analysis). But the vast majority of marijuana users are not in the grip of dependency; they use the drug because they want to use it.

About 40 percent of the days of use—which very likely means more than 40 percent of the marijuana consumed—in the United States involve people who self-report having tried to cut down or quit in the past year. Since not everyone who has a drug problem knows that he has a drug problem, and not everyone who knows he has a problem tries to quit, that likely understates how much marijuana is used by people who use too much of the drug. Still, at least a large minority of the stoned hours are hours of enjoyment rather than entrapment. Counting people rather than hours, most users aren't abusers.

Prohibition raises prices and imposes nonmonetary costs. Those are sources of loss to actual and potential consumers—at least those who are not dependent. Removing those costs—letting people do more of what they like doing, at lower cost and with fewer risks, fears, and penalties—ought to count, by all the canons of ordinary economic reasoning, as potential benefits of making marijuana legally available. The sum of those gains, were the United States to legalize marijuana, must be at least in the billions of dollars per year—perhaps in the tens of billions. (This is further discussed in chapter 11.)

Additional Reading

Erowid. "Cannabis Effects."

Grinspoon, Lester. *Marihuana Reconsidered*.

Huestis Marilyn A., et al. "Cannabis in Sport: Anti-doping Perspective."

Weil, Andrew. *The Natural Mind*.

7

WHAT ARE THE MEDICINAL BENEFITS OF USING MARIJUANA?

Does marijuana have medical value?

It depends who you ask. The U.S. federal government unwaveringly argues that marijuana has no medicinal value, the states' positions are mixed, pro-marijuana advocacy groups often paint it as a wonder drug, the public is mostly positive, and expert medical opinion falls somewhere in the middle of this muddle.

Federal law and regulations require that a drug meet five conditions in order to be accepted as a medicine in the United States:

1. The drug's chemistry must be known and reproducible.
2. There must be adequate safety studies.
3. There must be adequate and well-controlled studies proving efficacy.
4. The drug must be accepted by qualified experts.
5. The scientific evidence must be widely available.

The federal government insists that marijuana does not meet these conditions.

Sixteen states and the District of Columbia feel differently. They allow approved patients to possess marijuana for medical purposes without the risk of state-level criminal penalties. Doctors in these states may not prescribe marijuana, and these states' pharmacies may not dispense it (that would violate federal law). Instead, doctors provide *recommendations* to their patients, who then obtain marijuana products through diverse channels, including cooperatives and other dispensaries, or by growing it themselves or having a caregiver grow on their behalf. (The states' laws vary considerably regarding what sources of medical marijuana supply—if any—are shielded from state and local enforcement.)

The American public overwhelmingly supports making marijuana legal for medical purposes. This support cuts across party affiliation and ideology. Polls conducted in 2010 by ABC News/Washington Post and the Pew Center on the States showed that roughly 8 in 10 respondents supported medical marijuana, and this support is increasing. These polls also show that Americans tend to be quite liberal in deciding who should qualify for medical marijuana; the majority supports providing medical marijuana to anyone who might derive benefit from it (as opposed to defining eligibility more narrowly such as for those with serious diseases or terminal illnesses).

Proponents point to marijuana as having therapeutic value in treating a range of symptoms; among the most common are appetite loss, nausea, chronic pain, anxiety, sleeping disorders, muscle spasms, and intraocular pressure. A (relatively small) number of controlled studies show marijuana or cannabis-based medicines relieve some of these symptoms. Opponents counter that other approved therapies for these conditions exist and are as effective, or more effective, than marijuana.

A comprehensive review was published in 1999 by the Institute of Medicine (IOM), the medical arm of the prestigious National Academy of Sciences. Concerning the efficacy of *cannabinoids isolated from marijuana*, the IOM found therapeutic value "particularly for symptoms such as pain relief, control of nausea and vomiting, and appetite stimulation," although the effects are "generally modest, and in most cases there are more effective medications. However, people vary in their responses to medications, and there will likely always be a subpopulation of patients who do not respond well to other medications." So the IOM concludes that "scientific data indicate the potential therapeutic value of cannabinoid drugs, primarily THC, for pain relief, control of nausea and vomiting, and appetite stimulation."

In contrast, the IOM viewed *smoked marijuana* as a "crude THC delivery system that also delivers harmful substances," so "smoked marijuana should generally not be recommended for long-term medical use. Nonetheless, for certain patients, such as the terminally ill or those with debilitating symptoms, the long-term risks are not of great concern." It recommended limited clinical trials of smoked marijuana, but the goal "would not be to develop marijuana as a licensed drug but rather to serve as a first step toward the possible development of non-smoked rapid-onset cannabinoid delivery systems." Since that would take some years, it recommended that in the meantime "patients with debilitating symptoms (such as intractable pain or vomiting)" could be provided with smoked marijuana on a short-term basis (less than six months)—perhaps as single-patient clinical trials—if:

- failure of all approved medications to provide relief has been documented;
- the symptoms can reasonably be expected to be relieved by rapid-onset cannabinoid drugs;
- such treatment is administered under medical supervision in a manner that allows for assessment of treatment effectiveness; and
- involves an oversight strategy comparable to an institutional review board process.

Critics condemn the IOM review for not considering the possibility that some standardized mixture of the full range of chemicals in the cannabis plant might be more therapeutically useful than a single chemical in isolation (such as THC) or the possibility that vaporization could provide the benefits of quick uptake through the lungs without the unhealthy smoke. (A vaporizer is a device that uses heat—for example, from an electrical resistance element—to transform the active chemicals in marijuana from solids to gasses without combustion, allowing the patient or other user to inhale the chemicals without the mix of toxic chemicals in smoke.)

MedicalMarijuanaProCon.org summarizes peer-reviewed research on cannabis and cannabis extracts from 1990 to 2011. (The site uses the term cannabis so we do here as well.) The site includes twenty-one double-blind clinical trials, nineteen of which were published after the IOM review. (Double-blind studies are the most authoritative because both the patient and the doctor are kept in the dark regarding whether the patient has been assigned to the cannabis study condition.) Of these studies, twelve (57 percent) were classified as "pro," two as "con," and seven (33 percent) as neither clearly pro nor con in terms of potential medical benefits. Two-thirds of the studies pertained to cannabis extracts, such as Sativex; one-third to smoked cannabis. The "pro" proportions were the same for extracts and for smoked cannabis, meaning there were four "pro" studies concerning smoked cannabis. In all four, the positive effects cited pertained to alleviating neuropathic pain. That is significant because there are other effective analgesics already in routine use.

Considering studies of extracts as well as smoked cannabis, the trials show mixed evidence regarding cannabis use for patients suffering from spasticity from multiple sclerosis (one trial shows improved outcomes and another shows no effect). Studies of intraocular pressure associated with glaucoma found mixed results, as did studies of cancer-related wasting syndrome. And there were no definitive findings for patients receiving cannabis-based medication for Parkinson's disease or Huntington's disease.

Why isn't marijuana available as a regular prescription drug?

Those who believe marijuana can confer important medical benefits may ask why it has not been made available as a prescription drug. The narrow answer is that the federal government has placed marijuana in Schedule I, the category of substances with no accepted medical use. But substances can be rescheduled; seven have been removed from Schedule I status since the Controlled Substances Act was passed. So a more fundamental answer is:

1. Because no one has done the work necessary to make it a prescription drug;
2. Because "marijuana" isn't the name of a specific drug; and
3. Because the federal government obstructs the process.

Prescription drugs must be approved as "safe and effective" by the Food and Drug Administration (FDA). The FDA doesn't do its own testing. It's up to the sponsor of a New Drug Application—usually a pharmaceutical company—to conduct, or pay for, the research to show safety and efficacy.

The drug must succeed in two large-scale ("Phase III") clinical trials. These are usually randomized controlled trials (RCTs), in which the candidate drug is compared either to a placebo or some active comparison drug in treating a group of patients randomly assigned to the experimental condition (the new drug) or the control condition (the placebo or comparison drug).

Running two big RCTs can be a multi-million-dollar enterprise. In the usual case, the sponsor has a patent on the candidate drug, and expects to make that money back by charging monopoly prices from the time the drug is approved to the time the patent expires. However, one cannot get a patent on material from a plant that already exists (as opposed to one that has been genetically engineered). So it is not clear how the sponsor of clinical trials with whole marijuana could recoup that investment. Furthermore, the symptoms for which there is the strongest evidence of efficacy—pain relief—are ones for which there already exist good medicines, including various opioid analgesics. And the symptoms for which there are fewer competitors tend to be ones for which the potential market is smaller.

Furthermore, those trials need to be run with exactly the medicine that would be used by patients if the proposed drug were approved, and the sponsor needs to demonstrate its capacity to produce the medicine such that each unit has, within very tight tolerances, the same amount of the active agent or agents as every other unit. That's part of what the FDA calls GMP: "Good Manufacturing Practice."

This has been done for particular psychoactive chemicals found in marijuana including THC (available as Marinol) and a blend of THC and CBD (available as Sativex). It is harder to do for plant material.

So the first step in developing prescription marijuana would be to decide on a level of THC and other active agents, including CBD, that will constitute a dose of the new medicine. Next would be to develop a method of growing and blending cannabis so that every gram has precisely that mix of chemicals. (The growing and blending process might be patentable.)

To get to that point—the point at which clinical trials could be designed—the sponsor would need a supply of marijuana from a source willing to develop the relevant Good Manufacturing Practice, or permission to produce its own. But the federal government has only licensed a single producer of research cannabis, and that producer is forbidden to sell to anyone but the government. So you can't get a New Drug Application to make marijuana a medicine without getting some marijuana first, and you can't get the marijuana because it has no recognized use as a medicine.

Thus the official opponents of "marijuana as medicine" are hardly acting in good faith when they argue that it hasn't passed FDA scrutiny.

On the other hand, other countries don't have the same barriers to medical-marijuana research, and yet those places don't have such research, either. In the Netherlands, where cannabis is easily available, physicians rarely tell their patients to use it therapeutically. That may reflect a bias against herbal remedies more than a bias against intoxicants; the Netherlands does approve heroin maintenance as a form of treatment for opiate dependence. Inasmuch as the United States is not the only possible venue for medical research, skeptics can accuse medical marijuana proponents of having demonstrated more enthusiasm for publicity campaigns and ballot initiatives than for medical research.

But isn't smoking unhealthy?

Yes, smoking is unhealthy. So is exposure to X-rays. Every medicine and medical procedure involves weighing potential adverse side effects against beneficial therapeutic effects.

If it turned out that some patients with neuromuscular spasm got substantial relief from marijuana, the lung damage from smoking wouldn't be an automatic veto on using it, just as the stomach irritation from aspirin is not a strong reason not to take it when you have a headache.

Still, medicines (or delivery mechanisms) with fewer harmful side effects are preferred to those with more harmful side effects. That is one reason for favoring marijuana extracts in pill or spray form over whole smoked marijuana. (There are also practical complications with smoked medicines in an oxygen-rich hospital setting with shared rooms, etc.)

However, as noted in chapter 2, smoking is not the only mode of administration for whole marijuana, and vaporization might avoid many of the harmful effects of smoking.

Nor does marijuana need to be delivered by lung. Swallowing the drug (as a pill) can be problematic because of the long and variable time to onset, which frustrates any attempt to "self-titrate" the dose. But the active agents can also be extracted in liquid form and used as a nasal spray or as drops under the tongue. So the fear of smoking need not be a bar to the use of marijuana as a medicine.

One argument for legalizing marijuana for recreational use is that it might encourage users to substitute vaporizers for joints or blunts. It is widely believed that marijuana smoked in a water pipe—a hookah or a bong—is less unhealthy than a joint, but a study sponsored by the Multidisciplinary Association for Psychedelic Studies showed that the water filters out an even greater proportion of the THC and other cannabinoids as it does of the tars, so the lung damage per stoned hour could actually be higher for a bong than for a joint.

How about using one or more cannabinoids instead of the whole plant?

It is entirely possible that one of the active agents in marijuana, or some combination of them, will turn out to be therapeutically effective, and either more effective, safer, or just simpler to administer than the more complicated (and less predictable) mixture in natural marijuana.

For example, Marinol, a pill consisting of pure synthetic delta-nine-tetrahydrocannabinol (THC), has been on the market in the United States for many years now, though it isn't widely used. Its chemical composition and its oral delivery mechanism are probably both disadvantages for most patients compared to inhaling the vapor of crude marijuana.

Sativex, a liquid containing THC and cannabidiol (CBD) extracted from the cannabis plant (in roughly a 1:1 ratio) and designed for use as a nasal or mouth spray, is now an approved medicine in Canada, the United Kingdom, and Spain. CBD by itself has been studied for possible use as an antianxiety agent and an antidepressant.

Approving plant-based chemicals but not the plant from which they are derived may seem hypocritical, but it is not unique to marijuana. Indeed, Western pharmacology often takes advantage of plant-based medicines only after isolating, or isolating and modifying, the active agents in the plant materials and producing pure extracts to be given in pill form. That is in part a fact of medical anthropology—the practices of the officially recognized healers in the currently dominant culture. But it's also scientifically easier to study the effects of pure chemicals than of plant materials. There are also real clinical advantages to the more precise dosage control available when every pill in a bottle is exactly the same as every other pill in that bottle.

Certainly the history of the nutritional supplement industry, with its plethora of scientifically dubious claims and its paucity of reliable information, is a warning of the risks of straying too far from rigorous experimental technique.

Still it is entirely possible that the mixture of dozens of different cannabinoids in the natural plant might outperform any one or two or three cannabinoids in isolation. Marinol has proven disappointingly unhelpful to patients; pure THC, taken by mouth, is simply not a very good medicine for most people. Sativex, with its CBD content potentially reducing the risk of dysphoria and panic, seems better, at least in some uses. Yet nothing guarantees that something else—perhaps the crude material, extracted or vaporized—wouldn't be better still.

How much "medical marijuana" use is actually medical?

Some, but by no means all. Almost certainly much less than half in places such as California, but probably more in places with tighter rules. Just how much depends in part on what you mean by "medical."

No doubt marijuana makes some people who buy it at dispensaries feel better. But in some cases the only disease they are managing is their dependency on marijuana, just as a morning drink can make an alcoholic feel better (temporarily).

Proponents of medical marijuana tend to cite a few uses with both medical logic and strong emotional appeal. Marijuana is known to enhance appetite, so reports by people getting cancer chemotherapy or suffering from HIV/AIDS that marijuana relieves nausea and helps them eat more make perfect sense. Glaucoma, which can lead to blindness, involves an increase in intraocular pressure, and there's evidence that marijuana relieves that pressure (though often only temporarily). Multiple sclerosis and related diseases can cause painful muscle spasms, and, again, there's some evidence that marijuana can help relax those spasms.

In California, with its very loose rules, less than 5 percent of those seeking medical marijuana recommendations have any of those conditions. Most have nonspecific complaints of anxiety, pain, or insomnia, and most have been smoking marijuana illegally for many years before they apply for legal permission. Moreover, there is only the slightest medical evidence that marijuana helps relieve those conditions (let alone relieves them better than alternative therapies). In loose-regulation states, the number of "medical" users can be half the estimated number of *total* current marijuana users (see chapter 14). And some "patients" buy for resale: Christian Thurstone and colleagues at the University of Colorado studied adolescents entering treatment for marijuana dependence in Colorado and showed that about half reported obtaining marijuana from someone with a medical-marijuana card.

In California, the process of getting a "recommendation" for medical marijuana is an open mockery. Actual medical practice starts with a patient coming to a physician with a symptom and the physician examining the patient, taking a medical history, diagnosing the underlying disease, and then (sometimes) prescribing a medicine to treat that disease. Those prescriptions tend to be precise: "Take 3 each day, with meals, for 21 days." And responsible physicians follow up to find out whether the medicine is doing its job.

The medical-marijuana-recommendation business starts with permission to use marijuana as its goal. The physicians who write most of the recommendations openly advertise, promising not to diagnose and treat illness but simply to provide a recommendation. Some even advertise that the visit is free unless it results in a recommendation. Others have advertisements, or even storefronts, that list a range of conditions for which they will write marijuana recommendations. It's hard to take this seriously as the practice of medicine.

Additional Reading

Eddy, Mark. *Medical Marijuana.*

International Association for Cannabinoid Medicine. "Clinical Studies and Case Reports."

Joy, Janet E., Stanley J. Watson Jr., and John A. Benson Jr. *Marijuana and Medicine.*

Thurstone, Christian, Shane A. Lieberman, and Sarah J. Schmiege. "Medical Marijuana Diversion and Associated Problems in Adolescent Substance Treatment."

PART II

LEGALIZATION AND ITS CONSEQUENCES

8

WHAT ARE THE PROS AND CONS OF LEGALIZATION GENERALLY?

What does it mean to legalize a drug?

Legalization is the opposite of prohibition. It avoids the costs of prohibition—loss of liberty, criminal enterprise, and the need for enforcement—at the risk of increased drug abuse.

Legalization means treating a drug (not necessarily all drugs) more or less the way we treat other commodities: production, distribution, retail sale, possession, and use would all be legal for all or most people (e.g., for adults but not for minors).

That's a gain for those who want to use that drug and can do so without losing control of their drug taking or intoxicated behavior: they gain the liberty of doing as they choose and whatever benefits flow from their drug use, and in most cases get access to cheaper and safer products of known quality. It's also a gain to all those who suffer from the illicit markets and from drug law enforcement.

However, compared to prohibition, legalization is likely to increase the number of people who wind up abusing or becoming dependent on the newly legalized drug.

To legalize a drug, then—as the U.S. federal government did with alcohol in 1933 and a state or nation may do with marijuana sometime in the near future—is to choose the problems associated with increased levels of excessive consumption over the problems associated with illicit dealing and enforcement.

Are there shades of legalization?

In a market society, most things are freely bought, sold, and used. But "freely" shouldn't be taken too literally. There are still rules designed to prevent fraud in the marketplace, damage to third parties, and harm to children. For a legal commodity, though, those rules are meant to shape the market, not to shrink the amount of market activity. (Changes in smoking policy over the past generation have led to an interesting intermediate case: while cigarettes remain legal, reducing cigarette smoking is now the proclaimed object of national health policy in the United States.)

A relatively few commodities and services—mostly linked to danger, or pleasure, or both—are restricted or banned entirely. It is currently a crime, for example, to grow marijuana, import it, sell it, or possess it. That wasn't always so: while some states started passing antimarijuana laws in the 1910s, the drug wasn't effectively banned nationally until 1937.

Drugs are not the only prohibited goods. There are also prohibitions against trade in certain endangered species and weapons; recently a man was sentenced to five years' probation, six months' home confinement, and 150 hours of community service for selling eleven eagle feathers: the law exists to prevent the bald eagle from being hunted to extinction. Child pornography is banned both to protect the children in the pictures and (it is hoped) to prevent the viewers of such material from going out and molesting children. There are laws against prostitution, gambling, and usury (loan-sharking), as well as bans on selling human organs. Most prohibitions generate some gray market or black market evasion of the laws; there are even organ-selling syndicates. But the black markets for illegal drugs are unusually large and destructive.

Legalization could mean treating a currently banned drug as an ordinary article of commerce. Or the newly legalized drug could be subject to some specialized rules, perhaps of the sort that now apply to alcohol: limits on times and place of sale, special licenses for sellers, labeling rules, a ban on sales to minors, and special excise taxes over and above normal sales taxes. But those regulations wouldn't enforce themselves, any more than the current prohibition does. The tighter the restrictions and the higher the taxes, the greater the risk that an illicit market will develop to evade them; there are markets for untaxed cigarettes in some high-tax states and countries.

In most states, current drug laws criminalize the behavior of users as well as dealers: simply possessing marijuana constitutes a crime. Removing criminal penalties for possessing amounts of a drug suitable for personal use—and thus freeing users from the consequences of a criminal sanction—is called "decriminalization." In states that have decriminalized possession, it is still illegal to possess marijuana, but those who are caught are given a civil sanction, such as a fine. If a state removes both criminal and civil penalties for possession, it has legalized possession, but that is still far short of full legalization, which encompasses production and distribution as well.

Confusingly, the National Prohibition Act for alcohol, better known as the Volstead Act, had no penalties for drinkers, as opposed to manufacturers and sellers of alcoholic beverages. Thus, instead of thinking of the U.S. experience with alcohol prohibition as similar to marijuana prohibition, it is better to compare it to a regime that has decriminalized or, more accurately, legalized possession.

The logical problem with reducing the penalties for possession is that it suggests to users that it is not a criminal offense to buy what dealers are forbidden to sell. That logical problem is also a practical problem if the reduction increases demand for the still-illicit product and therefore creates more customers for criminal enterprises, more dealing-related violence and corruption, and potentially even more incarceration. Reducing arrest risk for marijuana users in the United States might be good for them but not so good for Mexico. So in order to judge the outcome of reducing enforcement risks for users, we would have to know how great an effect the threat of arrest has on potential drug buyers. That in turn depends on how vigorously the current prohibition is being enforced and on how aware the users and potential users are of the legal risks they run.

Another regulatory option is availability for medical but not recreational use. Methamphetamine, for example, is a legal drug when prescribed by a physician and sold by a pharmacist, but it's still a crime to manufacture or sell it outside of pharmaceutical channels or to have it in your possession other than as prescribed.

Why have drug laws in the first place?

Ideally, drug laws aim either to protect drug users from the risks of drug taking, or to protect other people (including users' family members) from the risks some drug users create. But it doesn't always work out that way. Drug laws, like drug abuse, can cause harm. Policies intended to reduce the unwanted consequences of drug use can create the unwanted consequences of illicit markets and enforcement.

The stated goal of U.S. drug policy is to reduce "drug use and drug-related consequences" (where "drug" means "illicit drug"; reduced drinking by adults—as opposed to reduced alcoholism or reduced drunk driving—is not an official policy goal).

Intoxicating drugs, like other commodities, are often used without doing any harm to the user or to others. But they can also be used in ways that subject their users and others to risk or actual harm.

Drugs can damage users' health. The wrong dose, the wrong mix of drugs, or the wrong combination of drug and user can lead to injury or even death, and chronic use can lead to chronic illness: smoking, for example, is bad for the lungs. Intoxication can lead to dangerous behavior that harms the user, or to reckless or criminal behavior that damages other people. And users can lose control of their drug taking, slipping into drug abuse, drug dependency, or drug addiction.

Prohibition makes drugs more expensive and less convenient to buy, and largely eliminates the marketing efforts that boost sales of licit goods. It also prevents the drug producing industry from lobbying for policies that promote addiction. The result is reduced consumption, including reduced abuse and dependency.

Hence the extent of harm caused by using a substance is a crucial variable in determining how much benefit is created by prohibition's (partial) suppression of use. That makes the case for marijuana prohibition weaker than the comparable case for cocaine or heroin; marijuana use does create harms, but at a much lower rate than any of the other major illegal drugs (see chapter 5).

Why even consider legalizing a substance whose use creates harm?

The liberty to make our own decisions about our own lives—including decisions that seem unwise to other people—is valuable, and allows us to learn from our own mistakes and those of others. Intoxicating drugs are hardly the only potentially dangerous consumer items or recreational activities. People get killed and crippled climbing mountains, jumping out of airplanes, sailing, scuba diving, playing football, and riding motorcycles. Marijuana use may well be less risky than any of those other forms of recreation, yet a proposal to ban any of them would generate outrage.

It isn't obvious that the majority of the users who do not, and would not, abuse the drug deserve to be inconvenienced—to say the least—to protect against the consequences of less responsible users.

Moreover, drug laws create risks and harms of their own—most of all, the harms associated with illicit markets. Illicit markets are less consumer-friendly than regulated licit markets; it's much harder for a marijuana smoker than a beer drinker to determine precisely what he or she is about to ingest. Buyers and sellers in illicit markets cannot resolve their disputes through the courts or complain to the police if they are the victims of robbery or violence. As a result, they sometimes resolve their conflicts with firearms. The illicit markets can easily become social problems comparable to or greater than drug abuse itself. It is hard to know how much of the approximately $20 billion a year that is spent on marijuana in the United States ends up in the pockets of large-scale criminals, but the answer is surely in the billions, and some criminal organizations involved in the trade (such as the notorious Mexican drug-trafficking groups) are highly violent.

Laws need to be enforced; otherwise they become dead letters. And enforcing the drug laws is inevitably an ugly process; without the victim-witness who testifies in a robbery or assault case, the drug police must engage in intrusive means of detecting crime and gathering evidence: undercover operations, the use of paid informants, or surveillance by technical means such as wiretapping. Because the evidence in a drug dealing case is easy to destroy, police engage in surprise "dynamic-entry" raids, crashing through doors early in the morning or late at night, guns drawn. Sometimes the raid is on the wrong house. As journalist Radley Balko has documented, more than one innocent homeowner has drawn his gun in an effort to repel what seemed to be a violent home invasion and been shot dead by the police as a result; at least one killed a police officer and wound up on death row.

Less dramatic, but far more common, are marijuana-possession arrests, of which there were about 750,000 in the United States in 2010. That does not mean there are 750,000 instances of vice squads intentionally building a case against a marijuana user or retail seller; many marijuana arrests are the by-product of routine policing or enforcement of other laws. Nevertheless, an arrest sometimes means spending a night or more in jail awaiting arraignment; spending time in jail is arguably more dangerous than smoking pot.

Jail risk for possession varies by state; roughly one-third of Americans live in states that have already decriminalized marijuana. Since 2011, marijuana possession in California— which had generated about 60,000 possession arrests per year—has been merely an infraction, akin to a parking ticket. Even before 2011, first-time possession in California had already carried no possible jail sentence and a maximum fine of $100. In many places, "arrest" usually means receiving a notice to appear in court, not a trip to the booking facility or the jail.

Efforts to deter use seem a natural adjunct to prohibition; after all, if there were no users, there could be no dealers. But the result is that laws designed in part to protect people from their own behavior wind up making some of those who are not deterred worse off than they would have been in the absence of the laws. That's the argument for decriminalizing possession for personal use even if sales remain against the law. No one has attempted to tally up the damage done to marijuana users by being arrested and jailed, or from the re-sulting criminal record. But it's possible that, right now, the laws are doing more damage to users than marijuana abuse itself does, or than the damage averted by deterring people from use.

Users, simply as users, rarely spend much time behind bars. But marijuana growers, importers, and dealers risk felony con-victions and prison terms, some of them very long; at any one time, there are about forty thousand such prisoners. That's a modest share of the half million people incarcerated for drug-law violations all told, but it's still an enormous amount of potentially avoidable suffering.

Thus in deciding whether to make marijuana legal—and just how "legal" to make it—citizens and officials are constantly trading off one set of costs and risks against another. The right choice is not obvious.

Wouldn't the results of a policy that treated marijuana like alcohol be an improvement over the current mess?

It might. Or, then again, it might not. And what is "better" depends on judgments about the relative importance of different kinds of harm and benefit as well as estimates of the likely results of alternative policies. We can observe what marijuana use looks like when it's prohibited; we can only conjecture what it would look like if it were legal. Alas, there's no way of finding out for sure except by trying a new set of policies; quantitative estimates about a hypothetical world so different from the one we can actually observe are subject to too much uncertainty.

Two abusable drugs are already offered for sale more or less freely: nicotine and alcohol. (Some might add caffeine as a third instance.) The results aren't entirely encouraging: those two drugs alone far exceed all the illicit drugs combined in the number of problem users and the resulting ill health and death (see chapter 11). Tobacco is thought to kill about 440,000 Americans each year and alcohol 100,000. Nicotine doesn't generate many crimes or accidents, but alcohol does so in massive numbers, accounting for a third to a half of violent crimes and motor-vehicle deaths in the United States. Marijuana is, in many ways, less behaviorally risky than alcohol, primarily because it has no measured tendency to unleash aggression. Still, "less risky" isn't the same as "safe."

And making a drug legal does not entirely eliminate the law-enforcement problem. Any regulation or any tax strict enough or high enough to actually restrict or change behavior will face defiance and require enforcement. About a million and a half arrests are made each year on the charge of driving under the influence of alcohol: nearly twice as many as for all marijuana violations combined. That's in addition to arrests for sales to minors, possession by minors, drinking in public, and drunk and disorderly conduct. The law against alcohol use by minors is massively evaded, creating both large numbers of arrests and contempt for a law that seems so unreasonable to many—if a twenty-year-old can get married or enlist, why can't he buy a beer?—and is so widely defied.

But are we really prepared to let people drive stoned, or authorize sales to minors? The risks to minors from heavy marijuana use are graver than the risks to adults. So a pure "no-coercion" regime doesn't seem very attractive, while a policy that included bans on driving and on sales to minors wouldn't eliminate law enforcement from the picture.

The right comparison isn't between the burden of marijuana abuse under prohibition and the burden of prohibition itself; the right comparison is between the marijuana abuse problem *as it would be under some alternative policy* and the combined damage from drug abuse and the illicit markets under current policy.

But wasn't alcohol prohibition in the United States a complete failure?

Eventually the prohibition regime collapsed as the enforcement machinery failed to keep up with the growth of the illicit market. And the growth of massive criminal enterprises created profound, and lasting, damage. But in the early years of the "Noble Experiment," deaths from cirrhosis of the liver—a good measure of heavy drinking by long-term heavy drinkers—fell by about a third as prices approximately tripled. No one back then kept count of domestic violence, but everything we know about that phenomenon suggests that it probably fell along with heavy drinking.

But doesn't everyone know that Prohibition led to a big increase in homicides?

Yes, "everyone knows" that. But that doesn't make it so. That Prohibition helped foster the rise of large criminal organizations can't be denied. And there were certainly killings among rival alcohol distributors. However, the data do not support the claim that Prohibition increased the murder rate overall; to some extent, the rise in beer-baron violence was compensated for by reductions in ordinary drunken murders.

The Roaring Twenties were a period of urbanization, and big-city homicide rates have always been higher than rural homicide rates, so the move to the cities was accompanied by an increase in murder. But the largest part of the purported "Prohibition effect" on homicide is a mere data artifact: the number of jurisdictions whose homicides were being counted centrally rose over the period.

How much of the increase in consumption after legalization would reflect increased heavy use rather than increased casual use?

For any newly legalized substance, most of the new users would be casual users. But most of the increased volume would reflect increased use by people who use frequently. The volume of drug consumption doesn't depend very strongly on the total number of users. What's crucial is the number of heavy users. One eight-joint-a-day smoker (and there are at least hundreds of thousands of such people) is more important to the marijuana industry—legal or illegal—than fifty people who smoke a joint a week.

Statistics on alcohol consumption in the United States dramatize this phenomenon. Drinkers can then be categorized by their consumption, measured in average "standard drinks" per day. Averaging four or more drinks a day, year round, puts someone in the top tenth among drinkers, even ignoring the 44 percent of American adults who do not have as much as a single drink in any given month. That top 10 percent, as a group, puts away half of all the alcohol consumed. The next 10 percent—people who average between two and four drinks per day—accounts for another 30 percent of drinking.

So the top 20 percent of the drinkers consume four out of five drinks sold. The other 80 percent of the drinking population—drinkers whose average consumption is two drinks per day or less, making them what most people would consider "social drinkers"—represent only one-fifth of the total volume of alcohol sales. Except for those very few who drink expensive wine or very old Scotch, moderate drinkers make a comparably modest contribution to the revenues of the brewers, vintners, and distillers.

Similar arithmetic applies to marijuana. In household survey data, those consuming it weekly or less often account for only 8 percent of all days of marijuana use. Since frequent users probably also consume more per day of use, those weekly-or-less users likely account for an even smaller share of the quantity consumed—and perhaps a yet smaller share of spending, since three-quarters of them report getting marijuana for free the last time they obtained marijuana.

So the more-than-weekly users account for more than 90 percent of marijuana demand. That has a frightening implication: if we create a licit industry to grow and sell marijuana, the resulting businesses will have a strong profit incentive to create and sustain frequent and abusive consumption patterns, because the heaviest users consume so much of the product. So if we create a licit market, we should expect the industry's product design, pricing, and marketing to be devoted to creating as much addiction as possible.

If you think that marketing executives earn their large salaries, and TV networks earn their huge per-second rates for advertising time, by actually influencing consumer choices, that thought should make you nervous about all-out legalization of commerce in marijuana.

Can't the effects of marketing be reined in by regulations and taxes?

To some extent. But taxes and regulations also require enforcement, which is exactly what we were trying to get away from with legalization. In theory we could legalize marijuana and tax it back to its current illicit-market price, but then the financial reward from successfully selling untaxed marijuana would be as large as the current reward for selling illicit marijuana. The required excise tax would be about $10 per gram for high-potency marijuana (see chapter 11). To put that in perspective, a pack of cigarettes weighs about 20 grams. So the tax on something as easy to conceal as a pack of cigarettes would be about $200. In the mid-1990s widespread tax evasion forced Canada to repeal a cigarette tax of less than $5 per pack.

Moreover, the taxation and regulation effort would have to contend with a licit industry, which would attempt to mobilize its employees, shareholders, and consumers as a lobby against any effective restriction. Since the industry would be as dependent on problem users as the problem users are on their drug, we could expect all that lobbying effort to be devoted to preventing the adoption of policies that would effectively control addiction. The alcohol, tobacco, and gambling industries provide good examples.

True, the tobacco makers have slowly been forced back—partly because cigarettes, unlike most other drugs, do not create a large number of happy, nonproblem users who are grateful to their suppliers. But that success is not universal—smoking rates continue to rise in many other countries—and only looks good in relative terms; even now, more than a thousand Americans a day die of smoking-related causes.

The alcoholic-beverage industry, with its legion of not very profitable moderate users providing political cover for the relative handful of very profitable problem users, is having great success in resisting the adoption of effective policies to reduce problem drinking. Adjusted for inflation, alcohol taxes have fallen by four-fifths over the past sixty years, and it's still perfectly legal to sell alcohol to people who chronically get drunk and break the law. Those who claim that "regulation and taxation" could provide the benefits of prohibition without its costs might reasonably be asked why that doesn't seem to have happened with the one intoxicant that has actually been legalized.

What about legal availability without free trade? Couldn't that work?

Maybe. There could be a government monopoly, with the officials in charge being tasked with making drugs available but not promoting their use. Users could be allowed to produce their own drugs, or to form small consumer-owned cooperative groups, as they now do in Spain. In theory, physicians could be allowed to prescribe drugs for nonmedical use and given the responsibility for ensuring that their patients didn't slip into abuse or dependency. (The record with opiate pain-relievers, which have become a major abuse problem even though they are, by law, to be prescribed only for medical use, is far from reassuring with respect to physicians' capacity to do that job.) Users could be allowed to set monthly purchase quotas for themselves, enforced by sellers.

Those are all imaginable options (see chapter 14). Whether they are practical alternatives would have to be worked out in the real world rather than on paper. The details of implementation can matter quite a bit, and there is no guarantee the political process would settle on a scheme as well-crafted as the ones that can be drawn up as an academic exercise by scholars who can safely ignore political realities.

Isn't it impossible to make someone better off by coercing behavioral change?

If you define well-being as getting what you want when you want it, then by definition restrictions make people worse off.

If human beings were the perfectly rational actors depicted in elementary economics textbooks—Spock-like beings with perfect foresight and perfect self-command—that definition would make sense. In the actual world, with actual human beings, it is often false. That's the problem with John Stuart Mill's famous "Harm Principle":

> That the only purpose for which power can be rightfully exercised over any member of a civilized community, against his will, is to prevent harm to others. His own good, either physical or moral, is not sufficient warrant. He cannot rightfully be compelled to do or forbear because it will be better for him to do so, because it will make him happier, because, in the opinion of others, to do so would be wise, or even right.

When Mill wrote *On Liberty* in 1859 (partly as a protest against the recent enactment of alcohol prohibition in Maine), the Harm Principle represented a strikingly radical viewpoint. A century and a half later, it has come to seem like common sense. Lots of people who have never read, or even heard of, Mill think that individuals should be free to choose their own lifestyles.

But the Harm Principle hides an important assumption: that every "member of a civilized community" is temptation-proof. For most of us, a moment of introspection suffices to refute that claim as it applies to ourselves. Few of us always act as we would like to act.

Drugs are a difficult policy problem precisely because drug taking is an activity more prone than most to escaping rational self-command. That being so, the case for protecting people from themselves—when it can be done at an acceptable cost in terms of intrusive enforcement—seems attractive, Mr. Mill's views to the contrary notwithstanding. As Mill himself says: "If anyone saw a person attempting to cross a bridge which had been ascertained to be unsafe, and there were no time to warn him of his danger, they might seize him and turn him back without any real infringement of his liberty; for liberty consists in doing what one desires, and he does not desire to fall into the river."

By the same token, while many people desire to use marijuana, no one desires to become addicted. This argument doesn't answer the practical question about how much drug control is enough, but the Harm Principle in the abstract does not answer that question either. Facts are needed.

If people choose to harm themselves with drugs, why is that anyone else's business?

As a practical matter, those harming themselves often also harm others, at least when the behaviors involve losing control over intoxicants. Nevertheless, imagining the pure case of someone who inflicts no tangible harms on the public generally is a useful thought experiment for challenging propensities to constrain others' behavior merely because it is different or unconventional.

That challenge encapsulates the central argument against any sort of paternalistic intervention in private behavior. To some libertarians and advocates of laissez-faire, it seems axiomatic. But it is subject to at least three substantive responses; how persuasive they seem will vary from case to case depending on the facts, and from reader to reader depending on differing values.

First, by some reckonings, self-damage to a human being is still damage, and if it can be prevented at reasonable cost—including some restrictions on the freedom to engage in self-damaging behavior, as in Mill's bridge example—that's a good enough reason to interfere.

Second, only a hermit could ever truly engage in purely self-regarding behavior as Mill defines it. The rest of us have families, friends, neighbors, and coworkers, all of whom are likely to pay some sort of price if we get ourselves into profound trouble. If "any man's death diminishes me," then is self-destructive behavior ever fully self-regarding?

Obviously, these two claims could be carried to the extreme of requiring everyone to eat a healthy diet and take sufficient exercise. But the fact that a given principle of action could be extended to the point of absurdity does not taint its less absurd applications. The practical claim that interventions in private consumption choices are likely to prove difficult to implement and often have damaging side effects is no doubt true, and it constitutes a good argument for moderation in drug control. But the sweeping assertion that self-damage should always be ignored in policy making is hard to justify, at least on the pragmatic, utilitarian grounds on which Mill in particular chose to take his stand. The claim that there is a "human right" to regulate one's own mental processes—chemically or otherwise—would, if accepted, be decisive. But Mill makes no such argument.

The third answer to the question is that people do not, in fact, make their decisions about drug consumption merely as individuals, without reference to the drug-consumption choices of others, any more than they decide how to dress without reference to how others dress. Fashion is a ferociously potent force, and a person's belief—true or false—about the drug-taking patterns of others turns out to have important causal power over his or her own drug taking, to the point where one proven technique of preventing drug abuse among adolescents is to correct their often overinflated ideas about how many of their peers are using various drugs and how much they are using.

Abraham Lincoln, as a very young member of the Illinois legislature, laid out this argument in his astounding Temperance Address, which may be the wisest, wittiest, and most eloquent set of reflections on drugs and drug abuse ever offered. (The sample below does not do full justice to Lincoln's argument; the full text, available online, repays close study.)

> But it is said by some, that men will think and act for themselves; that none will disuse spirits or anything else, merely because his neighbors do; and that moral influence is not that powerful engine contended for. Let us examine this. Let me ask the man who could maintain this position most stiffly, what compensation he will accept to go to church some Sunday and sit during the sermon with his wife's bonnet upon his head? Not a trifle, I'll venture. And why not? There would be nothing irreligious in it: nothing immoral, nothing uncomfortable. Then why not? Is it not because there would be something egregiously *unfashionable* in it?
>
> Then it is the influence of fashion; and what is the influence of fashion, but the influence that other people's actions have on our own actions, the strong inclination each of us feels to do as we see all our neighbors do? Nor is the influence of fashion confined to any particular thing or class of things. It is just as strong on one subject as another. Let us make it as unfashionable to withhold our names from the temperance cause as for husbands to wear their wives' bonnets to church, and instances will be just as rare in the one case as the other.

Nor does it help matters to scoff at the influence of fashion and to demand that every individual stand on his or her own two moral legs. Even if it were true—which it is not—that the example of others provides no evidence whatever about what is and what is not a prudent course of action, it would remain true that whoever departs greatly from the pattern of others exposes himself to their negative judgments, often with important and unpleasant consequences.

Again, the current state of the world concerning alcohol allows us to predict some of the likely consequences of legalizing marijuana. A nondrinker in a group of drinkers will not only feel uncomfortable—if he has a normal degree of social sensitivity—he will also, as often as not, be unwelcome. (The genius of the "designated driver" idea is that it provides a social role for the teetotaler. But that does not work in every social setting.) And if that group of drinkers consists of his workmates, teammates, schoolmates, neighbors, or kinsfolk, his exclusion may carry a cost well beyond hurt feelings.

Since, then, drug taking is profoundly fashion-driven, the claim that it is "self-regarding behavior" cannot stand.

Today, there are relatively few social settings in which *not* smoking pot would single someone out for unfavorable attention. But surely that fact results in part from the current prohibition. If marijuana were legal, some people who do not now use it, and would prefer not to use it, would find it more socially comfortable to go along with the crowd: possibly to their detriment.

None of that proves that any particular drug regulation is prudent, or justifies the majority in quashing minority patterns of drug taking "just because." But the notion that John Stuart Mill somehow offered logical proof that all restrictions on drug taking must, in principle, be unjustified does not stand up to close inspection.

But isn't everyone with an addictive personality already addicted to something?

Sorry, but this argument for legalization is mere wishful thinking. While it's true that people with drug addictions tend to have some personality traits in common, many of those traits (such as secretiveness) tend to develop and become entrenched only *after* the addictions—as effects, not causes. Certainly there are differences across individuals and population groups in susceptibility to specific addictive behaviors, and some of those differences seem to have a genetic basis. But those are tendencies, not the irrevocable decrees of fate. When drugs are cheaper and more available, more people use more of them, and some of those people get caught up in bad habits and/or experience or cause acute harm (e.g., having a car accident while driving stoned even if they are not dependent).

As will be discussed further in chapter 9 with reference to alcohol and marijuana in particular, while one drug can substitute for another, two drugs can also be mutually complementary—like printers and ink cartridges—so that making either one cheaper increases the desirability of the other. At present, there is simply no scientific basis for any confident assertion about how legalizing any one drug would affect heavy drinking or how it would affect dependence on other illegal drugs.

If the results of legalization are uncertain, why not just try it out, and go back to the current system if legalization doesn't work?

Some processes are reversible; some are not. If you melt an ice cube and then put it in the freezer, you get an ice cube back. But if you toast a piece of bread and put it in the freezer, you get cold toast, not fresh bread. Legalization is more like toasting bread than melting an ice cube.

If we tried out legalization just for a limited time or only in one area, we might not learn much about the effects of a permanent, national policy change. (The number of problem users in the experimental area would surely go up, but how much of that would be "drug tourism" from elsewhere?)

But "experimenting" with legalization nationally may be effectively impossible. If the result were little or no change in problem use—some would say anything up to a doubling—the experiment could be deemed a success and there would be no reason to change back. But if the level of marijuana abuse were to quadruple or quintuple, and if problem drinking simultaneously increased, rather than decreasing—outcomes that cannot be ruled out based on any knowledge currently available—then there would be strong pressure to return to prohibition. But reinstituting a ban could create problems worse than the current situation. Those newly dependent users would not magically cease to be dependent if the law changed back, and the problems created by illicit markets and by enforcement are roughly proportional to the number of dependent users.

Alcohol prohibition in the United States revealed the difficulty of trying to change the ingrained habits of tens of millions of people. It's not clear that marijuana re-prohibition after a failed legalization experiment would do any better.

Additional Reading

Kaplan, John. *Marijuana: The New Prohibition.*

Kleiman, Mark A. R. *Against Excess.*

Kleiman, Mark A. R., Jonathan P. Caulkins, and Angela Hawken. *Drugs and Drug Policy.*

Lincoln, Abraham. "Temperance Address."

MacCoun, Robert J., and Peter Reuter. "Assessing Drug Prohibition and Its Alternatives: A Guide for Agnostics."

Rolles, Stephen. *Blueprint for Regulation.*

Zimring, Franklin E., and Gordon Hawkins. *The Search for Rational Drug Control.*

9

HOW IS LEGALIZATION OF MARIJUANA DIFFERENT FROM LEGALIZATION OF OTHER DRUGS?

How does legalizing marijuana compare to legalizing all drugs?

Legalizing marijuana involves both lower stakes and less uncertainty than legalizing any of the other major illicit drugs (cocaine/crack, heroin, and meth). Not that the consequences of marijuana legalization would be small or easy to project; legalization would be a big change with unpredictable results. But the stakes are even higher and the uncertainties even greater when contemplating legalization of these other drugs.

A principal argument for legalization of drugs generally is the anticipated reduction in crime, violence, corruption, and other problems associated with black markets. However, within the U.S. borders, most of those problems stem from black markets associated with cocaine/crack, heroin, and meth, not marijuana, so legalizing marijuana would not do much to solve those problems.

Marijuana legalization would also represent a smaller change from current policy than, for example, legalizing cocaine. While no modern industrial country has legalized marijuana, quite a few jurisdictions—including some within the United States—have substantially relaxed their marijuana policies. For more than a generation, one-third of the U.S. population has lived in states that have decriminalized marijuana possession. Furthermore, even in the other states, enforcement against users has been gentle enough that survey respondents have only a vague idea whether they live in a state that has decriminalized or not.

Indeed, while Berkeley public policy and law professor Rob MacCoun coined the phrase "slouching toward Amsterdam" to describe marijuana policy in California, one might argue California has slouched past Amsterdam in some respects. The Netherlands has quasi-legalized only retail sales, not commercial production and distribution; there are no billboards or weekly newspapers plastered with back-page dispensary ads offering free edibles. And as of summer 2011, there were many more medical marijuana dispensaries in California than there were marijuana-selling coffee shops in the Netherlands.

Isn't marijuana different from other drugs? It's natural, it's not addictive, and it's not toxic

On many dimensions marijuana is less risky than, say, methamphetamine.

However, there's nothing about a "natural" substance that guarantees it's safer than a synthetic. Nightshade, water hemlock, monkshood, and castor beans are all natural, and all quite poisonous. Alcohol is a natural product; any fruit juice will ferment if left standing. Yet alcohol is still a terribly dangerous drug.

It's true that refined chemicals can be more harmful than their natural sources (e.g., cocaine vs. coca leaves), and some processed forms of natural products (such as tobacco cigarettes) include harmful additives. But the health effects of marijuana have to be determined by evidence, not by assumption or assertion. Chapters 5 and 7 review that evidence. The basic finding is that smoking marijuana has adverse health effects, but the effects are generally not thought to be severe. Likewise, marijuana use can escalate to dependence. Indeed, currently about 4.4 million people in the United States self-report on surveys experiencing problems sufficient to warrant a diagnosis of abuse or dependence.

If marijuana accounts for half of all drug arrests, would legalizing marijuana free up half of our prison cells?

No, not even close.

First of all, drug law violators account for only about one-fifth to one-quarter of those in prison—though that is still a considerable share. One sometimes hears figures in the 50–60 percent range, but those pertain either to federal prisons or to the number of prisoners whose incarceration is linked in some way to their drug abuse (e.g., they committed a burglary to get money to buy drugs). The state prison systems collectively house roughly ten times as many inmates as federal prisons, so the proportion in state facilities dominates the national (combined state and federal) figure.

The proportions are about the same in jails. Media accounts do not always differentiate between the two, but jails are not the same as prisons. To simplify, prisons are state and federal institutions that house people who have been convicted of a felony and received sentences of a year or longer. Jails are usually city or county facilities holding a mixture of people awaiting trial and those serving shorter sentences.

Would legalizing marijuana at least cut in half the number of drug law violators behind bars? Again, no; not even close. University of South Carolina criminologist Eric Sevigny estimates that only about 8 percent of state and federal prison inmates serving time for drug law violations were marijuana-only offenders. (Some caught trafficking cocaine, meth, or heroin also possessed marijuana when arrested. But those individuals would still have been imprisoned even if marijuana were legal.) Some other cases involve a mix of drug and non-drug violations. For example, there are convicted robbers who violated the terms of their probation or parole by getting caught with marijuana. Their "controlling offense" would be robbery, but if marijuana were legal they might still be on community release. (Or not. Probationers and parolees are sometimes forbidden to use alcohol; such a rule might apply to marijuana after legalization.)

So the counting gets complicated, particularly for jails as opposed to prisons, but in round terms, drug violations account for about a fifth of incarceration and marijuana-only violations account for less than 10 percent of that.

This might seem puzzling to those who have read claims that marijuana legalization would create big criminal justice savings. For example, Harvard economist Jeff Miron has estimated that marijuana accounted for $13.7 billion of spending to enforce drug prohibition. But Miron did not have data breaking down inmates by drug. So he assumed that the corrections budget for marijuana was the budget for all drug offenses multiplied by marijuana's share of arrests for drug sale or manufacture. This overestimates marijuana-related incarceration, because those arrested for marijuana are less likely than those arrested for other drugs to be convicted and sentenced to long prison terms.

How much drug-related crime, violence, and corruption would marijuana legalization eliminate?

Not much.

Arguably the greatest social cost of prohibiting most substances is the crime, violence, and corruption engendered by the resulting black markets. However, the great bulk of those problems stem from the markets for illegal stimulants (cocaine/

crack and methamphetamine) and opiates (specifically heroin), not marijuana. One does not read about many drive-by shootings between rival marijuana gangs.

This is not an inevitable consequence of pharmacology. Violent gangs are involved in cannabis production and trafficking in British Columbia and, most notoriously, in Mexico. Rather, it is mostly a matter of economics. Marijuana production, distribution, and consumption in the U.S. usually do not involve transactions or penalties with stakes high enough to make it worth killing someone.

Cocaine shipments entering the U.S. might weigh 250 kilograms and be worth $10,000–$15,000 per kilogram, for a total value of $3 million, yet that shipment can be hidden in the trunk of a large sedan. Marijuana entering the U.S. costs about $400 per pound, so $3 million worth of marijuana would weigh 7,500 pounds, or enough to fill a medium-sized truck. There is not much point trying to shoot one's way out of a traffic stop when the get-away vehicle is a semi.

Another difference is that most retail and even low-level wholesale marijuana sales occur between friends indoors rather than strangers on street-corners. Eighty-nine percent of survey respondents report obtaining marijuana most recently from a friend or relative, and more than half (58 percent) say they obtained it for free. That stands in marked contrast to low-level distribution of heroin and crack which often occurs in violent, place-based markets controlled by armed gangs.

Would legalization increase marijuana use and dependence by as much as legalization of crack and other drugs would increase their markets?

Probably not.

It is very hard to predict how legalization of any substance will affect use and dependence. But most of the factors suggest bigger changes in consumption for cocaine/crack, heroin, and meth than for marijuana. So common sense and armchair analysis point to smaller changes for cannabis than for the other drugs.

The three most salient mechanisms are availability, price, and enforcement risk for users.

Legalization, at least on the alcohol model, would generally increase availability; it's easier to make a purchase at a store than to find an illegal dealer. However, youth already report substantially greater availability for marijuana than for other drugs, so there is less room for change for marijuana. (More than four out of five 12th graders describe marijuana as "fairly easy" or "very easy" to get. The corresponding proportions are only slightly higher for alcohol (90.4 percent) but much lower for cocaine (36 percent), crack (26 percent), heroin (24 percent), and meth (18 percent).)

Likewise, legalization would reduce production costs dramatically for marijuana, but less than it would for the other major illegal drugs. Furthermore, at less than a dollar per stoned hour, today's cannabis prices may already be low enough not to represent much of a barrier to use.

And as argued above, current user penalties may already not be high enough to deter much marijuana use: again, especially among juveniles.

On the other hand, the effect on consumption of legalizing more dangerous drugs might tend to be self-limiting. Adolescents' rates of crack use in the 2000s were particularly low in demographic groups that crack hit particularly hard in the 1980s; watching one's aunt sell her body to buy crack may be a more potent warning than any conventional drug prevention message. So perhaps legalization would lead to greater increases in marijuana dependence precisely because marijuana dependence is so much less debilitating than is dependence on some of the other illegal drugs. On the other hand, insofar as marijuana use is currently a symbol of rebellion, legalizing it might actually eliminate one motive for adolescents to light up.

Overall, then, it seems very likely—but not certain—that legalizing marijuana would produce a smaller percentage increase in use and abuse than would legalizing other illicit drugs.

Would more marijuana use lead to more alcohol abuse, or less?

There could be effects in both directions, and it's not possible to predict which would dominate. The answer might be different for different groups of people, and might not remain the same over time.

It might seem intuitive that making marijuana more available would tend to decrease alcohol use; as competing means of altering one's mood, one drug can substitute for the other. No doubt if cannabis were legal some of today's alcoholics would be daily pot-smokers instead; that would, on average, make them and those around them better off.

But two drugs can also be mutually complementary. When two commodities are economic complements—like cell phones and cell phone apps—making either one cheaper or more available increases demand for the other. Most people with substance-abuse disorders who aren't exclusively alcohol abusers use at least two drugs; much of the folklore of drug use involves the effects of various drug combinations.

Economists have tried to estimate what they call the "cross-price elasticities of demand" between marijuana and alcohol—that is, the effect that cheaper or more expensive alcohol has on marijuana use, and the effect that cheaper or more expensive marijuana has on alcohol use. Alas, different studies reach opposing conclusions, and some studies reach opposing conclusions for different population groups. Furthermore, these studies estimate contemporaneous effects through the price mechanism but miss any longer-term effects and those through other mechanisms (e.g., reputation and custom).

The uncertainties are amplified when considering legalization for the simple reason that no country in the modern era has legalized marijuana, so there are no historical data pertaining to the effect of large declines in marijuana prices on alcohol use. Hence, there is truly no scientific basis for any confident assertion about what would happen to heavy drinking if marijuana were legalized.

This lack of knowledge matters enormously. The magnitudes of the various alcohol-related problems in the United States are much greater than the corresponding marijuana-related problems. The disparity varies by outcome; alcohol causes three to four times as much dependence as marijuana (8.8 million vs. 2.7 million dependent users by one measure), but more than ten times as much crime and violence. "Cost of illness" studies provide one relevant yardstick. The figure for alcohol (one estimate placed it at $185 billion in 1998) is comparable to that of all illicit drugs combined (estimated at $181 billion in 2002 by a similar methodology). Since marijuana probably accounts for no more than one-sixth of all illicit-drug damage, the "cost of illness" associated with alcohol is likely at least six times the corresponding figure for marijuana.

Hence, in policy terms, a small change in alcohol abuse and dependence could outweigh a large change in marijuana abuse and dependence. Imagine—and again, we don't know—that policy changes that led to doubling marijuana abuse and dependence would cut alcohol abuse and dependence by 10 percent. In cost-of-illness terms, those two effects would roughly cancel out; the losses from more potheads would be matched by the gains from fewer drunks. On the other hand, if the effect went the other way—if doubling marijuana use were to increase alcohol abuse and dependence by 10 percent—it's hard to see how any of the gains on the marijuana side could balance out the harms from increased heavy drinking. And yet, based on what is now known, it's not possible to rule out even bigger changes, in either direction.

Interactions with other drugs could also make a difference. Suppose doubling marijuana use also doubled marijuana abuse and dependence, leading to 4.4 million more people having a marijuana abuse or dependence problem. If even a modest proportion of them subsequently started abusing cocaine, then that would be a sizable increase in cocaine abuse. By most measures, even complete elimination of all marijuana-related social costs would not be enough to offset a 33 percent increase in cocaine-related harms. On the other hand, if cheaper marijuana prompted cocaine or meth abusers to "trade down" to a less disruptive dependence on marijuana, that would be a huge social gain.

Even interactions with tobacco could matter. If a doubling in marijuana smoking led to even a 1 percent increase or decrease in tobacco use, that could be a swing of 4,000 more or 4,000 fewer tobacco related deaths per year; those are large numbers compared to the (quite small) number of deaths associated with marijuana.

This uncertainty makes it simply impossible at present to produce a solid benefit-cost analysis of marijuana legalization. Even if one could somehow pin down all the marijuana-related outcomes, there is no way to do the same for indirect effects mediated through changes in the use of other substances. (See chapter 11.)

If alcohol is more dangerous than marijuana, what's the logical justification for one being legal and the other illegal?

If we were making laws for a planet whose population had never experienced either marijuana or alcohol, and we had to choose one of the two drugs to make available, there would be a strong case for choosing marijuana, which has lower organic toxicity, lower addictive risk, and a much weaker link with accidents and violence.

But that's not the planet we inhabit. Here on this planet, alcohol has been an ingrained part of many cultures since the Neolithic revolution (which may have been driven in part by the discovery that grain could be brewed into beer). People have used cannabis plant products for thousands of years, but its widespread use as an intoxicant in the United States is a phenomenon of the last hundred years. Even today only about one in sixteen American adults uses marijuana at all in the course of a typical year; for alcohol, that figure is more than half.

History matters. Custom matters. Practicality matters. Even if there were public support for it, going back to Prohibition wouldn't work—without a truly ferocious degree of law enforcement—precisely because centuries of tradition and decades of marketing have left alcohol use a deeply ingrained feature of most social systems outside the Islamic world.

The technical term for this is "path dependence." If alcohol had just been invented and no one was yet using it, it would go straight into Schedule I: high potential for abuse and no accepted medical value. And that ban might make sense. But once there is an established user base, prohibition becomes impractical. Marijuana is not, or at least not yet, equally entrenched.

It's true that the arguments for maintaining marijuana prohibition also point strongly toward tighter controls on alcohol: higher taxes, limits on marketing, bans on sales to people convicted of driving drunk or other crimes committed under the influence. So it's fair to mock the "drug warriors" who worry about every drug except the one that does the most damage. But, by the same token, advocates of marijuana legalization who point to the horrible amount of damage alcohol does are pointing to precisely the strongest argument for maintaining marijuana prohibition: the one drug we legalized is the most harmful of all despite all our efforts at regulation.

Could it be reasonable to support legalizing marijuana but not other drugs?

Absolutely.

There is no logical reason to apply the same policies to all psychoactives. Most people support prohibiting crack but not caffeine, and that is an entirely defensible position.

A key reason someone might be more willing to legalize marijuana than the other major drugs is that legalizing marijuana is less risky. Relative to the other major drugs, marijuana enforcement is already lax, and as a result prices are much less inflated. Also, social disapprobation is rather modest, and dependence is easier to break. So legalizing marijuana is far less likely to produce highly problematic increases in dependence than legalizing any of those other substances.

Can two reasonable people sensibly disagree about marijuana legalization?

Certainly.

Even if we could accurately estimate all the gains and losses—which we can't—there's no reason two people holding different values couldn't reasonably disagree on whether that change represented progress. One person might care enormously about reducing dependence for the sake of the children of those who are dependent; another might place greater emphasis on reducing violence or incarceration. Those two people could make the same predictions about the likely consequences of legalization but reach different conclusions about its desirability (see chapter 16).

Additional Reading

Kleiman, Mark A. R. *Against Excess.*
MacCoun, Robert J., and Peter Reuter. *Drug War Heresies.*

10

WHAT IS THE CONTEXT OF THE MARIJUANA LEGALIZATION DEBATE?

How does legalization differ from decriminalization
or depenalization?

One reason the debate gets so furious is that people sometimes use the same words to refer to different things. "Legalization," as we use it here, means allowing marijuana to be produced as well as possessed by anyone (within age restrictions) who follows relevant rules and regulations. "Decriminalization" maintains the prohibition against production and sale but not on use or possession of small quantities. Most jurisdictions that decriminalize retain civil or administrative sanctions for possession, perhaps in deference to international treaties. As a result there is no agreed-on term for fully legalizing possession while still prohibiting production and distribution. The term "depenalization" encompasses both decriminalization and the lesser step of reducing but not eliminating criminal penalties. By this definition, many of the U.S. states which are usually referred to as having "decriminalized" marijuana have only depenalized it. Unfortunately, outside the scholarly literature, this distinction is rarely made, and the term decriminalization is used to describe any situation that leaves first-time offenders facing minimal sanction risk for possession of amounts suitable only for personal consumption.

How many countries allow commercial marijuana production?

None for use as a drug, though some allow industrial hemp.

Historically, legal commerce was the original state, and prohibition came later—even later in the United States for marijuana than for the opiates or cocaine.

There was little or no use of marijuana for intoxication in many countries before the late nineteenth century. Commerce pertained primarily to medicines and to the nondrug uses of the cannabis plant as a source of food, fuel, and fiber (see chapter 15). So absence of prohibition did not indicate a liberal stance toward recreational pot smoking.

Marijuana as a prohibited substance is largely a twentieth-century creation. Greece in 1890 was one of the first countries to ban the cultivation and use of marijuana, due to concerns about hashish use among the poor. Most other European countries did not begin outlawing marijuana until the 1920s. In the United States, the Marijuana Tax Act of 1937 effectively prohibited marijuana nationally, but many states had already banned production and possession of marijuana. Starting in the 1960s, prohibition was globalized by the international drug conventions (discussed below); by the end of the twentieth century most countries had made it a criminal offense to produce and distribute marijuana.

A notable exception is India. In 1985 India's central government passed a law prohibiting the production and consumption of cannabis resin (*charas*) and flowers (*ganja*), but made an exception for cannabis leaves and seeds (*bhang*), which have been used in religious ceremonies for centuries. The law allows state governments to permit, control, and regulate "the cultivation of any cannabis plant, production, manufacture, possession, transport, import inter-State, export inter-State, sale, purchase, consumption or use of cannabis (excluding charas)." In some states there are government-authorized shops selling *bhang*-infused drinks and foods.

While Latin American countries have enacted a flurry of measures to reduce the penalties for drug offenses in recent years, no country currently allows commercial production of marijuana for sale for nonmedical use. Quite a few countries have experimented with "middle ground" positions between strict prohibition and commercial legalization (see chapter 14).

Has support for legalization in the United States been growing?

Yes. Support among the American public for legalizing marijuana use grew from the mid-1960s to the late 1970s, fell sharply through 1990, and has since rebounded to an all-time high; the latest poll shows the country just about evenly split. Not surprisingly, state-level attempts to liberalize are more common during periods of greater public support for legalization.

Figure 10.1 shows the number of state-level actions (bars, with counts indicated on the left-hand vertical axis) alongside public opinion poll results (line and dots, with levels indicated

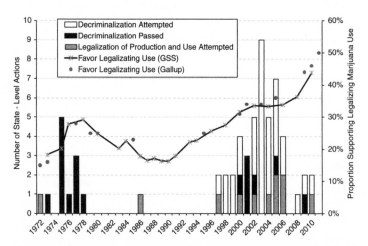

Figure 10.1 Trends over Time in Public Support for Legalizing Marijuana Use and in State-Level Actions (Passed or Failed) to Legalize or Decriminalize Marijuana in the United States.

on the right-hand vertical axis). The solid line is the proportion of people answering "yes" to the General Social Survey (GSS) question "Do you think the use of marijuana should be made legal or not?" The dots come from similar but not identical questions on Gallup Poll surveys.

However, these surveys did not ask respondents whether they supported legalizing marijuana use *and production*. Simply legalizing use is much closer to what is known as decriminalization than what we normally refer to as legalization. How many people would have agreed with the proposition "It should be legal to sell marijuana" is an open question.

Who supports and opposes marijuana legalization in the United States?

The demographic patterns mostly conform to stereotypes: greater support among those born after 1950, men, those without children, those with weaker ties to organized religion, liberals, and Westerners (see figure 10.2). And of course marijuana users—particularly long-term users—are more likely to support legalization. But there are some unexpected twists.

As one would expect, liberals are more likely to support legalization than conservatives. Yet the association is stronger for political ideology than for party affiliation. Conservative Democrats are no more likely to support legalization than conservative Republicans.

Younger respondents are more favorable to marijuana than their elders. In the 1970s this showed up as a generation gap between "baby boomers" (those born between 1945 and 1965) and both their parents and grandparents. But times changed. While the generation born before 1925 (the "greatest" or "GI" generation) remains staunchly opposed, support for legalization among the "silent generation" (those born between 1925 and 1945) has grown substantially. In contrast, support among baby boomers fell sharply during the 1980s and then rebounded.

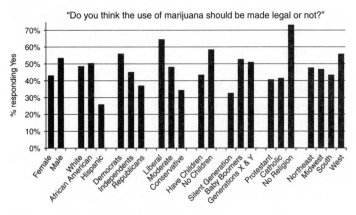

Figure 10.2 Support for Marijuana Legalization among Respondents to the 2010 General Social Survey.

Parents with children living at home are substantially less likely to support legalization; thus the baby boomers' vacillation may stem from their becoming parents. Generally, the gap between parents and those without children is most pronounced in groups with higher rates of overall support for legalization (e.g., males and liberals). To simplify, conservatives oppose legalization regardless of whether they have kids; liberals tend to change their position depending on whether or not they are thinking about the issue from a parent's perspective.

In terms of religious affiliations, fundamentalist Christians are less likely to support legalization than liberal Christians. But the largest gap is between those who self-identify as having no religion and those who report some denominational affiliation.

Most demographic groups' support for marijuana legalization follows the V-shaped pattern over time shown in figure 10.1, but the recent growth in support has been particularly pronounced among African Americans. A decade ago non-Hispanic whites stood out from the rest of the population in their high rates of support; now Hispanics and Asian Americans stand out from both non-Hispanic whites and African Americans by having lower levels of support.

Arguably the most consequential variation is not across demographic groups but across states. Even if national polls reveal ambivalence or slight opposition, there may be individual states with enough support to pass legalization, especially if advocates raise enough money to purchase media time and opponents do not. (How much funding would be "enough" depends on the state; more for California, for example, than for Colorado.) If even one state legalizes marijuana, that will have important effects for the country as a whole (see chapter 12).

Who supported Proposition 19 and why?

In the fall of 2010, California voters defeated Proposition 19, an initiative to legalize marijuana, by a vote of 53.5 percent to 46.5 percent. Variations in support across demographic groups provide fodder for "what if" analyses. Proposition 19 came close enough to passing that one can devise scenarios under which it would have passed. Suppose Californians had voted on Proposition 19 in a presidential election year, when more voters under thirty typically turn out? Or suppose it were voted on a decade from now, when generational replacement erodes the effect of continued opposition among the pre-boomer cohorts?

Indeed, Proposition 19 might have passed if it had simply been able to win support of all those who favor legalization. In a postelection poll conducted by the Public Policy Institute of California, 6 percent of respondents reported that they supported legalization generally but nonetheless voted against Proposition 19. (The most common reason they gave was that the initiative was poorly written.) Adding that 6 percent to those who did vote yes would have tipped the balance.

On the other hand, 2010 was a particularly opportune time to propose a new source of tax revenue in a state facing massive budget deficits. Three-quarters of California voters cited the economy, jobs/unemployment, or the state budget/deficit as the most important issue of the day, versus 4 percent for the next most cited concern (education). Not surprisingly, potential tax revenue was the most common reason cited by those voting for Proposition 19 (29 percent, versus 10–12 percent each for the three next most cited arguments: personal freedom, saving police resources, and reducing drug-related crime and violence).

Donations for and against Proposition 19 were not large, totaling in the low millions of dollars. Initial funding for Prop 19 came largely from one of the entrepreneurs of California's large and free-wheeling medical marijuana industry, and George Soros, a long-time supporter of liberalized drug policies, donated $1 million in the final days of the campaign. The anti-Prop 19 campaign received significantly less in donations (estimates are in the low six figures), with some money coming from law enforcement groups.

Why are voters sometimes bolder than the people they elect?

While some politicians favor legalizing marijuana—Congressmen Barney Frank (D-MA) and Ron Paul (R-TX) introduced the Ending Federal Marijuana Prohibition Act in 2011—as a rule, the voters are more supportive of legalization than their representatives: more states have passed medical marijuana laws by referendum than by legislation.

This gap has many potential explanations, but one of them is the campaign consultant's maxim: "It's not what you say about the issues, it's what your issues say about you." Some voters take a politician's stances on culturally charged issues as gauges of the politician's personal character. In the context of negative political advertising, a legislator must consider how any given vote would look if presented in the worst possible light.

Since marijuana is a drug, voting to legalize marijuana can easily be spun as "voting for drug legalization" generally. And while support for marijuana legalization now enjoys rough parity with opposition in public opinion, support for legalizing all of the currently illicit drugs is confined to a very small minority.

Thus, a state legislator needs to consider the risk of being portrayed by a future opponent as being "soft on drugs." Even though a strong majority of voters now support medical marijuana, voting for that position in the legislature would not be without political risk. Some voters who themselves support medical availability might still vote against a candidate who had voted for such legislation if the candidate's vote—as portrayed by opponents—made them suspicious of the candidate's moral soundness or cultural loyalties.

Would marijuana legalization violate international conventions?

About a dozen international conventions—essentially, multilateral treaties—about psychoactive substances have entered into force since 1919. The early conventions focused on regulating the licit opiate trade for medicinal purposes, but over time additional conventions encompassed more substances. These early conventions also introduced the idea of classifying drugs into "schedules" according to their potential for addiction and their value in medical use.

The multiplicity of agreements stimulated proposals for a comprehensive treaty to merge and update all of them. This led to the Single Convention on Narcotic Drugs in 1961, the cornerstone of modern-day drug control. Currently 184 countries are parties to the 1972 version of the Single Convention.

If a signatory nation legalized marijuana possession and production for nonmedicinal purposes, that would violate the Single Convention. Parties to the Single Convention are required to make the production, trade, and possession for nonscientific and nonmedical purposes a "punishable offense," although there is room for debate about what "punishable" actually means. The convention explicitly states that "serious offences shall be liable to adequate punishment, particularly imprisonment or other penalties of deprivation of liberty," although "abusers" may undergo treatment, education, rehabilitation, or social reintegration instead. It is up to each country to make its own decision about what is serious and what the punishment will be. Another UN convention signed in 1988 provided more guidance, suggesting that possession of any prohibited substance for nonmedicinal or nonscientific use "was to be made not just a punishable offense, but specifically a criminal offence under domestic law."

There is a belief that international law will not change until the United States wants it to change, although the United States is hardly alone in its hawkish stance; many African and Middle Eastern countries that could only join the convention after shedding colonial rule also hold conservative positions with respect to intoxicating drugs, as do many Asian countries. With respect to these conventions, the United States is out of step with its usual European allies and many of its Latin American neighbors, but not with the world at large.

Does Dutch policy violate these international conventions?

No.

As discussed in greater detail in chapter 14, the Dutch did not legalize the production of marijuana. Rather, they have a formal policy of not enforcing their laws against those possessing small amounts or against coffee shops selling small amounts; the coffee-shop policy is what makes the Netherlands unique. Still, they are in compliance with the Single Convention since they have a law on the books indicating that production, trafficking, and possession are punishable offenses. As noted by Dutch researcher Jos Silvis, the obligation to the Single Convention is met in Dutch legislation, "but there are no clauses in the relevant UN conventions that concern the actual enforcement of the legislation." While this logic could just as easily be applied to the growers and middlemen who supply the coffee shops, the Dutch choose to actively enforce laws against production and wholesaling.

While the 1988 convention pushed countries to make possession a criminal offense, the Netherlands ratified with "reservation" this clause so they would not have to comply with this provision.

What are the consequences for violating international conventions?

The consequences to an individual of violating a drug law are generally clear. The U.S. Controlled Substances Act specifies that first-time possession offenses are punishable by up to one year in prison and/or a minimum fine of $1,000 unless the quantities involved are personal-consumption amounts, in which case they instead are liable only for a civil penalty of up to $10,000.

In contrast, there is no formula specifying the consequences for a country violating the international drug control treaties; it is not as if the UN can lock up the offending country's president or prime minister. (Countries that receive international aid may have more to fear, if moves that displease donor countries lead to reductions in aid. Countries that become centers of international trafficking may feel additional pressure.)

Furthermore, since none of the signatories have yet violated the Single Convention by legalizing marijuana (the convention does not prohibit industrial hemp), the first violator would be in uncharted territory. The convention does not specify a penalty for violators, but it does state that if a dispute arises about the interpretation or application of the convention, it could be referred to the International Court of Justice (ICJ). The ICJ may render a decision, but it really does not have any enforcement power in these matters. Indeed, some countries made reservations so they would not have to accept the jurisdiction of the ICJ in these matters.

A likely consequence would be public rebuke by some of the signatories and by the International Narcotics Control Board (INCB), the body tasked with monitoring adherence to the Single Convention and its successors.

At the extreme, some countries could punish the violating state by imposing economic sanctions. Indeed, the United States has had a mechanism for this called "certification," by which the president decides each year whether certain countries known for illegal drug production and/or trafficking are making progress combating drugs and cooperating with the United States. There are currently twenty countries that must be certified, including Brazil, Colombia, and Mexico. Those countries determined not to be cooperating with the United States to combat drugs are "decertified" and become ineligible for certain types of bilateral assistance from the United States. For Andean countries, decertification can also mean the removal of U.S. trade preferences. This is very much a political tool, and even if a country is decertified, the president can waive the prohibition on assistance. For example, both Bolivia and Venezuela were decertified in 2011 (along with Burma), but President Obama determined that "continued support for bilateral programs in Bolivia and limited programs in Venezuela are vital to the national interests of the United States."

Could these international treaties be changed?

Yes.

The Single Convention can be amended, as it was in 1971 to include new substances. Any of the parties can propose an amendment, and it will enter into force if no party rejects the amendment within eighteen months. If a party does reject the amendment, there may be a conference for the parties to discuss the matter, or the UN General Assembly could take up the amendment. No international consensus on liberalizing policy toward marijuana is in sight.

A number of amendments have been discussed over the years by academics and advocacy organizations, including the removal of marijuana from the list of scheduled drugs. Australian sociologist Robin Room and his colleagues conducted an in-depth analysis about how to change policy in the context of the Single Convention. Room and colleagues outline a number of actions that a country could take if it wanted to legalize marijuana and remain within the limits set by the Single Convention. For example, a country could simply withdraw from the convention (a step known as denunciation), though this is rare—less than 4 percent of ratifications involving multilateral treaties since 1945 have been denounced. But a country could also denounce the convention and then immediately re-ratify it with a reservation about marijuana, essentially saying that the country agrees to abide by the rest of the convention but not that specific article. The reservation takes effect if less than one-third of the signatories object to it within a year. In July 2011, Bolivia announced it would withdraw from the Single Convention on January 1, 2012, and attempt to rejoin with a formal objection to the ban on coca chewing. As expected, the INCB and United States claimed that this unprecedented action would weaken the integrity of the international drug conventions. It remains to be seen whether Bolivia's reservation is accepted. But if it isn't, this means Bolivia's reaccession to the treaty is also rejected; the INCB and United States would prefer to have all of the major coca producing countries as signatories, so Bolivia may have the stronger bargaining position. If the Bolivian effort succeeds, it might—or might not—set a precedent followed by other countries with respect to marijuana.

Additional Reading

Caulkins, Jonathan P., Carolyn Coulson, Christina Farber, and Joseph Vesely. "Marijuana Legalization: Certainty, Impossibility, Both or Neither?"

Courtwright, David T. *Forces of Habit*.

Musto, David F. *The American Disease*.

Room, Robin, et al. *Cannabis Policy*.

11

WHAT IF MARIJUANA WERE TREATED LIKE ALCOHOL?

There are major variations in how alcohol is regulated in the United States, and even larger differences internationally. Yet in most parts of the United States, the following rules apply to alcohol; they might be thought of as constituting the "alcohol model" for marijuana:

Private, for-profit enterprise may participate in production, distribution, and sale.

Commercial activities are subject to normal business regulations.

Commercial activities are subject to additional, substance-specific regulations.

Commercial producers and sellers need special licenses that can be revoked for violations of those regulations.

The substance-specific regulations are designed to manage the market, not to minimize intoxication (other than behind the wheel or on the job).

There are restrictions on who may use, when and where they use, and what they may do under the influence, but for the most part, any adult not visibly under the influence can buy in unlimited quantities.

This might also be called "legalization with commercialization" to distinguish it from "noncommercial legalization" via government monopoly, grow-your-own (perhaps with informal sharing), or with production and distribution limited to non-profits such as user co-ops.

What special regulations could apply to legal marijuana?

Prohibition is a blunt instrument; legalization plus regulation allows for finer distinctions. Different localities might adopt different approaches according to local circumstances.

For example, municipalities might regulate where marijuana can be used. Drinking alcohol on the street, in parks, and in other outdoor public places is illegal in most of the United States, but drinking is allowed in restaurants and bars. In much of the country, the opposite holds true for tobacco: most indoor use in public spaces is banned to protect nonsmokers from secondhand smoke, but outdoor use is permitted.

Marijuana is both intoxicating (like alcohol) and often smoked (like tobacco), creating the risk of secondhand exposure, or at least offense—some people find the aroma of marijuana very hard to take. So marijuana regulations could combine approaches taken with alcohol and tobacco. Many jurisdictions already have special sanctions for smoking marijuana "in the public view," and California's 2010 legislative attempt to legalize marijuana—the so-called Ammiano Bill—would have banned indoor marijuana smoking in places where tobacco smoking is banned. (What a user is to do where smoking is banned both indoors and outdoors is a different question; perhaps the laws might permit the use of vaporizers, which produce mist instead of smoke.)

Smoking marijuana while driving could still be illegal, even if use were legal in other settings; most states ban having an open container of alcohol in a moving car, or driving under the influence of any intoxicant. However, regulating marijuana-intoxicated driving faces a technical challenge: the most common marijuana tests cannot detect current intoxication or impairment, as breath tests do for alcohol; instead, they measure use over the past several days, or—for frequent users—even weeks. Determining current intoxication requires a blood test which measures actual THC (as opposed to THC metabolites). Some Australian jurisdictions enforcing marijuana-impaired driving ordinances fall back on a saliva test which detects recent use (within hours), though not current impairment.

The product itself could be regulated. For example, even if marijuana in its conventional form were legal, one could still ban selling it in candy bars and brownies, paralleling efforts to limit the sale of "alcopops" that appeal to youth. For that matter, one could ban selling alcoholic beverages containing THC (as distinct from beer that is merely flavored with hemp seeds), just as there are restrictions on adding caffeine to alcoholic beverages on the grounds that it is an "unsafe food additive." Flavorings and other additives could be banned or regulated, just as the Tobacco Control Act bans cigarettes containing fruit, candy, vanilla, or clove flavors.

Two particular targets of regulation are potency (as measured by THC content) and the mix of psychoactive components (e.g., the CBD-to-THC ratio; see chapter 2). Limiting potency has advantages and disadvantages; more potent strains may create greater risks of adverse side effects, but they also may limit lung damage per hour of intoxication. There is also emerging science concerning synergistic interactions of THC with other psychoactive components; perhaps the seemingly dangerous very-high-THC, very-low-CBD varieties could be banned even if other forms were permitted—as absinthe (containing the toxin thujone) has sometimes been banned even when other forms of alcohol are allowed. Indeed, the Netherlands is now discussing plans to treat marijuana containing more than 15 percent THC as a "hard drug," thus banning it from the coffee shops.

A less intrusive approach than regulating the chemical contents would be requiring testing and accurate labeling. It is hard to argue with efforts to better inform consumers, but there may be complications. The requirements might be disproportionately burdensome for small producers.

Thinking about regulations can be a Rorschach test for the observers' beliefs about legalization generally. Public-health-oriented advocates of legalization see great potential for careful regulation to mitigate the harms of marijuana use, while libertarian advocates are suspicious of regulation generally. Opponents of legalization see regulations as weak instruments in the face of the creative force of market innovation, particularly if the regulatory agencies get too cozy with marijuana industry lobbyists. The history of tobacco and alcohol regulation is hardly encouraging on this score.

Opinions also diverge with respect to the nature of products that will be offered. Optimists anticipate organically grown, carefully labeled forms that protect users from the risks of black-market products and allow them to choose the product that best matches their reasons for using. Pessimists believe such high-end products will exist but, like organic vegetables, will remain a niche market for the educated elite, with the bulk of what is sold being the equivalent of "store brand" foods or mass-market beer—consistent quality without frills at low cost. Likewise, pessimists worry that for-profit companies will promote blends designed to maximize frequent intoxication, while optimists hope the market pushes products more consistent with responsible use.

"Bundling" with other products may be particularly appealing, because the cost of adding marijuana to some other existing product line would generally be very low.

It is hard to predict how the dance among producers' marketing strategies, consumers' tastes, and regulators' control efforts would play out, and the answer might vary from jurisdiction to jurisdiction. The most likely outcome would be considerable variety and product proliferation, if for no other reason than that the producers will have a hard time making large profits if they sell only undifferentiated marijuana.

Could advertising be restricted in the United States?

Advertising restrictions are both important and controversial. Public-health-oriented advocates of legalization reassure skeptics that advertising and promotion would be banned; children's television shows wouldn't be sponsored by the marijuana growers' association. Skeptics warn that First Amendment free-speech protections make such controls difficult in the United States.

A quick aside on constitutional law: the United States is atypical in this regard. The U.S. Supreme Court does distinguish between what it calls "commercial speech" (marketing) and other forms of communication, but the gap is much narrower than in most other democracies. For example, the court has struck down bans on alcohol advertising. What the pharmaceutical industry calls direct-to-consumer advertising is currently used aggressively to market some strongly psychoactive medicines. But the Securities and Exchange Commission has imposed very tight limits on what underwriters can say about issues of new stock. So any strong prediction about what the courts would do seems unwarranted.

The extent of advertising would depend in part on whether the legal marijuana industry is dominated by a few large corporations with national advertising budgets. Of course industry structure is itself a function of advertising opportunities. The possibility of advertising might be exactly what leads to a small number of large firms promoting a few recognizable national brands; arguably, that describes how national television transformed the beer industry.

Complicating predictions, the worlds of media and advertising continue to expand and fragment. In the 1960s, broadcast television dominated advertising opportunities; today there are myriad other strategies, ranging from simple internet search-engine placements to social-media-based strategies, product placements, advergaming, and viral marketing strategies. It is much easier for regulators to monitor and control traditional advertising than it is to limit these newer marketing and promotional activities.

If production and distribution were restricted to nonprofit entities or government monopolies, that might remove the incentive for marketing. However, this might prove to be only a partial remedy, as the aggressive marketing of some state lotteries illustrates.

How could marijuana be taxed?

Discussions often assume marijuana taxes would be assessed per unit weight: so many dollars per gram or per ounce, as with the Ammiano Bill in California. However, taxing per unit weight gives an incentive to produce and sell higher-potency products, because that would lower the tax per hour of intoxication.

Taxes could instead be based on value, like a sales tax; Colorado's proposed (as of this writing) Regulate Marijuana Like Alcohol Act of 2012 would direct the General Assembly to assess a tax that was initially "up to 15 percent."

Taxes could also be based on potency (as distilled spirits are taxed more heavily than wine and beer). The THC content varies enormously; 4–6 percent is typical for commercial grade, 10–18 percent for sinsemilla, and in excess of 40 percent for hashish. This parallels the range for alcohol, which varies from beer (2–6 percent alcohol by weight) to distilled spirits (which are 20–80 percent alcohol). However, taxing marijuana potency might be more complicated. Alcohol has just one type of psychoactive molecule (ethanol). In contrast, marijuana contains many psychoactive chemicals besides THC, and their relative proportion can vary dramatically. (The "menu" of one marijuana dispensary advertises strains with THC/CBD ratios that vary from 1:2 to 100:1.)

It also matters where that tax gets collected. Marijuana is much more compact than alcohol or even tobacco. In terms of volume, hiding a year's worth of marijuana for a two-joint-a-day user would be like hiding a single six-pack, and the beer would be heavier. Compactness makes smuggling easier, whether to evade outright prohibition or to dodge taxes. There might be less tax evasion if taxes were collected at the point of production rather than the point of sale.

Would regulations and taxes in practice approach the public health ideal?

It isn't hard to design a tax and regulatory system that looks good on paper. But would the actual rules emerging from the messy political process look anything like these theoretical ideals? As Otto von Bismarck is (probably incorrectly) reputed to have said, no one who loves laws or sausages should watch them being made. Allowing a licit industry would create businesses with strong incentives to develop and sustain abusive consumption patterns, because people with bad habits consume a disproportionate share of the product—whether the product is alcohol, tobacco, opportunities to gamble, or any of the major illegal drugs. So if there is a licit, for-profit marijuana industry, one should expect its product design, pricing, and marketing actions to be designed to promote as much frequent use and addiction as possible.

Efforts to tax and regulate in ways that promote public health would have to contend with an industry mobilizing its employees, shareholders, and consumers against any effective restriction. Since the industry profits from problem users, we should expect that lobbying effort to be devoted to blocking policies that would effectively control addiction. The alcohol and tobacco industries provide good examples.

How much enforcement would regulation and taxation require?

That depends entirely on how much regulation and taxation gets imposed. If marijuana were legalized on a completely free-market basis, the minimal regulations would generate minimal regulatory costs. If the only tax on marijuana were the general sales tax, there would be no more reason to evade that tax than the sales tax on soap. The more regulations and the higher the taxes, the more expensive they would be to enforce. That would apply with special force if there were many market participants rather than a small number of licensees.

There is also the option of having a lot of taxes and regulations but not bothering to enforce them. But then you shouldn't expect them to have much effect. Any regulation tight enough and any tax high enough to actually change behavior is worth evading, and therefore needs to be enforced.

So the cost of regulation and tax collection is a choice to be made, not a result to be predicted. The cost depends entirely on the nature of the regulations, the level of the taxes, and how seriously we take their enforcement.

It is natural to ask what is now being spent regulating tobacco and alcohol; the answer is a bit complicated. Currently, the federal Bureau of Alcohol, Tobacco, Firearms, and Explosives (BATFE, often just called ATF) has an annual budget of more than $1 billion a year, but only about 2 percent of that gets spent on alcohol and tobacco control, and the ATF recommends only a few hundred alcohol and tobacco tax evaders for prosecution each year. The budget of the Treasury Department's Alcohol and Tobacco Tax and Trade Bureau is about $100 million per year. The states collectively may spend more; California's Alcohol Beverage Control Board alone has a budget of over $50 million per year.

Arguably those enforcement levels are woefully inadequate. Billions of dollars in alcohol and especially tobacco taxes go uncollected, and minors continue to have access to goods nominally forbidden to them. States and localities with high tobacco taxes face massive smuggling of cigarettes from low-taxed states. So enforcing marijuana taxes and regulations seriously enough to ensure compliance would be a significant task.

Consider, for example, the seemingly straightforward proposition that legal marijuana should be assayed and labeled with the content of its main psychoactives and tested for dangerous contaminants such as pesticides, molds, and fungi. If regulations required every kilogram to be tested individually, testing alone could cost hundreds of millions of dollars per year, or more. The less frequent the sampling, the greater the risk of quality variations or contamination, as repeated outbreaks of salmonella in fresh eggs demonstrate. The "no-free-lunch" rule applies everywhere.

Would there be any marijuana-related arrests after legalization?

Legalization for responsible use does not mean there won't be legal complications for those who abuse or are dependent, as alcohol amply demonstrates. There would be arrests for underage possession, distribution to minors, drugged driving, and consuming where use is banned. In addition, if abstention were required of someone on probation or parole, marijuana use could lead to technical violations.

Alcohol is now legal and has an estimated 8.8 million dependent users, while marijuana is illegal and has 2.7 million dependent users. Alcohol generates 2.6 million arrests per year (drunk and disorderly, DUI, open container, underage drinking, sales to minors)—about three arrests per year for every ten dependent users. Marijuana generates 860,000 arrests (possession and sale), also about three arrests per year for every ten dependent users. Alcohol probably generates more bad behavior per dependent user than marijuana does, but legalizing pot would not reduce those 860,000 arrests to anywhere near zero.

Why aren't prices in Dutch coffee shops and California medical dispensaries a good indicator of prices after legalization?

Because it isn't legal to grow the stuff commercially. Retail sellers face little or no legal risk—though federal enforcement may change that picture for dispensaries in California—but the growers and wholesale dealers still face potential prison time and therefore still have to hide. There's no such thing as open commercial-scale growing of marijuana for use as an intoxicating drug anywhere.

Since no industrialized nation in the modern era has legalized large-scale commercial production, there simply are no historical analogies one can draw on to estimate how legalization would affect production costs or prices. Instead, one has to work through the numbers, the same way a farmer would when considering the possibility of growing any other new crop.

How much would legal marijuana cost to produce?

One of the most dramatic effects of legalization would be much, much lower production costs. The size of the potential decline is not widely appreciated, so this and the next several sections examine it in some detail. But the punch line is that full legalization at the national level—as opposed to only legalizing possession and retail sale—could cut production costs to just 1 percent of current wholesale prices.

The simple reason why marijuana would be so cheap to produce is that marijuana is nothing more than the leaves and flowers of a plant that is easy to grow. Yet marijuana currently costs one hundred times as much per gram as even very fancy tea. That is primarily because prohibition forces producers to operate covertly, not because of any intrinsic difficulties with growing the cannabis plant.

Furthermore, a daily dose of marijuana is much, much smaller than the quantities of familiar plants eaten as food. A gram a day of marijuana suffices for all but the heaviest users.

But a gram of apple a day wouldn't keep the doctor or hunger pangs away; it would amount to just one apple every three months.

Turning to the numbers, sinsemilla prices in the United States are now roughly $2,000 per pound when sold by the producer (the "farm gate" price), $2,500–$4,000 per pound in wholesale transactions, and $250–$450 per ounce (about $5,500 per pound) when sold to users. Prices for commercial-grade marijuana increase with distance from Mexico, from roughly $400 per pound near the border to $1,400 per pound further north; ounce prices are very roughly one-fifth to one-tenth the pound prices. (Prices reflect potencies: sinsemilla is several times as potent and several times as expensive.)

Agricultural experiments show that outdoor farming can readily achieve yields of 2,000–3,000 pounds of usable dry marijuana per acre per year, of which roughly 600 pounds would be buds, as opposed to leaves and other lower-quality material.

Marijuana is often grown from transplanted clones, not seeds, and production costs for crops that need to be transplanted, such as cherry tomatoes and asparagus, are generally in the range of $5,000–$20,000 per acre. This suggests production costs might be under $20 per pound of sinsemilla ($10,000 per acre divided by 600 pounds per acre) and under $5 per pound for commercial grade (same cost divided by 2,500 pounds per acre).

Production costs could be even lower. As chapter 15 explains, cannabis is already being farmed in Canada for industrial hemp; costs there are under $500 per acre. If similar costs applied to cannabis grown for psychoactive purposes, production costs could be below twenty cents a pound for commercial-grade marijuana (which is cheaper on a per-unit-THC basis than sinsemilla produced for $1 per pound). Likewise, professional farmers growing in black dirt might be able to coax out greater concentrations than can backyard hobbyists, let alone growers working marginal hillsides in national forests.

Marijuana must also be processed. Under current conditions of illegality, marijuana processing—manicuring, drying, curing, resin production, etc.—is as burdensome as growing. However, legalization, and the consequent mechanization, would change this dramatically; for tobacco, receiving, grading, stemming, and drying cost well under a dollar a pound. That suggests processing costs might be small compared to production costs.

So the $5 and $20 per pound figures for commercial grade and sinsemilla—including processing—are plausible, but they should not be construed as a forecast. Among other things, if farmers could grow in greenhouses or farm fields, it is not clear what form of marijuana would be the most economical to produce: commercial grade, sinsemilla, or either of those "fortified" with additional THC extracted from other parts of the plant or from other plants. In contrast, if just one state legalized (see chapter 12), then the need to evade ongoing federal enforcement would favor indoor growing that maximizes production per unit area, so one might expect sinsemilla to be the dominant form.

It is important to note, though, what production costs anywhere near these figures imply. The median marijuana user, smoking once a week, uses only an ounce or two a year. Production and processing costs to supply such a user would likely be below $5 per year. Even for someone consuming a gram of sinsemilla per day, production and processing costs would be below $25 per year.

This would make legal marijuana far and away the cheapest intoxicant on a per-hour basis. At current beer prices, getting drunk might cost $5 to $10—call it a dollar or two per drunken hour. The price of marijuana intoxication today is roughly comparable. But legalizing marijuana at the national level would allow a user to buy an hour's marijuana intoxication with a coin—probably a nickel or a dime—rather than a dollar bill.

FOUR ASIDES FOR POLICY WONKS

First: The calculations for commercial grade assume that the leaves, as well as the buds, can be sold; in some markets, the leaves are discarded and only the buds are sold. But that seems to be more typical of Canada than it is of Mexico, where most commercial grade cannabis used in the U.S. is grown.

Second: Yes, it is possible to produce sinsemilla outdoors, though perhaps the larger the growing operation the harder it becomes to prevent pollination. Outdoor sinsemilla growing is happening right now.

Third: If only buds are harvested, that squanders roughly half of a plant's THC. (Buds have 3–5 times as much THC per unit weight, but the leaves weigh 3–5 times as much as the buds.) Extracting and concentrating THC from leaves would be easy to mechanize after legalization. So even if outdoor grown buds fell short of THC concentrations now achieved indoors, it might be possible to augment ("fortify") them with additional extracted THC, further reducing the cost of producing the marijuana required to produce a stoned hour.

Fourth: Hashish, which now has only a tiny share of the U.S. cannabis market, might get much cheaper to produce if the process of extracting the trichomes were mechanized. There's no way of telling whether a hashish-dominated market would actually emerge, or what the effects would be on the risks and benefits to cannabis users.

How many people would be employed in marijuana production?

Not many.

Marijuana is not nearly as potent per gram as cocaine or heroin, but its production is far more potent per square foot.

The UN estimates that the world's 20 million opiate users are supplied by about 200,000 hectares of poppy cultivation, or a little over 1,000 square feet per user. It would take fifty very determined smokers to consume the fifty pounds of marijuana that could be produced on that amount of farmland. So production to supply today's consumption would take less than 10,000 acres out of the 400,000,000 acres of cropland in the United States.

Currently marijuana consumption in the United States is a few thousand metric tons per year, with perhaps about four-fifths of it the lower-potency commercial grade. At the lower costs associated with legal production, that mix of products might be produced for a total amount in the tens of millions of dollars, which means a market that would support perhaps five thousand full-time farmworkers. Even if legalization tripled consumption, the number of farmworkers employed in marijuana production would likely be under 15,000.

Hence, from the perspective of the farm sector, legal marijuana would be a minor specialty crop.

It is much harder to guess how many jobs would be created in the retail sales sector. The answer might depend on whether most marijuana would be sold in a basic, unbranded form (as fruits and vegetables are sold today), or whether branded and bundled forms would predominate. But the farm product itself would be of trivial economic significance.

What would the pretax retail price be for unbranded marijuana?

Nothing about marijuana production makes it a natural monopoly; the technical barriers to entry are low. So in a "regulate like alcohol" scenario, one possibility is a competitive market with many producers. The other possibility is that marijuana producers might convince consumers to place a high value on specific brands, as brewers and cigarette companies have done with similarly easy-to-produce commodities.

If the market remains fragmented, the (before-tax) retail price of standard (generic, unbranded) marijuana would be bid down to roughly what it costs to produce and distribute the marijuana, with costs defined broadly to include a competitive rate of profit.

If, as reckoned above, production costs would be under $20 per pound, the value-to-weight ratio of marijuana would be within the range of typical consumer goods: higher than most agricultural products sold at the grocery store (fruits and vegetables are a few dollars per pound, and liquid products like milk and juice cost less than a dollar a pound) but not as high as clothing or cigarettes. Mass-market tea, in teabags, sells for around $10 a pound; gourmet teas sell for $50 per pound. Fresh herbs such as basil go for a couple of dollars an ounce.

So distribution and retail markups for familiar goods may be relevant for thinking about marijuana after legalization, although one has to choose analogies carefully. The marijuana that could be shipped from the producer for $20 per pound would be ready to use. It would not need to be processed the way that bushels of wheat have to be processed to make bread or breakfast cereal. At most there might be some repackaging.

If production costs for commercial-grade marijuana were closer to $2 per pound, one analogy would be the markup on beef between the meat packer and grocery store. A 300-pound side of beef sells for $2–$2.50 per pound (after adjusting for fat and bone waste); beef at the supermarket costs $3–$15 per pound, depending on the cut.

Cigarettes might be a better analogy for sinsemilla. On line, a ten-pack carton of (possibly counterfeit) brand-name cigarettes costs under $25, making the wholesale price per pack ($2.50) about the same as our estimated wholesale price per ounce of legal sinsemilla. Average retail cigarette prices range from $4–$9 per pack, depending on the state, but much of that reflects excise and sales taxes. Subtracting out those taxes, most states' retail prices are close to $3.20 per pack.

So $3.20 would be one estimate of the untaxed retail price of an ounce of sinsemilla. Reasoning by analogy is a tricky business, and these figures are only very rough guides. They are, however, consistent with independent estimates offered by Dale Gieringer, director of the California chapter of NORML, a group that advocates legalization. Gieringer testified before the California Assembly that if marijuana was unregulated, the price "would presumably drop as low as that of other legal herbs such as tea or tobacco—on the order of a few dollars per ounce . . . or a few cents per joint."

Such figures are only about 1 percent of current prices, and it would be a huge surprise if such low prices didn't create a big increase in the quantity consumed, and in the number of dependent users.

Such a collapse in production costs would also have dramatic implications for the size of the marijuana industry. If retail marijuana sales are currently $20 billion, a 99 percent decline in prices would reduce that to $200 million. Even if legalization tripled consumption, retail sales would still be just $600 million per year, before taxes. In other words, providing run-of-the-mill marijuana intoxication would not be big business. As a result, this part of the market might not support the kind of marketing effort that goes into selling beer or tobacco.

What would the after-tax retail price be for unbranded marijuana?

The price with taxes might not be much higher than price without taxes. Colorado's proposed (as of this writing) Regulate Marijuana Like Alcohol Act of 2012 limits taxes to "up to 15 percent"; adding 15 percent to a very low price does not increase it much in absolute terms.

On the other hand, the potential for generating new tax revenues motivates much of the interest in marijuana legalization. As budget deficits loom ominously over all levels of government, and as the marijuana lobby does not yet have the power of the alcohol lobby, it is worth asking how large a tax the market could bear: How high a tax would not be undercut by tax evasion? The Ammiano bill that would have legalized marijuana in California proposed a tax of $50 an ounce, a small fraction of the current price of high-potency marijuana sold by drug dealers or medical dispensaries, but a large multiple of the likely free-market price for unbranded, unbundled marijuana.

A high tax per ounce would push the market toward high-potency products; that could be prevented if the tax were per milligram of THC, but that in turn would require a substantial amount of assaying. For simplicity, this section discusses taxes assessed per unit weight.

The highest excise taxes collected in the United States today on consumer goods are those on cigarettes, and cigarettes are also of interest because ounces of legal sinsemilla could be priced and taxed roughly like packs of cigarettes are today. The highest combined federal-plus-state excise taxes on cigarettes approach $5.50 per pack. (There are also local cigarette taxes, but when these are large, they are frequently evaded; University of Illinois at Chicago economist David Merriman found that only one-third of cigarette packs discarded in Chicago bore a tax stamp indicating payment of Cook County's $2-per-pack tax.)

These taxes result in substantial evasion, with cigarettes being smuggled from low-tax states or bought on Native American reservations. That is sobering, because a $5.50-per-pack tax on a 20-gram pack of cigarettes is only about $7.50 per ounce, far below the Ammiano Bill's proposal of $50 per ounce.

Problems collecting tobacco taxes are not unique to the United States. The situation in Europe is broadly similar, with wide variation across nations leading to substantial tax evasion. Australia appears to do a better job of collecting its high tobacco taxes, but geography matters for these purposes.

Another relevant benchmark is the markup when marijuana is smuggled into the United States from Mexico. People contemplating evading taxes weigh the benefits (money saved) against the cost (the risk of getting caught and punished), just as smugglers do. It seems doubtful that tax scofflaws would be punished more severely after legalization than international drug smugglers are today, and the likelihood of getting caught is greater at an international border, where Fourth Amendment protections against unwarranted search do not apply. So the intensity of prosecution of tax cheats probably will not support price gaps between taxed and untaxed marijuana greater than the price gap observed today across the U.S.-Mexico border. That price gap is about \$300–\$350 per pound, or about \$20 per ounce. So there is an argument for thinking of that as an upper limit on practicable taxation.

On the other hand, collecting high taxes on marijuana might be easier, because people use so little (by weight) that the tax burden might not motivate much evasion. The average pack-a-day smoker in the United States would spend about \$1,000 per year on state and federal taxes if all taxes were paid. In contrast, a gram-a-day marijuana user would only pay \$250 per year in taxes if the tax rate were \$20 per ounce.

So a guess, and it is only a guess, is that taxes up to \$5 per ounce could be collected without much difficultly; taxes of \$5–\$25 per ounce are possible but would be substantially undercut by tax evasion; and taxes above \$25 or \$50 per ounce might become uncollectable unless the regulatory regime were carefully designed to make tax evasion difficult (e.g., by restricting production to a small number of closely monitored operations).

This has important implications for potential tax revenues. Even if a \$20-per-ounce tax could be imposed in a way that generated no evasion, and legalization tripled the amount of marijuana intoxication, then a market dominated by high-potency marijuana would produce tax revenues of a few billion dollars per year nationwide (there might be greater potential for tax revenues from taxing branded and bundled forms of marijuana). By comparison, alcohol, tobacco, and the state lotteries each bring in $10 billion per year or more.

What would the retail price be for branded and other forms of marijuana?

After legalization, marijuana would cost very little to produce and distribute, some dollars or tens of dollars per user per year. But people value marijuana far more than that; many users today spend over $1,000 per year on it. So producers could make a lot more money if they can get users to pay what the marijuana is worth to them, not just the general competitive market price. To do that, producers would have to make their marijuana appear different or better or more appealing than the standard versions of the product.

There are myriad ways of doing this. High-end bottled water brands sell for more than common brands, and for vastly more than tap water, mostly because of the convenient package and advertising-induced associations with health and fitness. Mass-market beer, tobacco, and soft drink companies invest billions in advertising campaigns to cultivate an image of being different and better than their competitors and analogous generic or store-brand products. Purveyors of fine chocolates package their candies in elaborate golden boxes that even come with guidebooks describing each individual piece.

This is a mixed blessing from a public health perspective focused on constraining the increase in marijuana consumption, particularly by youth. On the one hand, if producers can moderate the price collapse, that will moderate the price-decline-induced increase in use. On the other hand, if they do so with billion-dollar marketing campaigns designed to promote their marijuana products and associate them with the glamorous life, they will also end up promoting marijuana use generally. (The public health community, with some justification, distrusts tobacco industry assurances that advertising merely shifts brands' market shares, without increasing smoking overall; comparable skepticism would be warranted if a legal marijuana industry that invested heavily in promotional activities made a comparable claim.)

We should also expect the creativity unleashed by a free market to pursue product innovation strategies. The portents already visible shatter notions that legalized marijuana use will be just like today, only without the arrests.

Malia Wollan reported in the *New York Times* ("Marijuana Web Names Snapped Up, in Case of Legalization," October 28, 2010) that people were snapping up internet domain names like icecreammarijuana.com and marijuanapastry.com in anticipation of the passage of Proposition 19. Indeed, medical marijuana dispensaries are already selling a range of edibles including brownies, gummi candies, chocolate bars, gingerbread, peanut butter, and cooking oils. (It is ironic that vitamins are sold in childproof bottles, but medical marijuana is sold in gummi candies.)

Take, for instance, Bhang Medicinal Chocolate bars, which are sold in California dispensaries and elsewhere. Bhang offers different types of chocolate with different cannabinoid levels. The bars with 60 mg of THC and close to 2 mg of CBD and CBN (or cannabinol, another psychoactive chemical found in marijuana), retail for about $10. The company web site boasts: "We promise to deliver you a medicinal product that you can count on, tested by third party Ph.D. scientists to contain no pesticides or harmful bacteria but most importantly, to have a precise amount of THC in every bite." And in true California style, they report using sustainably grown fair-trade ingredients.

Innovation may come not only from marijuana producers seeking to diversify but also from producers of conventional products. A chef, baker, confectioner, or microbrewer might jump at the chance to add an ingredient, in either trace or meaningful amounts, that is so cheap and yet would so dramatically distinguish his or her dish, cookie, candy, or beer from the competition.

To give one concrete example, Godiva makes a healthy profit selling brownies for $1 each (in packages of sixteen). After legalization it would cost a competitor only a few pennies to add to its brownies as much marijuana as there is in a brownie that dispensaries now sell for $10.

Such bundling could also occur at the service or experience level. Cafes with just the right atmosphere can charge far more for coffee and baguettes than soulless chains do, and both Napa Valley's wineries and Lancaster County's Amish farms support tourism that generates revenues that substantially supplement conventional product sales. It is not hard to imagine marijuana-based analogues.

The revenue potential from branded or bundled marijuana sales is virtually impossible to predict. But it's easy to imagine that a significant share of the marijuana industry's profits would come from such specialty products, even if the bulk of the intoxication comes from forms that provide more bong hits for the buck. Indeed, it is precisely because generic marijuana intoxication would be available for something like a dime an hour that the only sizable profits would be made by branding or by bundling the intoxicant with some other product or service.

Would businesses give legal marijuana away free?

Maybe. The cost numbers make it seem possible.

After legalization, producing a pound of high-quality marijuana might cost $20. Suppose, for the sake of argument, that after (machine) rolling into joints, modest taxes, producer margin, and delivery charges, a bar or restaurant could order a pound of sinsemilla joints from wholesale suppliers for $45. That would be $0.10 a gram, or four or five cents per joint.

A nickel a joint puts marijuana within the range of various things that restaurants and bars give away. Packets of artificial sweeteners such as Splenda can be purchased for $60 for a box of 2,000 packets ($0.03 per packet). Ketchup packets are about the same, while bulk prices of fortune cookies and packets of crayons that restaurants give kids are closer to $0.05 apiece. Unit costs for after-dinner mints range from $0.02–$0.07, and a one-ounce handful of salted nuts can cost between a dime (peanuts) and a quarter or more (cashews).

If smoking a joint made restaurant patrons hungrier or casino patrons more likely to gamble, would establishments give marijuana away as a loss leader? That seems hard to imagine, but it is also hard to argue that cost considerations would preclude it.

Thus, there are at least three pricing scenarios: users paying very low prices at stores for generic marijuana; users paying much higher prices for branded marijuana made alluring through expensive marketing campaigns; and users being comped free marijuana by companies trying to woo them into other purchases.

All three could occur together. Homeowners buy cheap water from the tap, while the affluent pay about five thousand times as much per unit for bottled water, and restaurants give you a glass for free. Likewise, grocery stores sell bags of chocolate morsels for $0.05 per bite-size piece, Godiva sells (slightly larger) morsels for more than $2 per piece, and fancy hotels leave them on your pillow for free.

How much would consumption increase?

No one knows how much nationwide legalization would increase consumption; we're in the realm of guessing, not forecasting.

Reasoning by historical analogy is tempting: "Lifting alcohol prohibition did this, so lifting marijuana prohibition will do that." Or "Consumption in the Netherlands is such-and-such a percentage of consumption in California, ergo this or that."

Ten years ago Rob MacCoun and Peter Reuter, two of the most respected scholars in drug policy, wrote a book called *Drug War Heresies*, the culmination of a decade-long systematic attempt to learn about legalization from comparisons with other times, places, and vices (such as prostitution and gambling). It still stands today as one of the five most important books ever written in the field, and we urge everyone to read it. Yet its ultimate stance is agnostic about the consequences of marijuana legalization; such comparisons simply do not provide definitive guidance. The RAND marijuana modeling project—in which two of us have been deeply involved—tried to generate estimates from quantitative modeling. It reached a similar conclusion. Legalized commercial production is so unlike what has been done in the Netherlands, Australia, Portugal, California, or anywhere else for which reliable data exist, that predictions cannot be made with any precision.

It can be instructive, though, to identify some of the mechanisms through which legalization may influence use.

The most tangible mechanism is price. There is a compelling body of empirical literature showing that drug consumption, like consumption of (almost) every other commodity, tends to rise when prices fall. Lower prices contribute to higher rates of initiation, greater consumption per year by those who consume, and lower rates of quitting. The effects are not small, but they are all estimated from observed data—that is, relatively modest price changes. There is simply no scientific way to extrapolate from that historical experience to project the consequences of the very dramatic declines that could accompany commercial legalization at the national level.

Different and equally plausible assumptions—all fully consistent with available data—can produce dramatically different predictions of the consequences of very large declines in price. When a RAND team considered the issue with respect to the more modest price declines that would follow a single state legalizing, their conclusion was that price effects could easily lead to a doubling of consumption, and it was hard to put an upper bound on the potential increase. The even greater price declines from national legalization would be expected to produce even greater increases in use, though probably not dramatically so; once the cost of intoxication falls into the pennies-per-hour-high range, it may not matter much if the cost is a nickel rather than a dime.

There are also a range of nonprice effects. After legalization, users would be subject to no legal risk and reduced social disapproval (perhaps reflected in the omission of marijuana from workplace and government drug testing). Better labeling and quality control would reduce health risks. And there would be advertising and promotion encouraging use. Based on comparison of a wide range of Dutch and U.S. indicators, and also drawing on other jurisdictions, MacCoun estimated that such effects might increase consumption by 5–50 percent over and above the increase caused by a fall in prices.

There is no guarantee that a doubling in use from price effects and/or an additional 50 percent increase due to nonprice effects is the upper limit, but to match alcohol, marijuana use would have to grow four to eight times, depending on the measure.

Additional factors could come into play as well. Greater variety generally increases total consumption, and unless regulations prevent it, we would anticipate users having convenient access to a greater variety of potencies, strains, and bundled products (e.g., edibles of various sorts). Social norms can also be important. The legal status of tobacco has changed little over the last seventy-five to a hundred years, but changing social customs led first to a massive increase in smoking and then to a large decline. Alcohol use in the United States seems to move up and down in long waves; the past generation has been on a "down" cycle, not much driven, apparently, by public policy, as regulations haven't tightened—except on drunk driving—and inflation-adjusted taxes have fallen substantially.

Drug taking is driven by personal habit and social custom. Anecdote suggests that most marijuana use today has as its goal getting stoned, while many people drink without getting, or intending to get, drunk. That may reflect nothing but differences in age; most marijuana is consumed by youth and young adults—age groups whose alcohol consumption is immoderate compared to that of their elders. However, optimists can hope that legalization might lead, over time, to social customs more favorable to moderation. On the other hand, marketing efforts by the newly licit industry might change attitudes in a direction favorable to chronic heavy use. Only time will tell.

At the end of the day, it is hard to imagine that commercial legalization would not lead to substantial increases in consumption, but there's no good reason to expect the increases to be catastrophic. A doubling or a tripling in the (potency-adjusted) quantity consumed seems like a reasonable guess, but that's all it is; if twenty years after legalization the ultimate change in consumption were greater or smaller, that wouldn't be a big surprise.

Does the marijuana trade fund drug violence in Mexico?

It has been widely asserted that Mexican drug trafficking organizations (DTOs) earn more than 60 percent of their revenue from marijuana. That figure has been used by advocates of strong enforcement policies as an argument for cracking down on marijuana users and by Proposition 19 advocates to bolster claims that marijuana legalization in California would diminish the profits of Mexican DTOs.

But the figure fits Ambrose Bierce's definition of a prejudice: "A vagrant opinion, living without visible means of support." The original source seems to have been a bar chart in the 2006 National Drug Control Strategy report displaying estimated Mexican DTO revenues from cocaine, heroin, marijuana, and methamphetamine. Without citing any data, the text accompanying that chart states that "61 percent of that revenue, or $8.5 billion, is directly tied to marijuana export sales."

The serious, documented analyses estimate the dollar value of the U.S. retail market for cocaine to be roughly twice as large as the marijuana market, and the bulk of the cocaine comes into the United States through Mexico. So it's hard to see how the 60 percent estimate could be true. Indeed, the Office of National Drug Control Policy has formally disavowed the 60 percent estimate, and RAND estimated that the actual figure was likely between 15 and 26 percent. Yet it would be overoptimistic to expect such an excitingly high figure to disappear from the discourse simply because it happens to be wrong; many years ago, Peter Reuter identified "the continuing vitality of mythical numbers" as one of the signal characteristics of drug policy debate.

Still, some DTO revenues do come from marijuana sales, and national legalization would reduce those sales to nearly zero (unless taxes were high enough to support continued smuggling for tax evasion). It is not clear how a 20 percent reduction in drug export revenue—to pick one plausible figure—would affect DTO violence. In the first place, a 20 percent reduction in *drug export* revenue does not imply a 20 percent reduction in *total* revenue. Despite the "D" in the acronym, DTOs are diversified criminal enterprises that parlay their capacity for violence into a variety of revenue streams including kidnapping, extortion, carjacking, and other activities.

It is not even clear that a 20 percent reduction in *total* revenue would lead to a proportionate reduction in violence. It might. Or it might prompt reallocation of "soldiers" from drug trafficking into other activities, some of which might generate greater violence per person or per million dollars than drug trafficking does. And even if the DTOs laid off these soldiers rather than reassigning them, the alternate work they sought might or might not be peaceful.

So there are many caveats about the effect of marijuana legalization in the United States on violence in Mexico. However, the basic point presumably holds that, at least in the long run, marijuana legalization would make a meaningful, but not decisive, contribution to reducing the flow of funds to violent Mexican DTOs.

Does legalization make sense from an overall social welfare (benefit-cost) perspective?

At one level, benefit-cost analysis is no more than common sense. If the sum of the advantages (benefits) of some proposed policy exceeds the sum of its disadvantages (costs), then making the change is better than preserving the status quo. This sounds simple, but there are serious debates about what to count as benefits and costs, and how to weigh them against one another.

Of particular relevance is whether and how the analysis counts the harm marijuana users impose on themselves. In many respects, alcohol is the natural comparison to marijuana, but the two drugs differ sharply in how their harms are distributed between users and others. Collectively, alcohol abusers impose great harms on other people, including egregious harms such as beating spouses and killing people while driving under the influence. Cigarette smokers also harm others, e.g., with secondhand smoke and fires, but the great bulk of tobacco's toll on society comes from smokers killing or sickening themselves. Marijuana is more like tobacco in this regard, not in terms of death toll—marijuana kills very few people—but in terms of who bears the brunt of marijuana abuse and dependence. While marijuana use can generate harms to non-smokers—"external costs," as the economists call them—most of the losses are to smokers themselves, or to family and friends concerned about their welfare.

Economists doing benefit-cost analysis typically adopt the principle of "consumer sovereignty," under which each consumer's preferences are accepted as an accurate measure of the consumer's welfare: in other words, consumers are assumed to know what they want and to want what they buy. From consumer sovereignty there follows the principle of "revealed preference," which infers preferences from actions. On this principle, if someone pays $10 for a drug, that act reveals that the consumer values the resulting experience at no less than $10. Thus consumer sovereignty implies that no consumer ever comes out behind by paying too much. The only question is how much more the consumer might have been willing to pay; the difference between actual price and willingness-to-pay is "consumer's surplus," a social gain. The net social benefit could still be negative—if the consumption harms others—but consumers are never harmed by their voluntary choices.

So it's not surprising that conventional benefit-cost analyses are favorable to marijuana legalization. Once it is accepted as axiomatic that all voluntary purchases improve consumers' welfare, then almost all government efforts to separate consumers from a consumption good—in this case, marijuana—stand condemned.

Those analyses may, however, be unpersuasive to people with less faith in shoppers' flawless wisdom. Some people, perhaps thinking of pet rocks, timeshares, and candy bought on impulse in the checkout line, are skeptical about consumer choice and the benefits of free markets generally. But an intermediate position accepts consumer sovereignty for most goods most of the time, yet still carves out an exception for intoxicating substances that induce dependence, especially for consumers who initiate as adolescents, not adults. (Three-quarters of past-year marijuana users initiated before age 18; over 90 percent initiated before turning 21.)

By this intermediate view, if someone has a drug abuse or dependency problem and finds his or her drug-taking behavior slipping away from voluntary control, then the axiom of revealed preference may not apply, making willingness to pay not a useful guide. Conventional benefit-cost analysis simply doesn't know what to make of the phenomenon of temptation.

Perhaps we should extend benefit-cost analysis to incorporate the idea of an "internality" or "excess internal cost"—the losses to individuals from their own ill-judged behavior. That would allow for the possibility of a "consumer's deficit" as well as the more usual "consumer's surplus." Thomas Schelling has written of the "divided self": someone, for example, who both wants to use marijuana and wishes not to have that desire. Such conflicting urges can lead to behavior that befuddles economic logic, such as flushing already-purchased drugs down the drain. Other economists and psychologists have shown that time-inconsistent preferences and inconsistencies between "hot" and "cold" emotional states also undermine the rationale underlying consumer sovereignty.

Once an exception has been made to the principle of consumer sovereignty, the clear "Yes" answer to the legalization question has to be replaced by a more cautious "It depends."

For marijuana, the answer depends crucially on how legalization would affect use, particularly heavy or dependent use. Those who believe use would go up only modestly (say 50 percent or less), will probably conclude that legalization would do more good than harm. Prohibition tends to reduce use and use-related problems, including dependence, but creates black markets and black-market-related problems. If the prohibition isn't delivering much in the way of reduced use and dependence, then it doesn't have much to say for itself in a benefit-cost analysis.

But it seems more reasonable to think of commercial legalization as having a fairly high likelihood of doubling or tripling use. There is great uncertainty, and much depends on details of how the legalization is done, but there is little basis for expecting only minimal increases in use and dependence if for-profit production and promotion are permitted.

Most of the things researchers spend time trying to estimate and monetize end up playing a modest role in the social welfare analysis. Yes, legalization will increase the number of users in need of treatment. Certainly legalization will reduce the workload of police and courts. But the monetary costs associated with those activities are not their most important effects. (Advocates produce some wildly inflated estimates of criminal justice costs; better estimates are in the low billions of dollars per year nationally, rather than in the tens of billions.)

The more important outcomes are so difficult to monetize that they tend to get left out of benefit-cost analyses. For example, some tens of thousands of marijuana distributors are in prison, and some hundreds of thousands of people are arrested and convicted of marijuana violations each year. Quite apart from the budgetary costs to enforcement agencies, there is a real, though hard-to-quantify, cost to those individuals' welfare, in terms of direct suffering, reduced job prospects, and other effects. What would you pay to keep your parent, sibling, spouse, or child from serving a year in prison? And what would the prisoner be willing to pay? Being a wrongdoer—accepting for the moment that illicit dealing is wrongdoing—doesn't make that person's suffering any less real.

On the other side, there are currently 1.2 million children living with a parent who meets clinical criteria for marijuana abuse or dependence. If marijuana use and dependence doubled or tripled, the number of children in that situation would presumably increase. There is no good way to quantify how a parent's substance abuse or dependence affects the children, but it's hard to imagine that it improves parenting (unless the increased marijuana dependence is substituting for dependence on alcohol or other drugs).

Most people would at least agree that reduced criminal punishment would be a benefit of legalization, and increased exposure of children to dependent parents would be a cost. However, for what is arguably the most salient consequence of legalization—the increase in marijuana intoxication—there is not even agreement as to whether it counts as a benefit or a cost.

Currently marijuana consumption in the United States produces very roughly 15 billion hours of intoxication every year. Legalization could add another 15–30 billion hours. It is not clear how that outcome scores in a benefit-cost analysis: some of those hours are intensely pleasurable and cause no harm to the user or anyone else; others contribute to dysfunction and personal failure. Either way, at a valuation—positive or negative—of even $1 per hour, the change in use would swamp all other gains and losses (leaving aside the equally unknown question of whether problem marijuana smoking would tend to increase or decrease problem drinking.)

As noted above, standard economic reasoning would hold that consumption necessarily generates a consumer surplus. A precise estimate would require some heroic assumptions, but people routinely pay several dollars per hour for various forms of entertainment ($11, for example, to watch a movie that lasts less than two hours), and prices after legalization would be low (perhaps a nickel or dime per hour of intoxication). So it is easy to imagine an average surplus of several dollars per hour, suggesting that legalization will bring new happiness to users measured in the many tens of billions of dollars.

But this rosy picture darkens once we consider the possibility of consumers' deficits. When people make poor choices and pay more than what something is worth, they end up regretting the purchase. Indeed, it's possible to regret consuming things received for free—a phenomenon familiar to anyone who has overeaten at a banquet or overindulged at a party. That the canons of standard economic analysis—including "consumer sovereignty" and "revealed preference"—rule out the very idea that people might ever make poor consumption decisions simply shows the limitations of that form of analysis.

Almost one third (31 percent) of days of marijuana use involve people who self-report enough problems with substance abuse to qualify as dependent on some drug—alcohol, marijuana, or another illegal drug. That proportion rises to almost half (47 percent) if one broadens the definition to abuse or dependence, and, inasmuch as denial is a hallmark of addiction, there are likely many who suffer such problems but do not report them. Furthermore, problem users probably consume more per day of use than controlled users.

The problem from an analyst's perspective is that we simply do not know how to score or value those hours of intoxication for either nondependent or for dependent users. Those are questions of personal values as much as they are matters for laboratory measurement; if you think—as some of the world's major spiritual traditions do—that intoxication is a violation of the natural order, then you're going to have a hard time ascribing benefit to it even if you understand that some people enjoy it. (Consider the parallel cases of erotically stimulating images or images of cruelty to humans or animals.)

But even if you accept that drug use can be beneficial, the question of whether some particular individual's drug use is broadening that person's range of experience and enriching his or her life, rather than narrowing and impoverishing it, is not a question with a formulaic answer, or even one on which the individual consumer necessarily has a settled view.

In the end, all the fancy benefit-cost analysis boils down to a rather simple proposition (but see chapter 9 for the possibility that the indirect effects of marijuana legalization on increasing or decreasing alcohol abuse might overwhelm its effects on marijuana use itself). If you think marijuana intoxication is, on average, a good thing—counting both the happy controlled users and the unhappy dependent users—then a benefit-cost analysis done in a way that reflects your values will probably conclude that legalization improves social welfare. If you think marijuana intoxication is, on average, a bad thing, then an analysis that reflects your values will probably conclude that legalization harms social welfare—because the dominant outcome of legalization will be more marijuana use.

Additional Reading

Kilmer, Beau, et al. *Altered State?*

Kleiman, Mark A. R. *Against Excess.*

MacCoun, Robert J., and Peter Reuter. *Drug War Heresies.*

Reuter, Peter. "The (Continued) Vitality of Mythical Numbers."

Schelling, Thomas C. "The Intimate Contest for Self-Command."

Schelling, Thomas C. "Ethics, Law, and the Exercise of Self-Command."

12

COULD ONE STATE LEGALIZE MARIJUANA IF THE FEDERAL GOVERNMENT DIDN'T?

Definitely. California came close to doing so with Proposition 19 in 2010, and legalization by one or more U.S. states in the face of continued federal prohibition appears to be the single most likely legalization scenario in the immediate future.

The question is not whether a state could change its own laws; under the Constitution, the states retain a degree of sovereignty. Rather, the question is how the conflict with the continued federal prohibition would play out. The federal government would clearly retain the right to enforce federal drug prohibitions within that state, but as a practical matter it is not clear whether the federal government would expand its efforts by enough to fully compensate for the elimination of state and local enforcement.

Could a state simply repeal its marijuana laws?

States cannot bar the application of federal laws within their borders; home growing is legal under Alaska law, but it's still a federal felony. Perhaps the clearest signal of this came in the Supreme Court case of *Gonzalez vs. Raich*, in which the Court concluded that the commerce clause allows the federal government to criminalize home production even in states that permit its medical use.

But the Constitution does not allow the federal government either to order state governments to create any particular criminal law or to require state and local police to enforce federal criminal laws.

The Eighteenth Amendment, and the Volstead Act passed under its authority, banned the production, transportation, and sale of alcohol nationally, and most states had their own legislation making violations of national Prohibition local crimes. But in 1923, the state of New York—under Governor Al Smith—repealed its own ban on alcohol. For the following decade, selling alcohol in New York was a violation of federal law but was not against the laws of New York State. Local police had no authority to arrest alcohol sellers. By the time national Prohibition was repealed in 1933, ten other states had followed New York's lead.

Enforcing Prohibition was largely a federal project, even in states that passed their own bans. The current drug war is different; about four-fifths of drug law enforcement takes place at the state and local level. Especially in a big state such as California, it's not clear that the federal government would have the capacity to replace the state and local marijuana enforcement effort. That's emphatically true with respect to punishing users for drug possession (which wasn't an issue with alcohol prohibition, since drinking was not a violation of the Volstead Act). Except in national parks and other federal lands, almost all possession arrests are made by state and local police.

A state that tried to tax and regulate marijuana commerce would run into all sorts of complications, given that the activity would remain illegal under federal law. But simple repeal faces no such problem. A state that wanted to do what New York did in 1923 would be perfectly free to do so.

Could a state regulate and tax a substance that the federal government still prohibited?

While the legal and constitutional issues are complex, the simple practical answer is "Yes, but only as long as the federal government decides not to thwart the effort."

State and local jurisdictions in the United States are currently collecting taxes and fees from medical marijuana. For example, the state of Colorado requires marijuana-related businesses to pay a license fee (up to $18,000), and in 2010 the state generated more than $2.2 million from the state sales taxes paid on medical marijuana. Further, some jurisdictions impose and collect special taxes on medical marijuana. Oakland, California, was the first city to do this in 2009, and a number of jurisdictions in California have followed suit, with taxes typically ranging from 2.5 percent to 7 percent of gross receipts.

It has been argued that the federal government could confiscate such revenues as the proceeds of illegal transactions, but as far as we know, the federal government has not touched a penny of the fees and tax revenues generated from medical marijuana. Whether the federal government would maintain this hands-off policy if marijuana was legalized for nonmedical purposes remains to be seen.

A distinct issue is whether the state employees enforcing state regulations could be in violation of federal laws, e.g., if state employees had to handle (possess) marijuana in the process of enforcing labeling or quality control regulations. It is very hard to predict what the federal government would or would not tolerate in this regard. It seems plausible to us that distinctions would be drawn between incidental possession in the process of quality control monitoring versus employees in state stores actually selling the marijuana, but that is just a guess. It is safer to predict that advocates and opponents would spar over this terrain than to lay odds on which side would prevail.

What about the reverse: If the federal government legalized marijuana, could a state still prohibit it?

Legally, yes. Practically, only with difficulty.

The Constitution leaves each state free to make its own laws, within fairly wide boundaries. Some states banned marijuana before the federal government did, just as some states remained dry after the repeal of Prohibition. The Frank-Paul bill to repeal federal marijuana prohibition would make it a federal crime to take marijuana into any state where it remained illegal.

But if at least one state followed the federal lead, that state would become a potential source of illegal marijuana for every other state, at prices far below current illicit-market prices. While the current federal penalties for growing and selling large quantities can be severe, the maximum penalty for illegal interstate shipment under the Frank-Paul bill would be one year in prison. The current multibillion-dollar market in smuggling cigarettes from low-tax states such as North Carolina to high-tax states such as New York—also a violation of federal law—illustrates the readiness of illicit entrepreneurs to take advantage of such opportunities. Residents in pot-prohibiting bordering pot-allowing states wouldn't have to rely on illicit markets; they could just drive across the state border to buy, as Massachusetts residents drive to New Hampshire for low-taxed liquor.

So, while states would be free to continue to prohibit marijuana, enforcing that prohibition would be a different matter. Prices would fall dramatically, and marijuana consumption would rise accordingly.

What could the federal government do if one state legalized marijuana for nonmedical use?

Restricting distribution to (nominally) medical users provides a justification for federal inaction: regulation of medical practice is primarily a state responsibility, and the international drug treaties contain exceptions for medical use.

It is not at all clear what the federal government would do if a state legalized the production, distribution, and possession of marijuana for nonmedical purposes. The federal response would likely depend on a number of factors, including the specifics of the policy, the particular state, and the political situation. Moreover, the federal government is not a unitary actor directed by a single will; there are a number of federal agencies and officials involved. In particular, the United States Attorneys (the chief federal prosecutors in each of the country's ninety-four judicial districts) have wide discretion; many of them have political connections and ambitions, and they may not all agree on the same approach.

Federal actions, or inaction, would be watched closely not only by residents and policymakers in the legalizing state but also by those in other states considering revising their state marijuana laws. Likewise, other countries will watch how the federal government deals with a potential breach of the international conventions that the United States insists that other countries uphold (see chapter 10).

The federal government will certainly still have the power to drug test and sanction federal employees in that state. Executive Order 12564 forbids federal employees from using illicit drugs on or off the job. The order gives the federal government the authority to test any employee if there is "reasonable suspicion" of illegal drug use, as well as anyone in a "sensitive" position regardless of suspicion. An employee who tests positive can be fired for continuing to use or refusing counseling and treatment. We do not know how many federal employees have been fired (or denied security clearances) because of marijuana use alone, but this order is on the books and could be used more frequently after legalization. If a state passed legalization with licensing and regulation, the U.S. Department of Justice could immediately crack down on those who receive these licenses and supply marijuana. Before the licenses were even distributed, the DEA and other federal law enforcement agencies could step up enforcement against marijuana traffickers in the state to send a signal that seizures could actually increase after legalization.

The federal government could also limit the profits of commercial enterprises by disallowing tax deductions. Business taxes are typically based on total revenues minus allowable business expenses and other deductions. Internal Revenue Service Code Sec. 280e forbids businesses from taking deductions if they traffic in schedule I or II drugs like marijuana and LSD. If the IRS applied this provision to entities producing and selling marijuana in states where it was legalized, these businesses could take a large financial hit.

These federal agencies could also use their discretion to help shape how marijuana is distributed, imposing a form of regulation by selective enforcement. For example, California's Proposition 19 would have allowed each of the state's more than five hundred jurisdictions to make its own decisions about taxes and rules for production and sale. Had Proposition 19 passed, federal enforcement agencies could have decided, for example, to only shut down marijuana-related businesses that advertised, sold to minors, did not impose a minimum price, did not test for mold and pesticides, etc.

The federal government could also use threats of sanctions to influence a state's decision about whether to legalize in the first place. For example, when the federal government wanted to strong-arm reluctant states into increasing the minimum purchase age for alcohol to 21, Congress passed a law that threatened to withhold a share of federal highway funds from states that did not comply. No such threats were issued during the Proposition 19 debate in California, but they could be used to derail a future proposition or—less plausibly—to "punish" a state after passage.

Threats could also be leveled at property owners, warning them that leasing to an illegal enterprise risks having that property seized and confiscated, or perhaps at banks, on the theory that holding accounts for marijuana businesses constitutes "money laundering."

What is the federal government doing in states that allow medical marijuana?

In states that allow medical marijuana, producing, distributing, and possessing the drug remains illegal under federal law. So federal agents could arrest, and U.S. Attorneys could prosecute, medical marijuana users. In practice, however, federal law enforcement officials do not go after medical marijuana patients or caregivers (unless they are also committing other crimes). For that matter, federal law enforcement also ignores marijuana users who do *not* have a medical recommendation; agents typically only pursue cases against people possessing hundreds of pounds or more, rather than just a few pounds, let alone a few ounces or joints.

Likewise, for years federal agents gave little attention even to the suppliers of medical marijuana. There are storefronts across the country where those with a medical marijuana "recommendation" from a physician (which is not, technically, a prescription) can openly buy marijuana. It would have been straightforward for the Drug Enforcement Administration to raid these places and chain their doors. That has happened occasionally, but usually when the outlet was believed to be involved in other crimes. Even large-scale distributors have been able to do business openly, their websites offering to make sales that count as felonies under federal law.

But it wasn't always this way, and it is not clear how long it will last. The federal government has great discretion in these matters; hence, it is hard to predict its response to a state that legalized nonmedical use.

Five years after California passed its medical marijuana initiative in 1996, Attorney General John Ashcroft tried to neutralize medical marijuana laws by threatening to revoke the federal drug-prescribing license of any physician who wrote a recommendation for marijuana use by a patient. While the DEA can regulate what doctors prescribe, federal courts ruled that trying to prevent doctors from "recommending" marijuana would violate the free speech protections of the First Amendment. While the doctors remained immune, dispensaries were targets of federal enforcement throughout the Bush administration.

In February 2009, U.S. Attorney General Eric Holder signaled that federal enforcement policy toward those operating legally under state laws would change. The reversal became more formal in October 2009 when Deputy Attorney General Ogden released a memo suggesting that as a general matter, U.S. Attorneys should not focus federal resources on "individuals whose actions are in clear and unambiguous compliance with existing state laws providing for the medical use of marijuana." The memo reserved the option of targeting those violating state laws or attempting to make a profit from selling medical marijuana, and federal agents have arrested dozens of individuals involved in supplying medical marijuana since the memo was released.

More recently, some United States Attorneys warned specific dispensaries to shut down or face enforcement, and in some cases have carried out those threats against operations that did not comply. A June 2011 memo from U.S. Deputy Attorney General Cole reiterated the warning of enforcement action against "commercial operations" and "persons in the business" of cultivating, selling, or distributing marijuana. It also argued that those "who engage in transactions involving the proceeds of such activity may also be in violation of federal money laundering statutes and other federal financial laws." Advocates saw this as a reversal of the Holder-Ogden policy. But the Ogden memo differentiated between individuals and their caregivers on the one hand and for-profit commercial enterprises on the other. Likewise, since California law recognizes only "cooperatives," and many of the medical marijuana dispensaries are actually for-profit businesses, it's not clear that any of them are in fact operating in compliance with state law.

In October 2011, the four U.S. Attorneys in California publicly described their plan to target the large, for-profit medical marijuana industry. Tactics will include criminal cases and civil forfeiture cases against those who own properties involved in drug trafficking (e.g., landlords who rent to dispensaries). It does not appear that all dispensaries are being targeted, but U.S. Attorney Melissa Haag suggests, "Although our initial efforts in the Northern District focus on only certain marijuana stores, we will almost certainly be taking action against others. None are immune from action by the federal government."

The moral of this back-and-forth saga is that the outcome of a state's making marijuana legally available depends on whether and how the federal government chooses to enforce federal laws.

How would production and production costs change if marijuana were legal in one state but not the entire country?

Freedom from state and local law enforcement would reduce production costs dramatically, but not as much as national legalization would.

If it were legal to farm marijuana the way other crops are grown, production costs would fall to a few dollars per ounce—a few cents per stoned hour. Prices would be determined largely by taxes, and might be so low as to make them largely irrelevant to consumer choice (see chapter 11).

However, farm fields and commercial greenhouses are easy for federal agents to find and seize. Above-board marijuana farming could be deterred merely by threatening to seize the farm land, without needing to impose expensive prison sentences. The effectiveness of such threats was made clear in early 2011 when the city of Oakland was about to allocate licenses for four large-scale medical marijuana production facilities. In a letter to the Oakland city attorney, the U.S. Attorney warned that "the Department [of Justice] is carefully considering civil and criminal legal remedies regarding those who seek to set up industrial marijuana growing warehouses in Oakland." The threat worked; Oakland tabled the discussion.

The message seems to be that the federal government (at least under the Obama administration) will tolerate small-scale growing of medical marijuana, but not massive commercial farming. Given the likely prospect of marijuana grown where it was legal under state law being exported to other states where it remained illegal, it's hard to believe that the federal government would not take similar steps to eliminate open commercial growing for nonmedical use. Marijuana can be grown discreetly at commercial scale in "grow houses" that look from the outside like ordinary family homes. If marijuana growers operated without fear of law enforcement but within the awkward confines of a residential structure, then their production costs would be somewhere between the very low costs of farming marijuana and the very high costs of growing illegally. There would be some economies of scale and mechanization of processing, but far short of what can be achieved by commercial agriculture. Low-skill labor could be obtained for wages typical of agricultural laborers, but light would still come from expensive electricity, not free sunlight.

The RAND *Altered State?* report estimates that such grow houses could profitably sell high-quality sinsemilla for $300–$400 per pound, or about one-tenth of current wholesale prices (but still about ten times the cost in open farming), and that the amount of THC currently consumed in the United States could be produced in fewer than 10,000 of the 90,000,000 single-family houses in the United States.

How would legalization in one state affect markets and use in other states?

Legalization in one state could influence consumption in other states via several mechanisms, although the magnitude of the effect depends on how marijuana is regulated in the legalizing state, whether the federal government and neighboring states step up enforcement to reduce cross-border smuggling, and how current and potential marijuana users will respond to large price decreases.

The first mechanism is "drug tourism": users crossing state lines to purchase where the drug is cheaper and/or involves less legal risk. This behavior can arise for any substance. Cheap alcohol in New Hampshire attracts buyers from Massachusetts, and drug tourists from France, Belgium, and Germany have been an important source of demand—and controversy—for Dutch coffee shops.

Cigarette tourism may have been a large contributor to the tax evasion documented by University of Illinois economist David Merriman. Merriman collected thousands of littered cigarette packages from the streets of Chicago, where a city tax adds 58 cents, and a county tax adds $2.00, to the cost of a pack of cigarettes. Only one in four packs bore a Chicago tax stamp, and just one in three bore the Cook County stamp.

Drug users are not the only ones who can cross state lines; drug dealers can too, as they already do. Currently, wholesale prices for commercial-grade marijuana increase fairly steadily with distance from the Mexican border at a rate of about $400 per pound per thousand miles. If drug dealers could buy sinsemilla legally in California for, say, $500 per pound, and drive it 2,500 miles to New York State for an additional $1,000 per pound, they could deliver wholesale quantities to New York for $1,500 per pound, or about one-third of the current New York wholesale price for sinsemilla.

California already exports marijuana to its neighbor states and beyond. If California legalized marijuana and thereby dramatically reduced production costs, people buying in California to smuggle out of state would benefit from lower prices. Competition would force prices in importing states down accordingly, probably enough to affect consumption levels.

Legalization in one state could also influence consumption in other states by changing attitudes. The legal change alone could make the drug seem less threatening and less stigmatized; if advertising were permitted, that too could "leak" across state lines.

Does it matter whether legalization is enacted by legislation or by voter proposition?

About half of the states in the United States allow their citizens to put initiatives on the state ballot; most require a small fee and some number of signatures from registered voters. In California the fee is only $200, but paying petition distributors to gather the roughly 500,000 signatures required can cost a few million dollars.

A number of drug-related proposals have been decided at the ballot box. Of the seventeen state laws (including Washington, DC) that allow for medical marijuana, ten were passed directly by voters rather than by legislators. And as of the fall of 2011, there have been four attempts to legalize marijuana for nonmedical purposes via ballot initiative; none have passed. Initiatives differ from normal legislation in two major ways. First, they do not go through the process of evidence gathering and political negotiation typically involved in legislation: there are no committee hearings, no staff work, no dueling witnesses, no officials explaining how the new law might be carried out, no body of expert drafters to make sure the i's are dotted and the t's crossed, and, for the most part, no element of bargaining and compromise. Second, what one legislature does its successors can modify, or undo. But under many state constitutions, a measure passed by the voters cannot be repealed—or even substantially modified—by their representatives. Those two facts make mistakes in initiatives more common and harder to fix than mistakes in legislation.

For example, California's Ballot Proposition 36 (P36), which allowed nonviolent drug offenders to accept drug treatment instead of receiving a traditional sentence of jail or prison, wound up generating far less actual treatment than its sponsors had promised the voters. Of the defendants who accepted the P36 deal of treatment instead of punishment, only a quarter completed the treatment, and very few of the rest suffered any punishment for violating program rules. In response, criminal justice agencies and even several treatment providers urged the legislature to allow brief jail terms as a way of punishing failures to appear for treatment, in order to create an incentive to comply. The legislature duly passed such a bill, but a court found it inconsistent with the spirit of P36 (which was anti-incarceration) and thus unconstitutional. In other words, the court found that making "mandatory drug treatment" actually *mandatory* was going too far. So the initiative process can leave a state stuck with an unworkable policy.

The extent of the problem depends in part on how the initiative is written. For example, if voters pass a legalization initiative that explicitly gives the legislature power to set the marijuana excise tax, then the legislature can set an initial tax and update it as needed. But if the tax is set in the language of the initiative itself, the legislature might be powerless to change it.

Since no jurisdiction has ever legalized marijuana, it is unlikely any will create the optimal regime on the first try. There will need to be midcourse corrections to address unanticipated consequences. Those voting on legalization should pay attention to how easy it will be to amend or repeal the law in light of experience.

Could states learn from one another's experience?

Yes.

There are many options for regulating marijuana, and the wide variation in alcohol laws illustrates some of the range of options. But for the states to serve as "laboratories of democracy," there needs to be some serious process for evaluating the results of the various experiments. Those developing legalization bills and initiatives may want to consider building an evaluation component directly into their proposals. Given the knowledge that will be gained from these research efforts observing the results of early efforts, there will be advantages to being the second or third state to legalize marijuana, rather than the first.

Additional Reading

Cole, James. "Guidance Regarding the Ogden Memo in Jurisdictions Seeking to Authorize Marijuana for Medical Use."

Kilmer, Beau, et al. *Altered State?*

Merriman, David. "The Micro-Geography of Tax Avoidance."

Mikos, Robert A. "A Critical Appraisal of the Department of Justice's New Approach to Medical Marijuana."

13

HOW WOULD MARIJUANA LEGALIZATION AFFECT ME PERSONALLY?

Those conducting benefit-cost analyses usually think in terms of the greatest good for the greatest number, perhaps augmented with observations about effects on traditionally disadvantaged populations. But what's good for the country as a whole is not necessarily good for every individual. This chapter highlights the effects of legalization—at the national level—for members of various interest groups.

How would legalization affect me if I'm an adult regular marijuana user?

It would simplify your life. You would be able walk the streets with an eighth in your pocket or drive with an ounce in your glove compartment, and never have to worry about getting arrested for possession. Of course, you could still be arrested for smoking and driving, using in public, or sharing a joint with someone who is under 21, but the police would not bother you for smoking on your porch or at a neighbor's barbeque.

With legalization you also wouldn't have to worry about the collateral consequences of being convicted of marijuana possession, which can include being denied federal student aid or access to public housing.

It would also increase the choices you have and somewhat reduce your cost of living. You'd have better access to higher potency marijuana at lower prices; if you're a near-daily smoker, you could save many hundreds of dollars a year on buying pot. If you live in a state that does not currently have a wide-open medical marijuana trade, you might be blown away by all of the strains, edibles, and hash oils that you will now be able to buy. That would improve your chances of finding a variety that fits your desires, or several varieties to fit different desires at different times; think Amsterdam, but much cheaper.

Legalization would reduce the stigma associated with marijuana smoking. Depending on where you live and with whom you socialize, you might find it more acceptable to use in front of nonusers. With a decrease in stigma, it might also be easier for you to talk to your friends, family, and employers if your marijuana use ends up causing you problems.

But with a decrease in stigma, increased availability, and the likely barrage of advertising, it could be harder for you to get away from marijuana if you wanted to quit. Insofar as the cost of pot, the inconvenience of buying it, the risk of possessing it, and the potential embarrassment of being known to use it currently lead you to smoke less than you otherwise would, legalization might increase your risk of developing a bad habit, abuse, or dependence. After legalization, simply avoiding your pot-smoking friends would not keep you away from the easy access and pro-marijuana messages that could tempt you.

Further, we still have a lot to learn about the high-potency marijuana likely to dominate the market after legalization. Most of what we know about health risks is based on people who first smoked marijuana in the 1960s, 1970s, and 1980s, when THC levels were lower. The story could be different for those who use high-potency sinsemilla. The risks of abuse and dependency do not only affect you alone; your family and friends may have to put up with your bad habits and possibly destructive behavior.

So legalization could significantly improve your quality of life and reduce your cost of living, as long as you don't abuse it or become dependent.

How would legalization affect me if I'm dependent on marijuana?

It would save you a bunch of money and free you from legal risk. But increased availability might also make it harder to quit. You'd be in the same position as an alcoholic trying to quit who has to deal with walking by bars every day and finding alcohol for sale in grocery stores and drugstores.

How would legalization affect me if I'm an occasional marijuana user?

It would widen your range of choices. As it is, you don't spend much on pot or face much risk of arrest or loss of employment. But legalization would mean that you no longer have to worry about being arrested and getting entered into a law enforcement database if a cop breaks up a party and finds you smoking a joint (unless you are under 21). If you hold a job, or have family responsibilities or social commitments that make it embarrassing to be seen breaking the law, legalization could allow you to use in more circumstances; you might, for example, want to offer it to friends with dinner, or smoke during an outdoor concert without looking around to see if there's a security guard watching you.

If you'd like to smoke more often than you now feel free to do, legalization might let you do so, and with the same enhanced options available to heavy users. If you are someone who likes to get stoned but does not like inhaling, then you will enjoy all of the options that marijuana legalization creates for you, including the candies, packaged foods, and baked goods infused with marijuana now available in medical marijuana outlets.

Legalization would mean a marijuana industry working hard to convert you into a heavy user, because heavy users are great customers. The alcohol and tobacco companies operate that way, and there is no reason to believe marijuana companies would be any different. State and federal officials might try to regulate these advertisements, but the free speech clause of the First Amendment, as extended to "commercial speech" by the courts, would be a barrier.

In conjunction with advertising and the reduced legal risk, the price reduction could increase the frequency with which you use and purchase marijuana. This is where you could run into problems.

There would also be short-run consequences of ramping up your marijuana use. For example, you might be more likely to drive under the influence, which is dangerous for you and others on the road, and especially dangerous if you have also been drinking. If you are currently a big drinker, legalization might influence how much alcohol you use, though no one really knows whether your alcohol use would be more likely to go up or down as a result.

For you, as for the heavy users, legalization would be a boon—if you kept your pot use under control.

How would legalization affect me if I'm not currently a marijuana user?

If you're not currently using because you're not interested in using, not much would change for you, unless marketing or changing social customs led you to change your mind. If you're not currently using out of respect for the law or fear of legal or social consequences, then you would have additional choices, which you could use well or badly. In some social settings, you might feel social pressure to smoke, just as some nondrinkers now feel social pressure to drink. And of course a rising level of marijuana abuse among your friends and neighbors might inconvenience you in various ways, though it seems unlikely to become a problem on the level of alcohol abuse.

There is debate about whether legalization will make our roads less safe, which could affect both users and nonusers. As discussed in chapter 5, stoned drivers may tend to be safer than drunk drivers, but driving under the influence of marijuana is more dangerous than driving sober.

The overall effect of marijuana legalization on your probability of getting in a crash will depend on how it affects driving under the influence of *alcohol*. If legalization increases the number of drivers who are under the influence of both alcohol and marijuana, that would likely increase traffic crashes; drivers under the influence of both are less safe than those who are only using either one. On the other hand, if legalization were to decrease the number of drunk drivers, because some users shifted from alcohol to marijuana, that would reduce crash risk; however, it is anybody's guess as to whether this would offset the crash risk associated with an increase in marijuana consumption.

How would legalization affect me if I'm a medical marijuana patient?

Legalization of marijuana for nonmedical purposes will most likely be great for you—greater availability at lower prices. If you already have access to medical marijuana dispensaries, the main effect will be no longer having to register with the state and/or pay a fee to get a recommendation from a doctor. And there will also no longer be a gray area surrounding the legality of delivery services. But don't expect marijuana to be covered by your health insurance plan, and don't forget that even medical use carries health risks. (See chapter 5.)

If you live in a state that does not allow medical dispensaries, you will now have access to a wide variety of products to address your symptoms or diseases. In particular, high-CBD strains would likely become more available.

Legalization would also make it easier for scientists to conduct research on the medical uses of marijuana and learn which strains and amounts are best for specific ailments.

How would legalization affect me if I'm a marijuana grower?

It would almost certainly put you out of business.

At first glance, legalization might seem like a great opportunity for you. It is usually the producers and traffickers who do serious prison time for marijuana, and legalization would allow you to work without fear of arrest and incarceration. In fact, you would be able to use the court system to address contract disputes and employee grievances. It would also be easier for you to acquire the electricity you need; you could work with the fire department and security companies to make sure that you are protected against fires and intruders. The days of paying trimmers $20–$25 an hour would be over (you could now hire folks at closer to minimum wage), and it would be easier for you to get access to technologies that will make harvesting more efficient.

But legalization will completely upend your industry, and the skills that made you successful at cultivating illegal crops will not have much value. A few dozen professional farmers could produce enough marijuana to meet U.S. consumption at prices small-scale producers couldn't possibly match. Hand cultivators would be relegated to niche markets for organic or specialty strains.

How would legalization affect me if I lead a Mexican drug trafficking organization (DTO)?

You would lose money, but not as much as is widely believed. You know better than anyone else that the claim that DTOs earn 60 percent of their drug export revenues from moving marijuana to the United States is just not true.

However, the revenues that you do derive from transporting marijuana to the United States would be severely impacted. You and your colleagues would not be able to compete with legal production. You may be good at committing ruthless murders and other atrocities, but you can't match farmers at farming. Even the still-illegal sales to minors would largely be made by friends and older siblings buying from legal suppliers.

So if the federal government legalizes, you can forget about the U.S. marijuana market. You and your colleagues would lose between 15 percent to 26 percent of your collective drug export revenues, or about $1–2 billion annually.

How would legalization affect me if I'm a parent of a teenager?

It is already easy for your teenager to get marijuana. Nationally, 82 percent of high school seniors report that it is "fairly easy" or "very easy" to get marijuana; the comparable figure for alcohol isn't much higher at 90 percent. In fact, perceived marijuana availability hasn't changed much since you were in high school; between 1975 and 2010, the share of high school seniors reporting that it was easy to get marijuana fluctuated between 81 percent and 90 percent.

Some advocates claim that legalization will make it harder for kids to get marijuana because drug dealers don't check IDs. You should be skeptical. The fact that it is easy for 90 percent of high school seniors to obtain alcohol, even with age restrictions, suggests that marijuana will still be readily available after legalization. Older siblings and friends, unscrupulous and naive cashiers, fake IDs, theft, and home cultivation will create leakages to the under-21 market.

Today most of the marijuana consumed in the United States is of low to medium potency; legalization would likely change that. High-potency marijuana would become so inexpensive to produce as to drive lower-potency marijuana out of the market. That would make it much easier for your kids to get access to the really strong stuff. Some research suggests that highly potent marijuana (especially if it's also low in CBD) can increase anxiety attacks and may have other negative consequences, but this remains an unsettled question (see chapter 5).

If marijuana is commercially legalized, you can expect to see pot-infused candy bars and baked goods hit the market. More importantly, with commercial legalization you should expect to see marijuana companies advertising these products and other forms of marijuana to your teens under the protection of the "commercial free speech" doctrine.

While most legalization proposals would keep marijuana illegal for those under 21, the sanctions might be reduced, making arrest less damaging to those who use and are caught. And it would surely reduce some of the stigma surrounding use for those below 21. On the other hand, reducing the stigma associated with marijuana might also make it easier to have honest conversations with your kids about using.

You would still have to worry about your kids getting intoxicated and ending up in a bad situation, and maybe more than you do today. Traffic accidents and date rape are the most salient risks, and it is unclear whether these will be more or less likely after legalization. Much depends on how legalization influences teen alcohol use, and how often your kids and their friends get stoned and drunk at the same time.

How would legalization affect me if I'm an employer?

Obviously, you do not want your employees coming to work intoxicated or hung over; it can hamper productivity and be both a liability and a security risk. If consumption of psychoactive substances causes at-will employees to not meet performance standards, you can terminate them regardless of whether the failure is attributable to alcohol, marijuana, or cocaine use. This would not change with legalization.

But legalization could create some administrative headaches for you. If the new law explicitly forbade you from testing applicants and employees for marijuana, you would have less information about the people you are hiring, and it would be harder for you to detect and deter marijuana use among your employees. If testing were allowed and you currently test for marijuana, you would need to decide whether to continue and, if you do continue, what to do with those who test positive.

Many states allow employers to test for alcohol, so there is a precedent for testing for legal substances. However, legalization would not by itself improve drug testing technology; it would be harder to determine which employees were under the influence of marijuana than to determine which were under the influence of alcohol. Saliva tests are becoming increasingly popular, and they do a better job of detecting only recent marijuana use, but they still cannot determine impairment.

In anticipation of an increase in postlegalization consumption, you could increase the intensity of marijuana testing for applicants and employees. On the other hand, you could find a niche by explicitly stating that you will not test for marijuana. Just as some people looking for a roommate on Craigslist will advertise that they are "420 friendly," employers could embrace a similar strategy to attract new talent to their firms.

In any case, it's very unlikely that marijuana use by employees will pose a problem for your firm at anything near the level alcohol now does.

Ultimately, the effect of marijuana legalization on your business will depend on the particulars of what is allowed and who allows it (i.e., the federal government or just individual states). After legalization, there would be a plethora of lawyers and consultants specialized in assisting employers like you with the transition. While some employers might appreciate the help, others would find the cure worse than the disease.

Additional Reading

Johnston, Lloyd D., et al. *Monitoring the Future.*

Kilmer, Beau, et al. *Reducing Drug Trafficking Revenues and Violence in Mexico.*

14

BETWEEN MARIJUANA PROHIBITION AND COMMERCIAL LEGALIZATION: IS THERE ANY MIDDLE GROUND?

Is there a middle ground between legalization and prohibition?

One can think about the choice between prohibition and legalization from two different perspectives: as a yes-or-no decision, or as a spectrum including many intermediate points between its extremes. Neither metaphor alone is "right"; both have value.

The spectrum perspective recognizes, for example, that cocaine is allowed for medical use, while heroin is not; in that sense cocaine is less strictly prohibited than heroin. Likewise, age restrictions and other special rules apply to alcohol but not to caffeine, so alcohol is less fully legalized than caffeine.

Yet it is misleading to think of the spectrum as a continuum that allows small adjustments up or down everywhere along it without crossing any threshold. There are important dividing lines between legalization and prohibition with respect to both use and production. For use, a key question is: can most people legally obtain and use the substance just for fun, without a prescription or medical justification? By that definition alcohol is legal in the United States, even though one must be 21 to purchase it, whereas marijuana is still illegal in California, despite the decriminalization of possession and a lenient medical marijuana system.

A key question for supply is: do the laws allow commercial production to serve nonmedical consumption?

Cast in these terms, the "middle ground" question asks whether it is possible to move a meaningful distance along the spectrum toward legalization without crossing over to full commercial availability. Yes, it is. Sometimes policy discussions implicitly define the middle ground as being limited to decriminalization, but that is just one among many intermediate positions short of truly legalizing production and sale as well as use.

What has been learned from depenalization and decriminalization?

Decriminalization typically refers to removing criminal penalties for possession of amounts suitable for personal consumption, at least for first time offenders; possessing 500 kilograms could still land one in prison. That does not require that possession of a small amount be made legal; it could still be punished with fines, treatment mandates, or other civil sanctions: just not criminal conviction or criminal penalties.

By this conventional interpretation, about a dozen U.S. states "decriminalized" marijuana possession in the 1970s, beginning with Oregon in 1973, and a few more have joined them since. The first thing we've learned from the experience is that— contrary to some alarmists' shrill warnings—one can decriminalize marijuana without having the world come to an end. Indeed, Berkeley public policy and law professor Rob Mac-Coun observes that the average citizen's awareness of the marijuana laws is pretty tenuous; in both decriminalized and nondecriminalized states, about the same proportion of survey respondents believed that marijuana possession could lead to a jail sentence (roughly one-third in each type of state).

A considerable literature tries to go further and estimate effects of decriminalization on marijuana use. One approach is to examine a panel of states over time to see if use is higher in those states after decriminalization than in other states or in earlier years. There is some evidence of increased use. For example, former RAND economist Karyn Model observed that emergency-room mentions for marijuana increased after decriminalization while mentions for other drugs fell, suggesting some substitution. However, the majority of the early studies found little if any effect.

More recently, Rosalie Pacula—another RAND economist—and her colleagues found that some states usually treated as having decriminalized had in fact merely reduced sanction severity while possession remained a criminal offense. Studies that use more nuanced categorizations of state control regimes often find effects of legal changes on consumption, but not large ones.

One challenge to such before-and-after comparisons is that enforcement intensity in practice may not correspond closely to the policy proclaimed in the law books; formal decriminalization may sometimes simply ratify practices already in place, giving statutory changes little impact on actual arrest patterns. Indeed, Pacula and colleagues found that by 2000, marijuana arrest rates were not systematically lower in the states that had eliminated criminal penalties for possession of small amounts than they were in other states.

Decriminalization experiences abroad have added to our knowledge of its results. For example, several jurisdictions in Australia implemented "infringement" schemes that substitute fines or education programs for criminal sanctions. In South Australia police responded to the option of giving "expiation notices," meaning they did not have to take the arrestee to the police station, by taking action against individuals they would previously have ignored altogether. (This effect is called "net widening.") Since many of those cited never paid their fines, and some subsequently went to jail for nonpayment, the actual effect of the "expiation notice" policy was to *increase* the number of incarcerations related to marijuana use. Whether decriminalization in Australia increased consumption is open to question; some studies say no (consumption went up everywhere, not just in places that decriminalized), while others find statistically significant effects of decriminalization on use in some subpopulations—more for older than for younger users, for example. A recent study by economists Anne-Line Bretteville Jensen and Jenny Williams suggests that Australian decriminalization shifted initiation to earlier ages, without affecting the proportion who initiate at some point.

Thus decriminalization may or may not increase use; where it does, it doesn't do so by much.

What about legalizing the way Portugal did (not do)?

Portugal is often held up as the poster child for successful legalization. It is better thought of as the poster child for misunderstandings about legalization.

Various people have studied Portugal's policies. The most influential analysis may be human rights lawyer Glenn Greenwald's report for the Cato Institute, entitled *Drug Decriminalization in Portugal: Lessons for Creating Fair and Successful Drug Policies*. Note the title: Portugal decriminalized; it did not legalize. Portugal was bolder than the decriminalizing U.S. states because its decriminalization pertains to all drugs, not just marijuana. It is bolder than various other European countries because in 2001 Portugal formalized its decriminalization by passing a law that explicitly makes acquisition, use, and possession of up to ten days' supply merely *administrative* offenses. So Portugal is an interesting case study—but of a middle path, not of legalization. (Italy and Spain also removed criminal penalties for possession of small quantities, but Portugal seems to get more attention.)

Portugal's approach is, nonetheless, qualitatively different from what people usually mean by decriminalization. Portugal did not merely reduce punitiveness; it also proactively expanded efforts to dissuade, treat, and reintegrate users. Portuguese police cannot arrest users, but they are still expected to issue citations to those they see using or possessing drugs. Those cited appear before "commissions for the dissuasion of drug addiction" (CDTs, in the Portuguese acronym). The CDTs have great latitude to impose a variety of sanctions including fines, community service, revocation of professional licenses, and what are essentially injunctions (e.g., against going to particular places). However, sanctions are usually suspended, though sometimes only if the violator complies with some condition, such as attending treatment; the CDTs' objective is behavior change, not punishment.

Evaluations of Portugal's 2001 law tend to compare drug use in 2001 to use in later years, sometimes noting whether that difference is greater or smaller than the corresponding difference in some comparison country, typically Spain or Italy. Data are scarce and their interpretation complicated, allowing both sides of the policy debate to make overstated claims.

Rates of treatment uptake, problematic use, and overall crime rates all moved in favorable directions. Overall drug prevalence, though, rose substantially in percentage terms, albeit from a very low initial level, and total homicides rose.

The results are sensitive to details such as the choice of starting dates. Greenwald observes that drug-related deaths fell from almost 400 in 1999 to 290 in 2006, which at first blush looks like a success for the new policy, but as Stanford psychiatry professor Keith Humphreys points out, deaths had begun falling before the law changed, having already declined to 280 by 2001. The fall continued for only another twelve months, stabilized for two years, and then headed back up, reaching 314 by 2007.

Criminologists Caitlin Hughes and Alex Stevens try to adjudicate the competing claims. They observe, for example, that counts of drug-related deaths in Portugal reported before 2010 are better thought of as deaths that involve a positive postmortem toxicological test, not deaths directly attributable to intoxication. They observe that none of the nightmare scenarios transpired (e.g., no hordes of drug tourists) and that reductions in HIV transmission and problem drug use and increases in treatment uptake could be viewed as offsetting any possible increases in overall reported drug use. They also caution that some changes may be due to other factors, such as expanded treatment funding and Portugal's natural transition from the explosive-growth phase to the stable, endemic stage of its heroin epidemic.

Sometimes lost in the welter of statistics is that Portugal wasn't arresting many drug users even before the new policy was formally instituted. By 1983, Portuguese law identified users as patients in need of medical care, and provided that contact with the criminal justice system should be designed to encourage treatment, not to punish. By 1993, Portuguese law indicated that drug users should only be punished in a "quasi-symbolic" manner in order to facilitate treatment seeking, that the element of disapproval implicit in the law be reduced to a minimum, and that occasional users "should, above all, not be labeled or marginalized." The number of users coming into contact with the criminal justice system under the pre-2001 regime was much smaller than the corresponding figure in the United States, even adjusting for differences in population. So although the law on the books before 2001 still allowed for criminal penalties, actual practice had become consistent with the 2001 law a decade before its passage. The bigger change in 2001 may have been not the reduction in penalties but the increase in proactive efforts to dissuade, treat, and reintegrate users.

Clearly, Portugal pioneered an innovative middle path, beginning in the 1980s. A decade's experience with CDTs proves the approach is feasible and produces no catastrophic consequences. But Portugal's experience cannot support specific projections about what would happen if the United States were to replicate Portugal's policies. Current U.S. policies are not much like those of Portugal in 2000, and programs and policies developed in one country or culture can play out dramatically differently if transplanted to another culture.

What about imitating the Dutch approach?

As discussed in chapter 10, the Netherlands has never formally legalized marijuana. Dutch law—in keeping with international agreements—criminalizes production and sale of the same drugs that are illegal elsewhere. However, an explicit, formal exception was created in 1976 for sale of limited quantities of marijuana. That activity, while nominally illegal, is not subject to enforcement, and about seven hundred "coffee shops" openly sell marijuana. The purchase limit was formerly 30 grams, a bit more than an ounce, but was reduced to 5 grams (enough for about ten joints) in 1996. As of this writing there are plans to restrict sales to Dutch nationals; both Dutch border towns and neighboring countries have been complaining about "drug tourism." There are also discussions about banning sales of products containing more than 15 percent THC.

Growing cannabis is still a crime in the Netherlands, as is importing it. Committing those crimes lands people in prison. As the Dutch say, the front door of the coffee shops—where the customers enter—is (almost) legal, but the back door—where the product comes in—is entirely illegal. As a result, coffee-shop cannabis costs about what fully illicit cannabis costs elsewhere in Europe or in the United States: about $10/gm for material of moderately high potency. By keeping production and wholesale distribution illegal, the Dutch have kept their cannabis prices high and marketing to a minimum. That situation is a far cry from legalization.

Nonetheless, marijuana use in the Netherlands roughly doubled—from a fairly low base—not when the policy was first passed but later, as coffee shops began to proliferate (roughly between 1984 and 1996). As Rob MacCoun of Berkeley has noted, Dutch prevalence subsequently fell back by about 20 percent between 1997 and 2005, a period during which the number of coffee shops was cut back by 40 percent (and when some other European countries were seeing continued increases). So it is plausible that the Dutch have a somewhat higher prevalence than they would with decriminalization but no such commercialization of retail availability.

Until recently the conventional wisdom was that the Dutch approach was successful at achieving its objectives, including making it possible for people to obtain marijuana without encountering purveyors of more dangerous drugs. There seems, though, to be an increasing sense of the inherent tensions in official approval of businesses that sell goods whose production the government seeks to suppress. This front-door/back-door inconsistency might be a workable compromise during a transition, but it is an awkward situation to face indefinitely.

What about just allowing home production, as Alaska does?

The central paradox of the Dutch approach is allowing people to buy and sell something that cannot be produced legally. Coffee shops paper over the paradox, because users themselves do not interact with criminals. But shop owners must. Some medical marijuana laws are similar. They grant immunity from enforcement to users possessing an ID card but say nothing about how dispensaries are to obtain the marijuana they sell.

The gentlest way to provide a legal source of supply is to allow individual users to grow their own and perhaps give to (but not sell to) friends. Marijuana is not particularly difficult to grow. One has to be a little conscientious, but almost anyone can develop the knack.

Allowing grow-your-own marijuana has clear appeal. It siphons demand away from the black market, reducing criminals' incomes. Yet, since grow-your-own activities are necessarily small, they do not enjoy the economies of scale that would accompany commercial production. So the effective cost of production—in terms of time and effort, not dollars—is much higher than it would be if commercial production were legal. That presumably limits any increase in consumption.

Note: this would be appealing from the public health perspective of wanting to moderate the increase in consumption and dependence. However, small-scale production would frustrate a free-market devotee who wanted to maximize efficiency and provide the widest possible variety of marijuana at the lowest possible cost.

There are also complications. It is not easy to set quantity limits. If the law limits the number of plants, people can grow very large plants. If the law limits weight, it might be hard for even well-meaning users to comply. One full-size outdoor plant can yield a pound of marijuana, which is roughly four times the average annual per capita consumption.

Allowing home cultivation for personal use also makes it harder to enforce laws against home cultivation for profit. If all cultivation is banned, the police merely need to find plants in order to build their case. If only the selling is illegal, the police must catch dealers in the act of selling, which is considerably harder.

The United States has some experience with allowing home growing. A 1975 Alaska State Supreme Court ruling effectively legalized growing one's own marijuana by determining that the state constitution's privacy rights cover possession of amounts suitable for personal consumption in one's own home. That threshold quantity was subsequently set at 4 ounces or twenty-five plants. Those (relatively high) limits and the entire constitutional premise were later challenged, starting with a 1990 voter initiative that sought to reverse the original case. There was a period of legal limbo, but it appears that a 2003 case reaffirming the 1975 ruling has now settled the issue:

Alaskan law allows Alaskans to grow at home; the activity is still banned under federal law, but federal agencies have other things to worry about.

Likewise, a number of states' medical marijuana laws allow registered patients or their care givers to grow their own, up to some limit (e.g., in California the limit is 8 ounces plus up to six mature or twelve immature plants).

The results of grow-your-own policies are hard to estimate. State-specific data on use in Alaska are limited, coming mostly from 2000 and later. They show higher rates of use in Alaska than in the rest of the United States (indeed, the highest in the country in the most recent household survey), but no trends or jumps associated with the 2003 ruling. Likewise, use rates in South Australia, which had at one point decriminalized growing as many as ten plants (later cut to three plants and now to one plant), paralleled those elsewhere in Australia, although that may be in part because South Australia became an important marijuana producing state, exporting to other Australian states.

Nevertheless, grow-your-own currently accounts for a tiny share of the market in the United States. Since 2002, the household survey has asked past-year marijuana users how they obtained the marijuana they used most recently. The vast majority got it for free or shared (54 percent) or bought it (40 percent). Slightly less than 1 percent report growing their own.

What about creating user co-ops, as in Spain?

A step beyond grow-your-own is allowing the growing, sharing, and trading to be conducted among members of formal user co-ops, such as those in Spain. Spanish law does not criminalize possession, only sale, so drug-sharing clubs inhabit a legal gray area.

Cannabis-sharing clubs solve a problem familiar to anyone who has grown zucchini; it is hard not to overproduce. A good grower can produce 300–400 grams per (outdoor) plant, so the exceptions for "amounts suitable for personal consumption" (usually defined as less than an ounce, or just over 28 grams) do not protect people growing their own. Furthermore, if that one plant died, the user would have no recourse but the illegal market. Also, there are many types of cannabis, varying in potency of THC, amount of CBD, and other attributes. One person growing for personal consumption could hardly have access to a variety of strains. In contrast, one club manager we talked to said his club grows fewer than three hundred (outdoor) plants per year for its three hundred members—i.e., less than one plant per person per year—but can still always offer members choices from a variety of strains.

The clubs operate on a nonprofit basis. That same manager estimated production cost—including the pay of the manager and of the people who tend the plants—of 2–3 Euros per gram of high-potency cannabis (at the time a Euro was worth about $1.40), and the club sells to members at about twice that amount, which is still below black-market prices. The net revenues are used to finance social activities and activism (e.g., renting buses to take members to protests in the capital).

A model club self-manages to control diversion. For example, a club might limit acquisitions to 2 grams per day, require participants to be 18, or have members sign a statement certifying they had already been using marijuana before joining the club and do not simultaneously belong to a second club.

However, each club has its own rules, and some serve as fronts for professional dealers. So it is not clear whether the co-op model will be sustainable. The Federation of Cannabis Associations, an umbrella group, is trying to find ways to certify the good behavior of responsible clubs before the shady operations undermine the overall concept.

But it is not clear whether a network of clubs could replace the illicit market without morphing into marketing enterprises.

What about a very liberal medical marijuana system?

A medical marijuana program with very liberal criteria for determining who is eligible to be a patient could serve a substantial share of the marijuana market. Something along those lines is already happening in some states. (Others states have implemented medical marijuana laws that restrict availability to the relatively small number of people who have the most serious conditions.)

If in addition the dispensaries were limited to something that looked like a co-op, with primarily volunteer staff and pure barter or sales at cost, then medical marijuana might be able to provide serious competition for black market activities. California's Medical Marijuana Program Act allows patients and caregivers to associate for purposes of collectively or cooperatively cultivating marijuana without being subject to state law enforcement if their aims are consistent with medical purposes. However, many if not most dispensaries in California do not operate in this manner; instead they effectively operate as businesses with full-time paid staff selling to anyone with a recommendation. But if the state or the federal government were to mount a consistent crack-down focused on the commercial outfits, co-ops might replace them.

California's "medical" system serves more than patients. Studies suggest the demographics of its buyers look more like those of drug users than of people receiving traditional health care services. They are mostly young, healthy men with long histories of marijuana use. For example, Thomas O'Connell and Ché Bou-Matar described 4,117 individuals who sought physicians' approval for marijuana use, mostly in the San Francisco Bay area. The typical patient was a thirty-two-year old male who started using marijuana as a teenager, and the rate of disability among the patients was actually below the overall national average.

Another study examined the medical charts and physician interview records of 1,655 applicants for medical-marijuana recommendations. Most sought marijuana to relieve pain, improve sleep, or relax. Almost all were approved, since California allows medical marijuana for any "illness for which marijuana provides relief," not just the diseases that motivated many voters to support compassionate use. Less than 5 percent were diagnosed with HIV/AIDS, cancer, or glaucoma.

California does not require patients to register, so it is hard to translate those studies into statewide estimates. However, until 2011, when Senate Bill 423 revamped its Medical Marijuana Act (MMA), Montana combined a mandatory registry with lax criteria for determining who was eligible. As of June 2011, Montana had 30,036 currently registered medical marijuana users. That was almost half the state's past-month users as estimated by the 2008–2009 household surveys (66,000). If the nation as a whole had the same number of patients per capita, that would total 9.5 million medical marijuana users, as compared to 16.7 million past-month marijuana users of all sorts.

The Montana experience shows that it is possible to create a program under the banner of medical marijuana that supplies a large share—on the order of half—of all marijuana users directly, and perhaps more indirectly if some of the holders of medical cards supply their friends. If such liberal policies for writing recommendations could be combined with regulations that ensured dispensaries looked more like user co-ops and less like drug dealers with storefronts, then it would appear possible to use medical marijuana to create a form of co-op based quasi-legalization.

What about limiting the quantity any user can buy?

People who use a little bit of marijuana mostly don't have problems or cause problems (and only "mostly" in that a single incident of foolish intoxicated behavior can cause a lifetime of damage). People who use two or three grams a day are likely in the grip of diagnosable substance abuse or dependence. So why not limit the quantity a user can purchase over the course of a month? Credit card companies already have the capacity to limit how much a cardholder spends, even though the cards are good at countless locations. It shouldn't be hard to put together a data system linking a finite number of sellers, and require that each purchase be subtracted from a monthly quota.

The problem is that those heavy users—the ones who would reach any externally imposed quota and then start looking for illicit supplies—use most of the marijuana. So forcing them back onto the black market would undermine the abolition of illegal dealing as an advantage of legalization.

An alternative would be to have a monthly quota but let the user him- or herself set it. (Some states have this system, on a voluntary basis, for gambling.) Every user could be required to get a license, just as some states currently issue licenses for medical marijuana buyers. Getting a license could require proof of age, and perhaps passing a short quiz—like a driver's license exam—designed to make sure buyers know the risks they face. When someone signed up for a license, he or she could be asked to specify a monthly quantity purchase limit. There might even be an absolute upper limit, subject to the need to avoid driving too many people away into the illicit market.

But why would anyone choose to set a limit, or choose less than the highest amount available? Because almost no one who starts using any drug intends to become dependent on it, and some of them are aware of the risks of picking up a habit that could spin out of control. Such a limit needn't be permanent; it just has to be fixed for a particular time period, and a little bit inconvenient to change. Just the need to do the paperwork to expand one's limit would serve as a warning sign. This is hardly a reliable way to prevent the development of addiction, but it is certainly better than nothing and probably worth the administrative effort.

(And yes, this could also work with alcohol, as used to be the case in Sweden, where it apparently had good results until the Swedish Prohibition Party demanded an end to what had been a government alcohol monopoly.)

Couldn't users go to physicians for nonmedical marijuana, making it the doctor's business to prevent problem-use patterns?

At first blush, this seems plausible. After all, doctors understand psychoactive chemicals better than the average person does, and the Hippocratic Oath binds them not to harm their patients. No doubt most would try to manage supply in such a way that patients do not escalate to abuse or dependence.

However, it would be an odd use of scarce and expensive medical resources, and it's not clear that medical education is the best preparation for acting as a rationing agent; after all, nonmedical use of prescription pharmaceuticals is already an enormous problem, especially in the United States. Initiation rates for pharmaceutical misuse now exceed those for marijuana. Emergency-room statistics and overdose deaths also reflect a fast-growing prescription-drug problem. The physicians in California who write "recommendations" for people who want to purchase (supposedly for medical use) at marijuana dispensaries haven't displayed much interest in monitoring their patients for signs of drug abuse or dependency.

What if distribution were controlled by a government monopoly?

In one sense, government-monopoly supply would be full legalization rather than a "middle path." But it belongs in this chapter because it is very different from legalization along the alcohol model. (In some states retail sales are restricted to government stores, but production and marketing are still done by for-profit enterprises with brand names and a strong interest in maximizing sales.) In particular, such a government monopoly would have a fighting chance of avoiding the drastic price decreases and aggressive marketing efforts that would likely result from commercial legalization.

Legal production costs are so far below current prices that taxes could not make up the difference without inviting a black market in tax evasion (see chapter 11). Government control of production and distribution can be seen as a mechanism for "collecting" the difference between retail prices and production costs. In theory a government monopoly could be limited to retail distribution, with production outsourced to the private sector, but that would require stringent oversight to prevent diversion from producers to the gray market. Even with strong diversion control, commercial production would create strong incentives for marketing efforts, and especially for efforts aimed at creating and sustaining drug abuse and dependency, because problem users account for most of the sales volume.

The great advantage of a government monopoly is that it undercuts black-market demand without undermining the effectiveness of drug enforcement. When a drug is fully illegal or can only be obtained from a government monopoly in small purchases, possession of more than personal-consumption amounts is prima facie evidence of law breaking. If private production is legal, then it becomes enormously more difficult for police to detect and prove illegal behavior, such as evading taxes or other regulations.

So prohibition makes enforcement against illegal supply activity easy, but forces all customers to patronize illegal suppliers. Legalization of private commercial activity destroys the efficiency of enforcement, allowing black market prices to fall; so it only siphons demand from illegal markets if the legal price falls. Government monopolies offer the happy possibility of eliminating (most of) the illegal market while keeping prices reasonably high.

Furthermore, a government monopoly could impose other conditions, such as requiring buyers to pass tests certifying their knowledge of the drug's dangers or limiting the amount sold to any given individual in a particular month. And there would be no incentive for anyone but the government to advertise, which it could choose not to do.

State lotteries already operate as government monopolies, so the model is not unknown in the United States. However, legalization via government monopoly is simply not a politically viable option in the short-run or medium-run in the United States. The U.S. federal government is not interested, and it would not be possible for a state to run a state-store system in the face of ongoing federal prohibition. Other countries could take this path, but many tend to worry about international political repercussions of deviating from the international conventions about illegal drugs (as discussed in chapter 10).

There are other concerns. Designing an ideal legalization regime is a popular academic exercise. The typical conclusion is that the author's design would be better than the status quo, and this is taken to prove that legalization is a good idea. The hidden assumption is that if drugs were legalized, they would be legalized in the socially optimal manner. One need only look in detail at California's Proposition 19—or for that matter many state lotteries—to realize that bad designs are possible; neither voter propositions nor laws passed by legislatures are written by civic-minded academics. They are usually written by activists who have agendas and are influenced by stakeholders with private interests. And once created, corporations participate in an ongoing dance with interest groups and officials that often tests the integrity of individuals and institutions.

Additional Reading

Caulkins et al. "Design Considerations for Legalizing Marijuana."
Decorte, Tom, Gary Potter, and Martin Bouchard. *World Wide Weed*.
Hughes, Caitlin Elizabeth, and Alex Stevens. "What Can We Learn from the Portuguese of Decriminalization of Illicit Drugs?"

MacCoun, Robert J., and Peter Reuter. "Assessing Drug Prohibition and Its Alternatives."

MacCoun, Robert J., and Peter Reuter. *Drug War Heresies.*

MacCoun, Robert J., Peter Reuter, and Thomas Schelling. "Assessing Alternative Drug Control Regimes."

15

CAN INDUSTRIAL HEMP SAVE THE PLANET?
(WRITTEN WITH CHRISTINA FARBER)

What is industrial hemp?

Industrial hemp is marijuana's sober cousin. The oil and seeds of the cannabis plant can be used as nonintoxicating food for animals and people, and the fiber can make rope, paper, and cloth. Or the whole plant can be burned for fuel. Cannabis grown for such purposes is called industrial hemp.

Hemp has been cultivated for thousands of years and on almost every continent. Both the cordage and the sails of sailing ships consisted largely of hemp; the word "canvas" is derived from "cannabis." Cloth made of hemp was inexpensive and was associated with commoners rather than gentry: in *A Midsummer Night's Dream* Puck refers to Nick Bottom the weaver and his fellow rustics as "hempen homespuns." A "hempen necktie" is a hangman's noose.

In colonial times and up through the late nineteenth century, the United States produced significant quantities of industrial hemp: it has been claimed that the paper on which the Declaration of Independence was written was made in part from hemp fiber. The industry subsequently declined but enjoyed a brief government-promoted resurgence during World War II, under the slogan "Hemp for Victory"; the United States had lost access to "Manila hemp" (derived from the abaca plant rather than cannabis) from the Philippines and needed cannabis hemp for rope.

Cannabis hemp had fallen into disuse well before World War II, as Manila hemp, nylon, cotton, and other substitutes became more functional or less expensive. Hemp advocates invoke corporate conspiracies to explain the fall of hemp around the turn of the last century, but there is no real evidence to support this. In particular, Jack Herer in *The Emperor Wears No Clothes* claimed that newspaper baron William Randolph Hearst and the DuPont Company joined forces to take down the hemp industry to reduce competition. But Herer's book provides no evidence to support the theory, and wood-pulp newsprint and nylon cordage replaced hemp in countries where industrial hemp was never banned.

Today hemp production is illegal in the United States, but it remains legal to import raw and refined hemp products. Indeed, the United States actually exports (very small amounts of) hemp products—clothing, food, and shampoo—made from imported hemp.

Do other countries allow legalized hemp?

About thirty countries around the world, including Canada, Australia, and a number of European countries, allow farmers to cultivate industrial hemp. China is the world's largest producer, growing 154,000 tons of hemp fiber on 50,000 acres. China exports most of its hemp and is the main supplier of hemp fiber to the United States, although Canada provides the bulk of hempseed oil to the United States. China bulks large enough in the hemp industry that its production can move prices worldwide, but hemp still represents only 0.3 percent of fiber crops grown in China and 0.01 percent of farm area in the country. For every acre of hemp planted in China, farmers plant 280 acres of cotton, the dominant fiber crop in China and around the world.

Growing industrial hemp outside China is a very small-scale activity. Canadian cultivation has varied but recently covered about 14,000 acres, and European farmers grew roughly 30,000 acres, or less than 50 square miles; the United States has almost two thousand times as much land as that planted in soybeans alone.

Could the United States allow industrial hemp without legalizing marijuana?

Certainly. Many nations legalized industrial hemp production in the 1990s while continuing prohibition of marijuana as a psychoactive drug.

Different strains of cannabis—and different parts of any given plant—produce very different levels of the plant's psychoactive agents. Typically, laws allowing industrial hemp require the use of very-low-THC strains (less than 1 percent or even 0.3 percent THC, compared to the 4–18 percent characteristic of cannabis produced and sold as a drug). So there's a reasonably bold line between industrial hemp and intoxicating marijuana.

But it's hard to imagine that the passionate advocacy of industrial hemp is unrelated to its link to drug policy. Groups such as the National Organization for the Reform of Marijuana Laws (NORML) have picked up the hemp crusade in order to claim the benefits of industrial hemp as an advantage of marijuana legalization.

Politics makes strange bedfellows, and the politics of marijuana are no exception. Oddly, the Drug Enforcement Administration (DEA) and other advocates of continued prohibition agree with hemp advocates in linking the industrial-hemp and drug-legalization questions. But they do so from the opposite perspective, arguing that industrial hemp should not be legalized because it would complicate efforts to enforce prohibition against use as an intoxicant.

One DEA concern is that farmers could line the outside of their fields with low-THC (industrial) cannabis while growing high-THC (intoxicating) cannabis in the middle. Since relatively few acres would be needed to supply the intoxicant market, allowing free cultivation of industrial hemp could indeed pose an enforcement challenge. (Even the upper estimate of 5,000 metric tons of intoxicating cannabis consumed in the United States could be supplied by less than a third of the acreage Canada cultivates for industrial hemp.)

However, unregulated, laissez-faire production is not the only alternative to complete prohibition. Authorities in other countries use stringent protocols for the licensure, seed selection, and inspection of hemp operations to monitor the hemp production process. Prospective growers have to submit substantial paperwork, complete a background check, and join a professional hemp association to become sanctioned producers. Governments also require farmers to grow specific approved hemp varieties that fall under the THC threshold. Farms are subject to annual visits by inspectors and sometimes to aerial surveillance. Farms are valuable assets that would be vulnerable to seizure and forfeiture if farmers were found to be producing illegal (intoxicating) forms of cannabis.

There are also purely technical barriers to hiding pot plants in fields of industrial hemp. For example, fiber hemp plants are planted close together to encourage tall vertical stalks with few leaves.

Moreover, hemp fiber is harvested early, before the intoxicant-bearing flowers are ready. Marijuana grown amid industrial hemp would probably have to be the low-value, relatively low-THC commercial grade rather than higher-value sinsemilla, because the pollen produced by the hemp plants would pollinate the drug plants. (Sinsemilla comes from unfertilized female cannabis plants.) Indeed, some medical marijuana growers in California oppose a proposed law permitting an industrial hemp pilot project because they fear hemp pollen might ruin their harvest. Canadian industrial hemp farmers try to ensure that their crops are at least three miles from any wild or culti-vated cannabis to ensure pedigreed hempseed production; studies show cannabis pollen can travel three to twelve miles.

The really convincing evidence is negative. Like Sherlock Hol-mes's dog that did not bark in the night, the absence of any reports from Europe of diversion from industrial hemp farms into the drug market argues for the success of these regulations.

In sum, while legal industrial hemp production could create a Trojan horse for the production of intoxicating marijuana, there is no real problem in creating regulations to limit diversion.

Would allowing industrial hemp in the United States save the planet?

No. If legalizing industrial hemp could save the planet, then Canada and China would already have taken care of it.

It seems silly even to entertain such a question, but some hemp enthusiasts make rather extravagant claims. In *The Emperor Wears No Clothes*—the Bible of the hemp movement—the late Jack Herer wrote that hemp "could substitute for all wood pulp paper, all fossil fuels, would make most of our fibers naturally, make everything from dynamite to plastic," and that "one acre of it would replace 4.1 acres of trees." According to its advocates, hemp could fuel automobiles, be a staple ingredient in super foods, and provide superior building materials for developed and developing countries alike.

It's certainly true that the hemp plant can meet a wide variety of needs. So why isn't it an important crop today, as it was in colonial times? Some hemp advocates place the blame on an irrational prohibition. But that doesn't explain why hemp remains a minor niche industry even in countries that do not ban it.

A more pedestrian explanation is simply that global trade and technological progress have produced superior alternatives to hemp for most of its historical uses. Plastics have replaced hemp in many of the primary industries where hemp fiber was once the leader, because plastic offers greater longevity and resilience. There are also other plant-based options. Bast-fiber plants, such as jute and abaca (Manila hemp), had already largely supplanted industrial hemp for making rope before they in turn were rendered obsolete first by nylon and then by other synthetics. The advent of the cotton gin allowed cotton to outpace hemp as the staple material for fabric and textiles.

Hemp does have some advantages. Hemp is biodegradable while plastic is not. Hemp has essential fatty acids while other oilseeds do not. However, one crop that consistently competes favorably with hemp across categories is flax. Flax provides comparable nutritional benefits and textile properties to hemp, and produces a high-quality fabric at lower processing costs than cannabis: converting flax stalk to linen is easier and less expensive than converting hemp to hemp fiber to hemp cloth. That's why Hanes, for example, plans to market a blend of cotton and linen rather than of cotton and hemp. Where does that leave hemp? Likely with a smaller market share than flax, which is itself a modest industry.

There are also competitors for hempseed and hempseed oil. Flaxseed matches hempseed on a number of factors, including nutrient profile and density. For example, both contain rare omega-3 fatty acids. Both oils also have short shelf lives and have to be packaged in dark colored bottles to prevent spoilage. Consumers who want the nutritional benefits from flax seeds and flaxseed oil can find those products in health food stores.

Hemp can also be turned into a biofuel, as corn can be converted to ethanol. In fact, hemp produces more fuel than corn per unit area—40 gallons per acre compared to 18 gallons per acre—and offers advantages in efficiency of conversion to oil and usage at low temperatures. But other energy crops eclipse hemp. Soy produces 48 gallons of biofuel per acre, and jatropha, a crop that, like hemp, can grow in poor soil, produces 200 gallons per acre. Likewise other energy crops beat hemp on conversion to biomass, which can be used for heating and electricity production. Switchgrass exceeds the other biomass materials, including hemp, in the amount of energy it generates from a given amount of mass, and it is a perennial crop that does not need to be planted every year.

Hemp is an impressively versatile plant, but it is not a panacea.

How big is the potential market if the United States legalized industrial hemp?

This is really two distinct questions: how much farming of industrial hemp would there be, and how much processing and production of hemp-containing products would there be?

About a decade ago a number of states commissioned studies by agricultural economists and agronomists asking them to estimate the commercial potential of industrial hemp farming. Most reached pessimistic conclusions. It is also sobering that Canadian and European production never reached appreciable scales and actually declined from initial peaks, even though European hemp production receives government subsidies; the United States offers no obvious advantages as a place to grow hemp.

Legalizing cultivation of industrial hemp might stimulate some growth in the processing and production of hemp-containing products if the price of domestically produced industrial hemp turned out to significantly undercut the cost of obtaining those materials from foreign producers on the international market. However, it would continue to be quite unlike the industry in colonial days both in terms of function and scale. The hemp-based cordage, cloth, and textile production of early America would not prosper again with global availability of cotton and polypropylene to fulfill those uses. If a modern American hemp industry developed, the most successful markets might be those best paired to a regional specialization. For instance, one study examined the market potential for hempseed-oil production in North Dakota, taking advantage of existing supplier expertise and equipment in seed-oil processing. Another study measured the potential production of hemp for animal bedding in Kentucky, which was a center of hemp cultivation after the Civil War and has maintained a strong equestrian and livestock sector throughout its history.

Another possibility is selling to customers who would buy hemp-based products even if, in terms of functionality, those products were inferior to ones made with alternative materials. That is, some customers might be willing to pay a premium just because the product carried a "made with hemp" label, in the same way that some people will pay more for products that carry a label that says "union made" or "made in the USA."

If global experience over the last twenty years is any indication, then hemp will remain a minor player, even in the industries to which it is best suited. Lovers of marijuana as a drug may have an emotional attachment to hemp as a fiber or a food source, but there's no reason to think industrial hemp is poised to take off even if its production in the United States were legalized.

Additional Reading

Herer, Jack. *The Emperor Wears No Clothes.*

Johnson, Renée. *Hemp as an Agricultural Commodity.*

United States Department of Agriculture. *Industrial Hemp in the United States.*

Vantreese, Valerie L. *Industrial Hemp: Global Markets and Prices.*

16

WHAT DO THE AUTHORS THINK ABOUT MARIJUANA LEGALIZATION?

Angela Hawken

Existing policies suit me well.

I enjoy wine with most meals; summer wouldn't be summer without a good gin and tonic; and I like to serve a signature seasonal cocktail when hosting dinner parties. But I don't drink and drive, and you'll never find me drunk. I have never been a problem drinker, and no one in my family has a history of alcohol or drug abuse.

So the current rules work for me. I am at liberty to enjoy my mind-altering drug of choice, paying only modest excise taxes; the combined California and federal taxes on a bottle of wine come to 25 cents, which hardly matters given my low level of consumption. And the ban on marijuana doesn't keep me from doing anything I want to do.

But the fact that these policies work for me, and for others who share my preferences, doesn't make them right.

Laws should be rational, consistent, and fair. Alcohol does more total harm than any other drug because of its widespread use and the dangers associated with its abuse: it causes more recklessness, accidents, aggressive behavior, criminality, and loss of life than all the illicit drugs combined. Yet there is no move to (re)prohibit its use. Given the relative harms of alcohol compared with marijuana, having permissive alcohol laws alongside marijuana prohibition makes no sense. We could tighten our laws governing alcohol use, but that is unlikely to happen anytime soon. Absent tighter restrictions on alcohol, the only way to inject some sort of proportion into our drug policy is to loosen controls on marijuana.

But this raises a troublesome question: if two policies are inconsistent mostly because one is too lenient, is loosening the other really the right solution? Is it better to be consistent when that means being consistently wrong? Yes, two wrongs don't make a right. That's a fine principle, but equal protection is also a fine principle, and with billions in illicit revenues and hundreds of thousands of arrests, plus tens of millions of people whose otherwise harmless behavior is criminalized, in this case I think it's pretty clear that the cost-benefit balance is in favor of loosening the reins on marijuana.

Sixteen states and the District of Columbia have moved in this direction by allowing marijuana for medical use. I am concerned with the exploitation of medical-marijuana laws. That's not because I want people who suffer from insomnia or pain or glaucoma or any of the other ailments medical marijuana may (or may not) address to be denied access to its therapeutic benefits. I want them to have access, but they should be allowed to do so in a way that does not damage the reputation of the medical profession.

Some states have well-controlled marijuana laws; others do not. My views on medical marijuana are colored by living under California's poorly designed law, and near the city of Los Angeles, which has hundreds of "dispensaries" (though there are efforts afoot to drastically reduce their number). While many doctors recommend medical marijuana in the spirit in which it is intended, far too many others provide a recommendation with a wink and a nod to anyone who slips them a fifty. Marijuana doctors are not the only physicians to tarnish the profession; "Dr. Feelgood" kept his celebrity clients stoked with Dexedrine, and many Beverly Hills cosmetic surgeons are less reputable than Dr. 420 with her pad of "medical recommendations." But the medical marijuana industry, through its links with "herbal recommendationists," actively *recruits* "patients" that it knows do not suffer from any of the conditions that medical marijuana laws were intended to cover. Those pot docs give the profession a bad reputation, and jeopardize marijuana provision for patients with legitimate needs.

Medical marijuana is open to abuse in some states because many of the ailments that qualify for treatment (such as pain or lethargy) cannot be confirmed by a physician. It is unfair that healthy recreational users who aren't willing to feign a symptom to obtain a medical marijuana card run the risk of being busted for possession (or having their probation or parole revoked if they are on community-corrections status and test "dirty"), while their less scrupulous friends, wielding cards, face no similar risks. Until we are better able to accurately measure pain and sleeplessness and many of the harder-to-diagnose medical problems that marijuana is claimed to treat, the opportunity to abuse medical marijuana laws will remain.

As we have no good way to separate the frauds from those in real need, I would rather we stop playing this game. This is different than the case of the opioid pain relievers, also prescribed for nonspecific conditions and also abused. Physicians are more careful with prescriptions than pot docs are with recommendations, in part because they risk legal and professional sanctions if they fool around. But we can't make marijuana a prescription drug because federal agencies effectively prevent doing the research. Legalization is more honest than nebulous medical marijuana laws.

Given already-widespread use among adults and kids, the enormous costs of marijuana prohibition, and the inconsistencies in our drug laws, it seems worthwhile to experiment with legalization in the United States. As a first step, the federal government should step aside and let the states determine their own fate. Local communities have control over the use and sale of alcohol; why should marijuana be any different? Yes, users would easily be able to cross jurisdictional lines, but so can drinkers. There are two added advantages of this approach. First, states could serve as testing laboratories to help shed light on what approaches to marijuana regulation work best for curbing problem use. Second, making policy at the state level empowers people in politics at a scale at which they can meaningfully participate in democratic rule. A sizeable share of our citizens has a strong interest in marijuana policy. Sending this "live" issue to localities might draw people into political debates and participation where they could learn how to be political creatures.

Our time and public monies would be better spent focusing on punishing negative behaviors associated with marijuana use rather than the production, sale, or use of the drug. Using in public, disorderly conduct, sales to minors, and driving under the influence should be punished, with heavy penalties for repeat offenders.

Some might argue that punishing only the problem behavior hasn't worked very well with alcohol. I am optimistic nonetheless, for two reasons. First, although DUI/DWI programs have a poor record of managing repeat violators, new programs show great promise, notably South Dakota's 24/7 Sobriety program for drunk drivers. As the name implies, the program requires that chronic DWI offenders remain sober all the time, rather than allowing them to drink but forbidding them to drive drunk. Offenders must present themselves twice daily to the sheriff's office and submit to a breath-alcohol test; anyone who tests positive is immediately jailed. For such a simple program, it has produced impressive results. Participants show up, sober, for more than 99 percent of their scheduled tests, and DUI recidivism has plunged. Second, it is easier to monitor compliance with abstinence from marijuana than from alcohol, as marijuana has a much longer window of detection. Monitoring abstinence for repeat marijuana-DUI offenders would be logistically much simpler; weekly rather than twice-daily testing would suffice. Thus we could simultaneously loosen up on harmless behavior and tighten down on harmful behavior.

We should also raise taxes on alcohol and establish controls on alcohol advertising at least as strict as for tobacco. I would then support removing the federal ban on marijuana, and managing marijuana with regulations similar to those that apply to alcohol. This would mean strict licensing rules for production and sale, controls on advertising and product labeling, penalties for negative behaviors following from use, and taxes high enough to avoid a spike in use. The marijuana industry emerging from legalization would have a strong incentive to promote heavy use and would lobby hard against tax and advertising restrictions. Strong legislation would be needed to keep this in check.

My greatest concern going into this social experiment would be the implications for children. But even now, roughly 85 percent of American youth report that marijuana is easy to get. And we don't understand well how early marijuana use affects development. We'll need to make it easier for parents to find drug treatment resources for kids with unhealthy patterns of use (more treatment would also be needed for adults) and do what we can to manage the uptick in use among youth. As a start, our courts should wield a heavy hammer on any adult providing the drug to minors. And there's an extensive body of research on the effects of taxes and advertising controls on youth drinking and smoking that could be mined for ideas about marijuana control. High prices—high enough to avoid a surge in demand but low enough to avoid a black market— ought to be preferred to lower prices.)

Two additional concerns:

First, legalization might be seen as an endorsement of marijuana as safe. We don't know how that might affect consumption patterns, either in the short run or in the long run.

Second is the slippery-slope argument. Legalize marijuana and what comes next? Are alcohol and marijuana categorically distinct from other psychoactive drugs that would remain illicit? We will need to assess all of our illegal drugs for relative harms and decide where to draw the line. The final placement of that line might turn out to be more permissive than I would prefer, but my vote is to put marijuana on the right side of the law.

Jon Caulkins

I would vote against legalizing marijuana. Most of what people dislike about the current prohibition can be fixed by reforming prohibition and/or pursuing "middle path" options. Among middle path options, decriminalization plus home growing and sharing (with or without user co-ops but without commercial production and sale) strikes me as having particular advantages for shrinking the black market.

This conclusion reflects my personal values. Marijuana legalization would bring benefits as well as costs; people with different values can look at the same projected outcomes and think the benefits outweigh the costs. (Relative to most people writing about the issue, I worry more about the children of dependent users and less about the costs of criminal-justice sanctions that do not involve prison terms.)

I would not say the same about legalizing all drugs. When people anticipate a net win from legalizing crack and methamphetamine, they inevitably have beliefs about effects on abuse and dependence that are (in my opinion) naively optimistic.

My best guess is that legalizing marijuana would only double, or perhaps triple, abuse and dependence, from 4 to 8 or even 12 million people in the United States. Those are big numbers, but I do not see marijuana dependence as debilitating in the way compulsive daily use of crack or methamphetamine is. People who abuse marijuana have a bad habit, but they mostly still function; people whose lives are dominated by crack and meth are often burdens on others, particularly their families.

I generally agree with libertarian notions of letting people harm themselves if that's what they choose: but only to a point. I also believe people can be fooled; we are heuristic decision makers, not mechanical optimizers. Certain products and activities fool a sizable minority of us. For those special cases, I think the majority who would use responsibly ought to be willing to give up their fun to protect the minority who would not.

In my judgment, the potent stimulants are such special cases. Heroin probably is. I think marijuana is, although it is a close call. Driving without wearing a seatbelt and riding a motorcycle without a helmet are not, but are also close calls. That is, for me, the dividing line between the government's trampling personal liberty and its exercising prudent paternalism falls somewhere between seatbelts and marijuana (although I am prepared to change my mind after we see how legalization works in the jurisdictions that experiment with it first).

I also think much of the debate about marijuana legalization misses the mark. Legalizing all drugs would reduce overcrowded prisons, rampant street crime, and corruption. Advocates try to associate those benefits with marijuana legalization, but since marijuana does not cause much crime, incarceration, or corruption in the United States, legalizing marijuana can't produce big wins in those domains. But it also wouldn't produce big losses; we have already slouched quite a ways down the path toward normalizing marijuana use, to adapt Rob Mac-Coun's phrase.

Likewise, effects on health-care costs would probably be relatively minor—some hundreds of millions of dollars per year out of total health spending of more than two trillion dollars. The cost to taxpayers of imprisoning marijuana offenders is a medium-scale issue—40,000 people in prison times $30,000 cost per inmate-year is $1.2 billion.

Contrast that with the change in use itself. Current consumption generates roughly 15 billion hours of intoxication each year in the United States. Legalization could double or triple that. Optimists would say most of those hours would bring pleasure, perhaps valued at $5 or $10 per hour. Pessimists would say most of those hours represent lost productivity at work, school, or household tasks, perhaps at a cost of $5 or $10 per hour. Neither view should be dismissed out of hand. Both represent outcomes whose value—when multiplied by an additional 15 or 30 billion hours of intoxication—could approach $100 billion per year, utterly dwarfing other considerations.

Likewise, if even one in four of the additional 4 million or so people who became dependent on marijuana then moved on to abuse alcohol, hard drugs, or tobacco as a result, that would generate social harms that dwarf a $1.2 billion savings on incarceration or most other marijuana-specific outcomes.

Thus, and oddly for a quantitative analyst, I think one's position on marijuana legalization boils down to values, not calculations. If you like marijuana intoxication, you should like marijuana legalization; if you don't, you shouldn't.

About half of all days of marijuana use come from people who self-report enough use-related problems to meet criteria for substance abuse or dependence with respect to marijuana or another substance. Does the happiness a controlled user derives from using marijuana on a typical day offset the unhappiness of someone else spending a day harmed by and/or struggling to control problem drug use? In my opinion, the answer is no. In a free society there are plenty of other ways to have fun without insisting on a right to use something that becomes a stumbling block for others.

Mark Kleiman

Marijuana can be a source of harmless pleasure and other benefits. Many millions of otherwise responsible and law-abiding

Americans enjoy it and would like to do so without breaking the law and taking the risk of getting arrested, or of losing a job for a positive drug test. Marijuana use can also become a rather nasty bad habit. Illegal businesses are an evil; so are arrests and prison terms.

Those, it seems to me, are the important stakes in marijuana policy. Neither public expenditure on control efforts nor public revenue from marijuana taxes is likely to be as important as the benefits to users on the one hand or, on the other hand, the costs of ongoing criminal enterprise, law enforcement, and the suffering caused by punishment. So the principles that ought to guide our choice of a marijuana policy ought to be:

More freedom is better than less freedom.
A smaller criminal sector of the economy is better than a larger one.
Fewer people in handcuffs and behind bars is better than more.
Less drug abuse is better than more drug abuse.

There seem to be, broadly speaking, six options:

1. Current policy: virtually everything associated with marijuana is illegal
2. Decriminalization of use, keeping production and distribution illegal
3. Permission to use marijuana, grow it, and give it away, but not to grow it professionally or sell it
4. Legalization without commercialization, allowing both home production and small consumer-owned cooperatives with paid employees
5. Commercialization with high taxes and tight restrictions on marketing, or the equivalent in the form of a state monopoly

6. Commercialization on the alcohol model, with low taxes and loose restrictions on marketing

The advantage of current policy, compared with any alternative, is some reduction in drug abuse. On all the other dimensions of choice current policy is worse than any of the alternatives. Marijuana dependency, while not as bad as dependency on alcohol or the "hard" illicit drugs, is plenty bad enough. But—unlike heavy drinking—marijuana intoxication doesn't generate much in the way of crime. Depriving millions of people of a freedom they value, generating $15–$30 billion a year in criminal income, making three-quarters of a million arrests, and keeping tens of thousands of people in prison or jail at any one time all seem to me like too high a price to pay for the substance abuse reduction we get from marijuana prohibition. Thus current policy would be my last choice.

Decriminalization would eliminate most of those arrests, but if it had any effect on the size of the dealing problem the effect would be to make the problem worse. It would free users from the fear of the law, while still forcing them either to do business with criminals to get their drug or to break the law themselves by growing their own. Better than the status quo, but not really very satisfactory.

At the other extreme, commercialization on the alcohol model would create an industry like the alcohol industry: a multibillion-dollar enterprise devoted to creating and sustaining as much addiction as possible—including among minors—because addiction is where the money is. Nevertheless, I think that might well be better than what we have now, but it could easily turn out to be worse, depending on the size of the increase in abuse (a 50 percent increase at least, and quite possibly a tripling), on whether abuse of alcohol and other drugs would go up or down as a result (there's no way to guess in advance), and on how you weigh the harms of drug abuse against the harms of prohibition and the benefits of responsible use. Of the legalization options, this seems to me quite clearly the worst. Unfortunately, it's also the most likely: if not right away, then once the legal industry created by some more restrictive form of legalization puts its lobbying muscle to work on the political process.

That leaves, as my preferred outcomes:

- permission to grow, use, and give away but not to sell;
- noncommercial legalization with small consumer-owned co-ops;
- a tight form of commercialization: taxes high enough to maintain prices at least half as high as current illicit prices, and a ban—if the courts would permit it—on any advertising except simple statements about the price and chemical content of the product; or
- a state monopoly to do the same job: making marijuana legally available without making it cheap or allowing it to be heavily promoted.

The problem with home growing is that not everyone who wants to use the drug can or will grow it, or find a friend to do so. That would bring back an illicit market—though perhaps a smaller, and surely a less harmful one, than now exists—and make it harder for people to get the varieties they desire; growing marijuana is fairly easy, but growing marijuana with your preferred ratio of active agents is much harder.

A commercial market with tight controls would be more convenient for consumers and would give them a wider range of choices. But I doubt that system would be politically stable; the industry would simply have too great an incentive to move it toward the alcohol model. State monopoly has many attractive features in principle, but it's hard to imagine the political process that would get us there.

So my first choice—not what I think will happen, but what I would like to see happen—is permission for production and use through small not-for-profit cooperatives, with a ban on commerce.

Beau Kilmer

Like alcohol, marijuana has provided pleasure to hundreds of millions of people around the world.

Personally, I do not see much difference between alcohol and marijuana when adults use either one in moderation. The vast majority of alcohol and marijuana users enjoy themselves and do not bother anyone else; not all users by any means, but most.

When used in excess, alcohol is clearly the bigger problem. Heavy marijuana use can lead to abuse and dependence, and this can create serious problems for users and their families (see chapter 5 for a discussion of the negative consequences). However, the scientific consensus is that heavy drinking is much more harmful than heavy marijuana use, largely because of alcohol's strong connection with violence, traffic fatalities, and chronic disease.

When it comes to teenagers, who are prone to rash decisions and are still developing—physically, mentally, and emotionally—heavy substance use can be especially risky. Thus I find some aspects of marijuana prohibition appealing: it inflates the price of marijuana and keeps out commercial promotion. We know that adolescents are especially sensitive to the price of intoxicating substances since they do not have a lot of money to spend. Prohibition thus serves as an effective, albeit imperfect, prevention program.

If marijuana were not prohibited and commercial enterprises got involved in the trade, those companies would likely target adolescents and young adults, trying to get them to use, and to use often. This is how the alcohol and tobacco companies operate, and there's no reason to believe that marijuana companies—or the new marijuana products divisions of existing consumer-products companies—would act differently. And once business interests get entrenched in an industry, toughening the laws related to that industry becomes more difficult. As we have seen with the alcohol lobby's successful efforts to keep alcohol taxes low (adjusting for inflation, my grandparents paid approximately 50 percent more for a drink in the 1950s than I currently do), private interests prioritize profit, not public health or public safety.

That said, I also have serious concerns about our current marijuana policies. Millions of adults have been caught up in the criminal justice system for simple possession of an intoxicant that research indicates is safer than alcohol. In addition to the short-term consequences of being arrested and possibly convicted, the long-term effects of being convicted of a misdemeanor drug charge can be significant. Among other consequences, a marijuana possession conviction can make one ineligible for federal student loan and grant programs, and makes it harder to obtain public housing. There is absolutely no evidence showing that these collateral consequences for a possession conviction deter consumption or improve social welfare.

So where does this leave me on the question of marijuana policy? Before answering, I need to make two points.

First, I work for a nonpartisan, nonprofit organization (RAND) that has researched and analyzed drug policy for more than twenty years. RAND's goal is to inform policy by illuminating the facts. We do not take official positions on ballot initiatives or pending legislation, so nothing I say here represents "the RAND position"—there is no such position. We pride ourselves on being able to put our personal opinions and differences aside in order to conduct objective research and analysis that is informative to decision makers.

Second, my thoughts about marijuana policy continue to evolve. The work behind this book and my research on the legalization question in California opened my eyes to how little we know about the full range of consequences of major marijuana reforms. My thoughts will continue to evolve on this issue, especially if a state or country implements meaningful change.

If I were approached for advice by a policymaker who represented a constituency seeking significant changes in their marijuana policies, today I would offer the following thoughts:

- Whatever you decide, incorporate a sunset provision. Given the enormous uncertainty about the outcomes of policy changes and the strong possibility of unintended consequences, it is reasonable to incorporate a sunset provision that makes the laws revert back to what they were before reform after a certain number of years unless extended by the voters or the legislature. As the sunset date approaches, the legislature or the voters could vote to sustain the reform if they thought it was a good policy, or they could try something different. This is especially important for policies that allow private companies to make money from the marijuana trade. The sunset provision would give pioneering jurisdictions an escape clause, a chance—by simply sitting still—to overcome the lobbying muscle of the new industry fighting hard to stay in business.

- Given the weak knowledge base, it is risky to implement the most extreme alternative to prohibition. Marijuana legalization can refer to legalizing any or all of at least five different activities: (1) possession of small amounts; (2) nonprofit production and sharing (in-home, co-ops); (3) retail sales; (4) commercial and/or government production; and (5) advertising and promotion. Given the dearth of evidence we have about legalizing *any* of these activities, I am not convinced that jumping from one end of the continuum (prohibition) to the other (commercial production and sale with advertising) is a good idea. Indeed, given the concerns about marijuana companies working hard to promote use, nurture heavy users, and keep taxes low, implementing the most extreme alternative to prohibition could be a really bad idea. Incremental approaches that experiment with different combinations of these activities are inherently less risky than implementing them all at the same time.

I expect that the knowledge base about marijuana legalization will improve over time. In ten to fifteen years we could have insights about commercial legalization from another country. There is also a strong possibility that a U.S. state will pass a marijuana reform initiative in the near future. As change occurs, I will assess the research findings on these reforms and incorporate them into my opinions about marijuana policy. I hope you do too.

BIBLIOGRAPHY

Caulkins, Jonathan P., Carolyn C. Coulson, Christina Farber, and Joseph V. Vesely. "Marijuana Legalization: Certainty, Impossibility, Both, or Neither?" *Journal of Drug Policy Analysis* 5 (2012): 1–27.

Cole, James. "Guidance Regarding the Ogden Memo in Jurisdictions Seeking to Authorize Marijuana for Medical Use." Memo to Paula Dow, Attorney General of the State of New Jersey, June 30, 2011. Available online at http://www.drugpolicy.org/sites/default/files/DOJ_Guidance_on_Medicinal_Marijuana_1.pdf.

Courtwright, David T. *Forces of Habit: Drugs and the Making of the Modern World*. Cambridge, MA: Harvard University Press, 2001.

Decorte, Tom, Gary Potter, and Martin Bouchard. *World Wide Weed: Global Trends in Cannabis Cultivation and Its Control*. Farnham, UK: Ashgate, 2011.

D'Souza, Deepak Cyril, Richard Andrew Sewell, and Mohini Ranganathan. "Cannabis and Psychosis/Schizophrenia: Human Studies." *European Archives of Psychiatry and Clinical Neuroscience* 259, no. 7 (2009): 413–31.

DuPont, Robert L., and Carl S. Selavka. "Testing to Identify Recent Drug Use." In *American Psychiatric Publishing Textbook of Substance Abuse Treatment*, edited by Marc Galanter and Herbert D. Kleber, 655–64. 4th ed. Washington, DC: American Psychiatric Press, 2008.

Eddy, Mark. *Medical Marijuana Review and Analysis of Federal and State Policies*. [Washington, DC]: Congressional Research Service, 2010.

Erowid. "Cannabis Effects." Available online at http://www.erowid.org/plants/cannabis/cannabis_effects.shtml.

Federal Bureau of Investigation. *Crime in the United States* 2010. Washington, DC: Federal Bureau of Investigation, Criminal Justice Information Services Division, 2010.

Grinspoon, Lester. *Marihuana Reconsidered*. 2nd ed. Cambridge, MA: Harvard University Press, 1977. Reprint, Oakland, CA: Quick American Archives, 1994.

Hall, Wayne, and Rosalie Liccardo Pacula. *Cannabis Use and Dependence: Public Health and Public Policy*. Cambridge, UK: Cambridge University Press, 2003.

Herer, Jack. *The Emperor Wears No Clothes: The Authoritative Historical Record of Cannabis and the Conspiracy against Marijuana*. Austin, TX: Ah Ha Publishing, 2000.

Huestis, Marilyn A., Irene Mazzoni, and Oliver Rabin. "Cannabis in Sport: Anti-Doping Perspective." *Sports Medicine* 41 (2011): 949–66.

Hughes, Caitlin Elizabeth, and Alex Stevens. "What Can We Learn from the Portuguese of Decriminalization of Illicit Drugs?" *British Journal of Criminology* 50 (2010): 999–1022.

International Association for Cannabinoid Medicine. "Clinical Studies and Case Reports." http://www.cannabis-med.org/studies/study.php.

Iversen, Leslie L. *The Science of Marijuana*. 2nd ed. New York: Oxford University Press, 2008.

Johnson, Renée. *Hemp as an Agricultural Commodity*. Washington, DC: U.S. Congressional Research Service, Library of Congress, 2010.

Johnston, Lloyd, Patrick M. O'Malley, Jerald G. Bachman, and John E. Schulenberg. *Monitoring the Future: National Survey Results on Adolescent Drug Use*. Rockville, MD: National Institute on Drug Abuse, U.S. Dept. of Health and Human Services, Public Health Service, National Institutes of Health (Annual).

Joy, Janet E., Stanley J. Watson Jr., and John A. Benson Jr. *Marijuana and Medicine: Assessing the Science Base*. Washington, DC: National Academy Press, 1999.

Kaplan, John. *Marijuana: The New Prohibition*. New York: World Publishing, 1970.

Kilmer, Beau, Jonathan P. Caulkins, Brittany Bond, and Peter Reuter. *Reducing Drug Trafficking Revenues and Violence in Mexico: Would Legalizing Marijuana in California Help?* OP-325-RC. Santa Monica, CA: RAND, 2010.

Kilmer, Beau, Jonathan P. Caulkins, Rosalie Pacula, and Peter Reuter. "Bringing Perspective to Illicit Markets: Estimating the Size of the U.S. Marijuana Market." *Drug and Alcohol Dependence* 119, nos. 1–2 (December 2011): 153–60.

Kilmer, Beau, Jonathan P. Caulkins, Rosalie Liccardo Pacula, Robert J. MacCoun, and Peter H. Reuter. *Altered State? Assessing How Marijuana Legalization in California Could Influence Marijuana Consumption and Public Budgets.* Santa Monica, CA: RAND, 2010. Available online at http://www.rand.org/pubs/occasional_papers/OP315.html.

Kleiman, Mark A. R. *Against Excess: Drug Policy for Results.* New York: Basic Books, 1992.

Kleiman, Mark A. R. *Marijuana: Costs of Abuse, Costs of Control.* New York: Greenwood, 1989.

Kleiman, Mark A. R., Jonathan P. Caulkins, and Angela Hawken. *Drugs and Drug Policy: What Everyone Needs to Know.* New York: Oxford University Press, 2011.

Leggett, Ted. "A Review of the World Cannabis Situation." *Bulletin on Narcotics* 58, nos. 1 and 2 (2006): 1–155. Available online at http://www.unodc.org/documents/data-and-analysis/bulletin/2006/Bulletin_on_Narcotics_2006_En.pdf.

Lincoln, Abraham. "Temperance Address (22 February 1842)." In *The Collected Works of Abraham Lincoln,* edited by Roy P. Basler, 1:271–79. New Brunswick, NJ: Rutgers University Press, 1953. Available online at http://showcase.netins.net/web/creative/lincoln/speeches/temperance.htm.

MacCoun, Robert J., and Peter Reuter. "Assessing Drug Prohibition and Its Alternatives: A Guide for Agnostics." *Annual Review of Law and Social Science* 7 (2011): 61–78.

MacCoun, Robert J., and Peter Reuter. *Drug War Heresies: Learning from Other Vices, Times, and Places.* New York: Cambridge University Press, 2001.

MacCoun, Robert, Peter Reuter, and Thomas Schelling. "Assessing Alternative Drug Control Regimes." *Journal of Policy Analysis and Management* 15.3 (1996): 330–52.

Merriman, David. "The Micro-Geography of Tax Avoidance: Evidence from Littered Cigarette Packs in Chicago." *American Economic Journal: Economic Policy* 2, no. 2 (2010): 61–84.

Mikos, Robert A. "A Critical Appraisal of the Department of Justice's New Approach to Medical Marijuana." *Stanford Law and Policy Review* 22 (2011): 633–69.

Musto, David F. *The American Disease: Origins of Narcotic Control.* 3rd ed. New York: Oxford University Press, 1999.

National Drug Intelligence Center. *Domestic Cannabis Cultivation Assessment.* Washington, DC: U.S. Department of Justice, 2009. Available online at http://www.justice.gov/ndic/pubs37/37035/index.htm.

Office of National Drug Control Policy. *Arrestee Drug Abuse Monitoring Program II: 2010 Annual Report.* Washington, DC: Office of National Drug Control Policy, 2011. Available online at http://www.whitehouse.gov/sites/default/files/ondcp/policy-and-research/adam2010.pdf.

Pollan, Michael. *The Botany of Desire: A Plant's Eye View of the World.* New York: Random House, 2001.

Ramchand, Rajeev, Rosalie Liccardo Pacula, and Martin Y. Iguchi. "Racial Differences in Marijuana-Users' Risk of Arrest in the United States." *Drug and Alcohol Dependence* 84.3 (2006): 264–72.

Reuter, Peter. "The (Continued) Vitality of Mythical Numbers." *Public Interest* 75 (Spring 1984): 135–47.

Rolles, Stephen. *Blueprint for Regulation.* London: Transform, 2009.

Room, Robin, Benedikt Fischer, Wayne Hall, Simon Lenton, and Peter Reuter. *Cannabis Policy: Moving Beyond Stalemate.* Oxford: Oxford University Press, 2010.

Schelling, Thomas C. "The Intimate Contest for Self-Command." In *Choice and Consequence*, 57–82. Cambridge, MA: Harvard University Press, 1984.

Schelling, Thomas C. "Ethics, Law, and the Exercise of Self-Command." In *Choice and Consequence*, 83–102. Cambridge, MA: Harvard University Press, 1984.

Sevigny, Eric L., and Jonathan P. Caulkins. "Kingpins or Mules: An Analysis of Drug Offenders Incarcerated in Federal and State Prisons." *Criminology and Public Policy* 3.3 (2004): 401–34.

Sewell, R. Andrew, James Poling, and Mehmet Sofuoglu. "The Effect of Cannabis Compared with Alcohol on Driving." *American Journal on Addictions* 18, no. 3 (2009): 185–93.

Thurstone, Christian, Shane A. Lieberman, and Sarah J. Schmiege. "Medical Marijuana Diversion and Associated Problems in Adolescent Substance Treatment." *Drug and Alcohol Dependence* 118, nos. 2–3 (November 2011): 489–92.

Toonen, Marcel, Simon Ribot, and Jac Thissen. "Yield of Illicit Indoor Cannabis Cultivation in the Netherlands." *Journal of Forensic Sciences* 51, no. 5 (September 2006): 1050–54.

United Nations Office on Drugs and Crime. *World Drug Report 2011.* New York: United Nations, 2011. Available online at http://www.unodc.org/documents/data-and-analysis/WDR2011/World_Drug_Report_2011_ebook.pdf.

United States Department of Health and Human Services. *State Estimates of Substance Use and Mental Disorders from the 2008–2009 National Surveys on Drug Use and Health.* Rockville, MD: Substance Abuse and Mental Health Services Administration, 2011. Available online at http://oas.samhsa.gov/2k9State/toc.cfm#All.

United States Department of Agriculture. *Industrial Hemp in the United States: Status and Market Potential.* Washington, DC: United States Department of Agriculture, 2000.

Vantreese, Valerie L. *Industrial Hemp: Global Markets and Prices.* Lexington: Department of Agricultural Economics, University of Kentucky, 1997.

Weil, Andrew. *The Natural Mind: A Revolutionary Approach to the Drug Problem.* Rev. ed. Boston: Houghton Mifflin, 2004.

Zimring, Franklin E., and Gordon Hawkins. *The Search for Rational Drug Control.* Cambridge, UK: Cambridge University Press, 1992.

INDEX

A page number in italics indicates a chart or table on that page.